W9-BNC-227

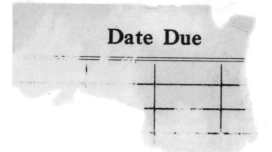

Date Due

VESTMENTS
AND VESTURE

PLATE I

THE ANGELS OF THE LITURGY

Observe the excellent vestments of the ministers as they walk in procession to the altar of sacrifice.

Simplicity, dignity, religious character. (Beuronese School)

Vestments and Vesture

A Manual of Liturgical Art

By

DOM E. A. ROULIN, O.S.B.

Monk of Ampleforth Abbey

Translated by

DOM JUSTIN McCANN, O.S.B.
of the same Abbey

SANDS & CO.
15 King Street, Covent Garden
LONDON, W.C.2
And at Glasgow and Edinburgh

B. HERDER BOOK CO.
15 and 17 South Broadway
ST. LOUIS, Mo.

1931

NIHIL OBSTAT: D. STEPHANUS MARRON,
CENSOR CONGR. ANGLIAE O.S.B.

IMPRIMERE LICET: RR. DD. EDMUNDUS KELLY,
ABBAS PRAESES

NIHIL OBSTAT: JOANNES GRAY,
CENSOR DEPUTATUS

IMPRIMATUR: ✠ ANDREAS JOSEPH,
ARCHIEP. S. ANDR. ET EDIM.

EDIMBURGI, ID. NOV. MCMXXX

MADE AND PRINTED
IN GREAT BRITAIN

PREFACE

THE book here presented to the reader is a translation of a work which I published earlier this year in French under the title of *Linges, Insignes et Vêtements Liturgiques* (Paris, Lethielleux, 1930). The translation has been made by a friend and colleague, not from the French edition, but from a text which I supplied to him, and a careful scrutiny will reveal some minor differences between the French edition and this English version. But the differences are only minor ones, and for vastly the greater part of their substance the books are identical. The French edition has a preface in which I explain the character and purpose of the book, an explanation which I may be allowed to repeat here.

The book does not pretend to be a learned and methodical treatise on its subject, but a practical manual. Hence it is not afraid to be incomplete on some points and (apparently) too full on others. Hence also it indulges not seldom in repetition of points which need special emphasis, and it sometimes adopts a conversational manner. This I say in order to forewarn the reader and to spare him any surprise or annoyance.

The history of practically all liturgical vestments and insignia has been written with consummate knowledge and care in the great *Dictionnaire d' archéologie chrétienne et de liturgie*, so far as that publication has reached. In that work, as is proper to a dictionary of pure archaeology, the history is brought down no further than the tenth century. For the complete history of the same articles of liturgical vesture, brought down to our modern times, there are the books of the German Jesuit, Father Joseph Braun. And since these are standard works and will probably long remain so, there would be no point in my attempting to cover the same ground. For the most part, therefore, I have abstained from giving a full history of the vestments which are discussed, and in one case only (the pallium) have I allowed myself any latitude. My purpose was in fact a very different one.

Yet the reader will find that history has not been entirely neglected. I have given introductory accounts of the vestments of the priest, as also of those of the deacon, sub-deacon and servers ; and I have something to say regarding the history of pontifical insignia, of the vesture of the sanctuary, altar, and tabernacle, and of banners.

The cassock is not a liturgical vestment, and yet a recent discussion regarding the red cassocks used for some altar servers and choir-boys—not to mention their red girdles and red slippers and red tippets—almost tempted me to insert a section on cassocks. But it would have been a digression from my proper subject and I refrained. However, I may perhaps be allowed to express my mind here and to say that I deprecate the use of these red garments. The use of red for such cassocks and accessories dates from the nineteenth century and no earlier, and however attractive red cassocks may be to some (and distracting to others) they do not really harmonise well with the dignity of Christian worship. As ministers of the altar the servers have dignity enough from their office without these red ornaments ; and I believe that both for them and for choir-boys the true and proper vestments are the black cassock and the full surplice.

My principal aim in writing has been to produce a practical guide to liturgical and beautiful vestments, in order to help not only the professional makers of vestments, but also those devout women who take up the work from religious motives, and especially priests, who are concerned to follow the best liturgical traditions and who have to deal with the serious question of costs. Some may be disposed to think that the work has been done already by the Benedictine nuns of the Rue Monsieur (Paris) in their *Guide pratique*. It is true that that publication treats excellently of the cut of vestments and the processes of manufacture, of making orfreys and embroideries, of the care of church linen, etc. And it seemed to me that this book too ought to deal with those points, and it has dealt with them. But my guide differs much from the other, in that it does not deal so much with technical processes of manufacture as with the aesthetics of vestments. It has much to say about the conditions of beauty, or at least of its salient qualities ; it has many comparisons to make between vestment and vestment, between this design and that design, between this style of ornamentation and that. It is my hope and desire that the book may prove a manual of "practical theory," such a theory of good vestments as will help to produce good vestments.

For many years now I have had practical acquaintance with the subject of this book, for I have been asked from the most various quarters to design vestments and their accessories. Now it was a parish, now an abbey, now a diocesan seminary ; another time the request

came from a Cardinal Archbishop and the vestments were to be made for
his metropolitan cathedral. In this way I have been compelled for
many years to be busy constantly with pen and pencil and brush ; and
I have experimented with many designs and with many ornaments,
from very various sources. It has been my business to prepare the
designs, to settle the cut, quality and ornament of every sort of vestment, and then to negotiate for their making and discuss their cost
with the firms who make such things. It has been a labour of love and I
have worked at it with all my heart, *corde et animo*. Indeed I feel bound
to thank all those who by their commissions have made me devote
myself to this liturgical work, and who have thus compelled me to study,
to compare and to learn.

Yet, even so, such knowledge and experience as I have thus acquired
would hardly justify me in writing down and publishing the results of
my labours, were there not other motives to urge me to that course.
But I am a religious, and my abbot has asked me to do it ; I am a
parish priest, and my bishop has continually encouraged me, pointing
out the usefulness, and even the urgent need of manuals of religious art
for the parochial clergy.

The perusal of a book of this sort is an intolerable and almost useless
task, if it be not adequately illustrated. For that reason the present
volume has more than three hundred illustrations, accompanied with
brief explanatory titles, and often so arranged as to show clearly the
contrast between good and bad. By this means even those who do no
more than skim the book will perhaps be interested and even benefited.

I have dared sometimes to criticise vestments made by firms which
are still in full vigour of production, but of course without mentioning
names. I have dared also to show the weakness of opinions which have
originated in friendliness or fellow-feeling, in the desire to please
designers and makers, writers and readers of magazines. *Fallax gratia et
vana est pulchritudo :* a fallacious thing is mere amiable praise and vain
are fine compliments. Praise and well-deserved compliments are many
times given in this book where they are due, and given with a good will ;
but the fear of displeasing ought never to check the pen of an author,
when it is his business to show faults of taste, composition and colour.
Therefore I speak what I believe to be the truth, in order to serve those
who have at heart the liturgy and its beauty. A good reviewer is one
who in his review of a book gives a sincere and truthful account of its
contents and value. I am reviewing liturgical art and it is my duty to
my readers to be sincere and truthful.

But human nature is so made that those whose works are judged reprehensible will be angry with the author ; while those who are praised will, of course, be pleased. In the meanwhile the neutrals, who prefer such free and unbiassed criticism, will perhaps be very well content, breathing an atmosphere no longer saturated with the usual fulsome compliments.

But, however that may be, I beg those who may be discontented to be pleased to pardon me, and themselves to take time for reflection. It may be that it will take weeks, or even months, before we can bring ourselves publicly to admit our faults of taste. But when criticism has pointed out faulty work, let us have the honesty to admit it in our own consciences and endeavour valiantly to do better for the future.

Some will perhaps tell me that my whole effort is a misguided one, because there is no discussing tastes or colours. *De gustibus* . . . How false is that poor adage ! What else is all art criticism but a discussion of tastes and of colours ? That criticism considers a work of art, analyses it, and then proclaims its judgment aloud, or publishes it in the press. The papers are full of such criticism : of films, of plays, of pictures, of schools of art and of artists. And by criticism we mean of course a rational and reasoned examination, consisting of approbation and of censure, since perfect work is infinitely rare, and since innate good taste and acquired knowledge do not prevent a critic having his preferences. Yet his criticism is based on precise laws and on solid principles, and at the very least on an educated taste. For a work of art, whatever it may be, whether statue, picture or liturgical vestment, is not produced at random, without rule or reason, like some purely accidental and arbitrary occurrence. It has its law and it has its reason.

And why should the making of chasubles and other such things be exempt from public criticism ? If they deserve praise, silence will not give it them ; and if they are vicious in form and make and ornament, silence will not hide their vices. Therefore criticism must deal with them; and perhaps it will oblige our artists and craftsmen, our vendors and their clients, to know what they should make and sell and buy. No longer shall we have the old spirit of "anything will do" ; we shall have work that conforms to precise rules of sincerity and beauty. Whether our vestments be very simple or very magnificent, they will be in good taste.

Nor shall we have that other noxious principle of "something for every taste" in the sense that there should be vestments of good character, others less good, and others again that are positively bad. A person of good taste will easily choose and buy a good vestment, even if it is surrounded by mediocre or bad ones. But the buyer who lacks discernment should not for all that be given the occasion of buying bad vestments as easily as good ones. Let our firms then have none but beautiful vestments in their stocks and all will be well. For long purses and exacting tastes, let them provide vestments that are expensive as well as beautiful ; for those who are neither rich nor of very exacting judgment, let them combine beauty with simple ornament and inexpensive materials. Such then is my answer to the catchwords which I have cited, and with that answer made I shall leave my book to its destiny.

But first let me be allowed to express my gratitude to the many friends who have helped me in the writing of this book. I thank Dom M. Bluté for many true and valuable criticisms, Dom Sylvester Fryer for the excellent drawings which the reader will be able to appreciate for himself, Miss Hilda Crump for her careful and accurate designs, and finally all those many persons who have sent me drawings and photographs. In this English edition I wish to thank Miss Mildred Vernon Harcourt for the very generous assistance which she has given to the translator, and the translator himself for the work which I now lay before the English reader.

E. A. ROULIN

August, 1930.

ANALYTICAL CONTENTS

CHAPTER V

Dom Guéranger, "liturgical doctor," and full chasubles. Indults granted by Rome. Cardinal Wiseman and Pugin. The First Provincial Council of Westminster prescribes "Gothic" chasubles ; which are approved by Rome. Dr. Adrian Fortescue explains that the skimped chasuble is not Roman. Pius IX, Pius X and Pius XI. The Exhibition of Liturgical Art at Rome in 1925. The Sovereign Pontiff blesses numerous vestments, all antique in form and character.

CHAPTER VI

The sequence : elaboration, comparative perfection, decadence, revival is characteristic of the worlds of thought, taste and art. Impossible to stand aside from the general movement towards thoughtful, sound and improved work. The art of sacred vesture shares in the revival. Practical examples, with at one end of the series the simplest of vestments, yet excellent ; at the other the elaborate "storied" vestment.

CHAPTER VII

A glance at the latest art. The spirit which animates the true liturgical artist : return to the classic fundamentals, combined with freedom of vision and æsthetic sensibility. Ultra-modern art devoid of the exact laws and principles which were accepted in the best periods ; expressing itself in cubism, quadrangulism, etc. Commentary on some products of this art. If it would serve the Church, the new art must get rid of its startling and fantastic effects.

CHAPTER VIII

Pronouncements of the Sacred Congregation of Rites and their interpretation. Sound authorities find in them no condemnation of full chasubles. Full chasubles abundantly supported by tradition, and by the implications of the ceremonies of the liturgy. Full chasubles gladden and edify the faithful ; while narrow chasubles distress all people of taste and knowledge. The appellations : Roman, Gothic, French, Belgian, etc., inexact ; better to speak of full, medium and small chasubles.

CHAPTER IX

Shapes, measurements and proportions. Full chasubles easy to wear and quite convenient. Advice regarding the care of them.

CHAPTER X

Stole and maniple : bad shapes and ornamentation. Dalmatic and tunic ; how to distinguish them. The cope and its hood : errors and uglinesses ; true qualities and beauty ; good copes described. Humeral veil. Chalice veil and burse.

CHAPTER XVII

Painting, appliqué-work, tapestry and embroidery. A chasuble ornamented with two thousand figures. Summary of this work : the least possible amount of ornament, but that well-conceived, thoroughly appropriate and well-executed. Our watchword : vestments not ornaments. Our ideal : simplicity and beauty.

APPENDIX

The Labarum of Constantine. Historical note on banners. Dreadful abuse of pennons and flags in some churches. Banners considered according to the principles of decorative art. Commercial horrors contrasted with good banners. A masterpiece among banners.

LIST OF PLATES

---

*The figures in the text (339 in number) are indexed at the end of the
book along with the subjects which they illustrate.*

VESTMENTS AND VESTURE

CHAPTER I

ESSENTIAL PRINCIPLES AND EVOLUTION OF LITURGICAL VESTURE

A MANUAL of liturgical art must of necessity deal with a great number of particulars, for art expresses itself only in and through such particulars. But, if the manual confines itself to detail and attempts to give no comprehensive view of its subject, there is a real danger that the student will not acquire any general principles and will fail to grasp the unity of the whole. He will not see the wood for the trees. For that reason, since the succeeding chapters of this book are to be devoted to a detailed study of the qualities of liturgical vestments and vesture, it will be appropriate and convenient if this first chapter should lay down some general, directive principles. With this object in view, some of the ideas which are put forward in various parts of the book are here brought together into one context, and an attempt is made also to give a rapid sketch of the development of liturgical vesture from one period to another of the Christian centuries. But first let us consider the general principles which should govern such vesture.

We all have a tendency to take things out of their context and isolate them. We confine ourselves to a more or less restricted field, and we isolate the things which we see and the things which we use from their proper setting. But this isolation is purely our own and is repudiated by the facts. No single piece of ecclesiastical vesture is isolated, it has an intimate relation with other vestments. And all the vestments used in the liturgy, those of priest, deacon, subdeacon, and servers, those also of the altar and of the sanctuary, all these form a whole which again is not isolated. They have a definite part to play in the life of the Church and a definite rôle to fulfil. They belong, in fact, to that great whole which is called the liturgy, a great and important thing, for it is concerned with religion and worship and with the mysteries of our faith. In consequence of this fact the vestments of the Church have a dependent character and a well-marked relativity ; their sphere is large, but it has definite limits ; and it is by recognising this dependence and these limits that we shall achieve liturgical balance and harmony.

In order to grasp what qualities are common to all vestments and what are distinctive of each, it is of the first importance to have a clear idea of the purpose of a vestment in the broadest sense of that word. We should endeavour, that is, to realize the nature of a vestment and to seize its salient, or rather essential, quality.

Now common sense tells us, and good taste confirms its finding, that the chief quality of liturgical vesture is to vest well, that is, to clothe him well who wears it. This is the essential nature and the chief quality of costume. Everything else : material, colour, cut, stitch, style, ornamentation, all these differentiate and specialize a vestment ; they put it in this or that category ; but they are nevertheless secondary to its essence. Primarily and essentially a vestment is a garment.

But if a vestment is a garment, we must however beware of regarding it as we would regard any secular garment. For our world is so small, our times so lacking in permanence, we are surrounded by so many styles and sub-styles, so many ephemeral forms and fashions, that we should do wrong if we measured the vestments of the Church by contemporary standards. Some will say that this is a fault which is seldom or never committed. But that is an error, or at least an illusion ; and one is justified in believing that fashion, whether of male or female dress, and of whatever degree of value or want of value, does exert its influence. Are there not good people who, when they have to choose a vestment, demand what they call a "practical" vestment, in a "reasonable" style and of a "moderate" size ? I am afraid that very many of us, when we visit our ecclesiastical outfitter—or ought I to say artist ?—in order to purchase a chasuble or a cope, think a great deal about rigid symmetry, standard size and fashionable cut ; we think a great deal about the opinion of those around us. And so, without perceiving it, we drift away from the ideal and lose sight of the essential qualities of a vestment.

Where then are we to find vestments which have this essential quality ? The answer is that they are to be found with security and certainty in the early Christian centuries. The Church of the Greco-Roman world shared in the artistic feeling of that world. The Greeks are our unquestioned masters in the realm of art and taste, in a reasoned and genuine culture. Now that sense of beauty which was theirs without effort was shared in some degree by the Romans, and through them passed into the possession of the Church. There is no reason why we

FIG. 1. THE PROTOMARTYR OF THE HOLY EUCHARIST, BY G. B. CONTI
A very modern work, yet with all the grace of Christian antiquity
Oratory of St. Tarcisius, Rome

should quarrel with the fact. If that beauty is pagan in its origin, yet it has been baptized, it has been purified, it has been transformed into the beauty of Christian antiquity. Instead therefore of rejecting that good which was the possession of Greeks and of Romans, we shall accept it and rejoice in it, and we shall draw our profit from it.

In the first centuries of the Christian era the ministers of the Church, when they were performing their official duties, did not wear any distinctive liturgical and symbolical costume. They used the garments which were worn in everyday life by the Romans of the period, that is to say the long tunic (now the alb, *alba*, *linea*) and the cloak or overcoat (the *paenula*, now the chasuble.) But it seems to be tolerably certain that they would, when celebrating the Holy Sacrifice, from a sense of the reverence due to its dignity, wear a whiter tunic and a more beautiful *paenula* than those which they used on ordinary occasions, in the street or on a journey.[1] And soon the vestments which had to be worn at the altar became the "sacred vestments", *vestes sacratae*, as Pope Stephen calls them as early as the middle of the third century.[2] When the old Roman dress was no longer used in ordinary life, Christian bishops and priests continued to wear it. And they did so because this dress was dignified and beautiful, and was therefore specially suitable for Christian worship. To the items which have been already mentioned, the dalmatic, stole and maniple were presently added. We may say, in brief, that our liturgical vestments derive by direct descent from the secular dress of the ancient world. A short study of each of the elements of this dress will be made in later chapters ; but the reader will know already, at least in general, how our fathers and brethren in the faith were dressed. He will know from ancient monuments and from modern designs what was the simplicity and what the nobility of their costume. Who does not delight, for instance, in the figures of Ceccarini's "Ordination," now familiar in reproductions to the whole world ? There we see a bishop clad in a full *paenula* imposing hands upon deacons in long tunics, the folds of these being accentuated by simple *clavi* (stripes). The Saint Tarcisius that we reproduce (fig. 1) wears a tunic of the same kind. The painting is quite a modern one, but it has all the grace of that antiquity which we cannot help but love.

Now this suggests some questions which every lover of liturgical art might well put to himself. Can we without the gravest inconsistency ad-

[1] Benedict XIV affirms this definitely: *De Sacrosancto Missae Sacrificio*, lib. I, CH. VII.

[2] Duchesne: *Liber Pontificalis*, p. 154.

mire these things in antiquity and yet refuse to imitate them in our own day ? Can we say that those qualities of fullness and flow and simplicity are very well for the costume of persons represented in fresco or mosaic or sculpture, but quite unsuited for the bishops and priests of the twentieth century ? Must these latter be arrayed in skimpy vestments, stiff and overloaded with ornament ? Must they be dressed in

FIG. 2. ARCHBISHOP MAXIMIAN
Clad in long tunic and ample
chasuble.   Mosaic of the sixth
century
Church of St. Vitale, Ravenna

FIG. 3.   POPE HONORIUS
In a mosaic of the sixth century
(*Sant' Agnese fuori le muri*). The
paenula is circular and falls all
round the pope

garments which have neither style nor taste, though we willingly admire these qualities in the vestments of antiquity ? Is not this an absurdity ? Surely there is evidence here that modern fashions and a certain prim correctness have invaded the Church.

The antique vestment was wide and long ; it draped the body flowingly, it was finely decorative by its fullness and natural folds (figs. 2 and 3) and not by any super-added ornament. Such ornament, as we have said already, is a secondary and comparatively unimportant element; the vestment ought before all else to be really a vestment. Such is the primitive, fundamental and outstanding characteristic of

FIG. 4.   SAINT MAURUS, BISHOP, clad in long paenula; SAINT SEPTIMIUS, in dalmatic; and other personages.   Seventh century
Baptistery of St. John Lateran

church vesture.   It speaks not to the eyes only, but to the reason and to the heart.   We see at once the effect which it produces, and we recognise its sincerity and its worth.   And so we may summarise what has been said in these few words: The ancient ecclesiastical vesture, from which derive our present liturgical vestments, clothed a man properly and clothed him tastefully, for the reasons which have been given. It was tasteful apparel. That was its outstanding character; that was what its designers aimed at ; that was sufficient and with that they were content (fig. 4).

To this essential character of liturgical costume there corresponds a character of stability and permanence, which may be called the result of its qualities of simplicity and beauty. Such then is our typical and ideal liturgical vesture. It has suffered much in the course of the centuries, but it has not wholly perished. It is to it that we must turn if we would acquire a notion of perfect ecclesiastical vesture.

In this matter of vestments we may say that the first Christian period ends with the eighth century. There followed a period of many changes and transformations, in which the vestments submit to novelties of make and of ornamentation. The spirit of the early Middle Age, of the Romanesque and pre-Romanesque period, was sometimes rather rude, and yet did not lack solidity and inspiration. The various items of the ecclesiastical wardrobe underwent the influence of this spirit, yet without losing all contact with tradition, which manifests itself in the survival of a taste for the antique style. But, speaking generally, simple and dignified costume

FIG 5.   DURANDUS, BISHOP OF TOULOUSE.   xiith century
Cloister of the Abbey of Moissac, France

seems no longer to be the ideal. Changes are introduced very freely. The vestments are always ample, but their cut and trimming, their ornamentation with orfreys of interlaced work, gems and floriated designs, these things vary with the artistic taste of each country. As an example of this, consider the chasuble that Durandus of Toulouse (twelfth century) is represented as wearing in a bas-relief of the Abbey of Moissac (fig. 5).

During the three centuries which follow, that is during the Gothic period, there are further and very considerable changes. We are familiar

enough with the spirit, culture, and art of those centuries, and it is not
necessary to say much about them. But, as an example of their style in vestments, we may call attention to the S. Firminus of Amiens Cathedral (fig. 6). The representation is thoroughly statuesque, yet the saint has real distinction with his small and beautifully proportioned mitre, his chasuble with folds draping so easily, his dalmatic and long stole. If we study this figure carefully we shall be in a position to understand the contemporary ideas about vestments. The statue was carved by an artist of the thirteenth century, it is true, but he has impressed on the stone a beautiful attitude and beautiful lines. He has arrayed his bishop in beautiful vestments, of which we have so many examples from this golden age of the Gothic period. We may say, speaking generally, that vestments of full and generous dimensions are still to be found in the fourteenth and fifteenth centuries, but they do not achieve that high quality of which we have spoken. The art of embroidery has covered them with orfreys and with masses of intricate

FIG. 6.   SAINT FIRMINUS, XIIIth century
Notice the small mitre, full chasuble, long
tunic, etc. From the liturgical standpoint
a thoroughly well-dressed bishop
Cathedral of Amiens

needlework. These are very skilfully executed and are very rich and costly; the designs are sometimes bold and clear, sometimes very pretty and delicate; but the skill is really too great, the knowledge too elaborate. The age had in fact become sophisticated. Simplicity of spirit had given place to complexity, simplicity of taste to a desire for elaboration ; and so, under the influence of this secular evolution and simultaneously with it, the antique simplicity of ecclesiastical vesture passed away.

During the three centuries next after the Gothic period, tailors, embroiderers and manufacturers did worse still. They diminished the length and width of vestments, and on the other hand exaggerated the accidental ornament. We have a riot of elaborate orfreys and crosses, on which are embroidered numerous figures in theatrical postures and with pathetic expressions Every sort of appliqué work is used, sometimes not inelegant, often very complicated. Gilt and lace and other finery— these things are used to excess, and ecclesiastical vesture groans under a heavy mass of ugly elaboration. Such was the disastrous performance of the craftsmen of this period. In their worth, or rather in their wretchedness, the chasubles, copes and other vestments of this period go hand in hand with the swaggering costume worn by the exquisites of the Renaissance, or with the elaborate dress of the great lords of the eighteenth century in its monumental affectation and pride, or with the lace frills, embroidered waistcoats and rose-tinted coats of the Revolution. And so we come to the end of the eighteenth century. The decadence is complete. The liturgical vestment has ceased to be a vestment and has become an ornament, and an ornament in a style either of pompous affectation or of stilted ugliness.

But this degradation could not last, and the nineteenth century saw the beginnings of a revival in the domain of ecclesiastical vesture. In proportion as the ancient monuments of the Church were examined, and the more her devoted sons studied the Catholic and Roman liturgy, so did there grow a practical zeal for the dignity and beauty of vestments. This revival has spread over the world ; we find it in Germany, England, Austria, Belgium, France, Holland, and even as far afield as in America. We hope presently to give numerous examples which will illustrate its character.

But let us never forget this, that a return to the usages of the ages of faith should be submitted to the guidance and approval of the Church, which has the right and the power to legislate even in matters of the least importance. To the Church does it belong to weigh the arguments which are put before her ; to her does it belong to pronounce judgment. If in her unceasing love for those liturgical arts which serve her so well, she deigns to bless the new which is also old (*nova et vetera servavi tibi*), they are legion who will thank her with a deep filial gratitude ; it will be the consecration of the revival. Even so in the year 1925 the Holy Father blessed a great number of vestments, of modern make yet fragrant with the beauty of Christian antiquity (*nova et vetera*). So and with such approval will this ecclesiastical renascence be able to proceed. So may it take us back to the glories of the Middle Ages, and, better still, past them to that first Christian period when the faithful lived a life of charity in an atmosphere of simplicity and dignity. We shall gain infinitely by contact with those antique brothers of ours, with their noble spirit and simple taste. We shall love to see once more those long linen vestments, those simple dalmatics with *clavi* (stripes) and true sleeves, those full chasubles which vested bishops and priests and vested them with grace and dignity.

Those early centuries, therefore, will appear again and again in our pages. We shall show them a marked predilection because, as we have seen, they offer and will ever offer an ideal. But we do not suggest that there should be any sort of servile imitation of the past, that we should merely copy the vestments of antiquity, any more than that we should copy those of the Middle Ages or of the eighteenth century. The world of thought and of taste does not want any more of that inferior and fossilized art which was so widely practised in the nineteenth century and which unfortunately is still practised in certain places. What it wants is that we should seize the *essential* character of liturgical vesture, and that we should be *inspired* by the best, without respect to style or epoch or country. The consequence of such a logical and sincere effort will inevitably be the production of vestments which are not of any rigorously exact style, whether that be antique, Romanesque, Byzantine, Gothic, or Renaissance. It will produce Catholic vestments, yet vestments which shall be in harmony with the individual spirit, taste and feeling of each nationality. If this revival is allowed and encouraged by the Sacred Congregation of Rites, it will give us a truly liturgical art, which in its productions will proclaim that variety in unity and unity in variety which are the characteristic notes of the universal Church. [3]

3 These points will be appreciated when we give examples of what has been done and of the new methods.

CHAPTER II

CHURCH LINEN

THE reader had better be warned at the beginning of this chapter that it will traverse some familiar ideas, ideas which are very generally accepted and in some quarters very warmly cherished. It needs some courage to undertake and pursue the task of opposing such favourite ideas, of censuring what deserves censure, and of praising what deserves praise, but is either little known or misunderstood. The story goes that a certain sculptor used to say that his material, whether stone or marble, "trembled" before him. Here, however, the exact contrary is true, for the writer trembles before his material. But he believes that his readers will appreciate his sincerity ; and he hopes also that they will share his love for all that is good in the domain of liturgical art, and join with him in his desire for the best.

THE MATERIAL.—Having said so much, by way of apology, let us proceed. The first step is easy. We have to settle what is the proper liturgical material for the articles about which we are going to speak, and we find that there is practically only one material, namely linen, good white linen. And under this name we would include that hempen fabric which is called canvas. [1] If the linen be particularly fine and closely woven, then it is lawn or cambric. Such then is the material, and of this must, or ought to be made all altar cloths, cloths used in Mass, amices, albs, and those garments which derive from, or are closely connected with, the alb. Stuffs woven wholly or in part of cotton or wool are not liturgical material.

It is, however, *permitted* to make surplices, towels and credence-table cloths of a mixed fabric, or even of cotton only. But such *toleration* and certain special indults do not invalidate the plain desire of the Church for linen cloth. We are very quick to allege our poverty when we have to provide for our own church, or present to another, the true liturgical material, and we satisfy ourselves by spending money on trivial ornament or absolutely superfluous lace.

[1] The Congregation of Rites has decreed that canvas is equivalent to linen for liturgical purposes. (15 May, 1819.)

11

BEAUTY of plain, unadorned linen.—This true liturgical material has beauty of itself without adornment. The reasons for this are not recondite. We have explained them intelligibly, we hope, in the preceding chapter, and we shall return to them more than once in the present chapter, and again in chapter xvi, where we have to speak of ornamentation. So we may be quite brief in this place.

Simplicity of fabric is beautiful ; at all events it is more beautiful than complexity, intricacy, finicality, prettiness, as exemplified by most of the petty ornament that is imposed so generally on church linen. The linen cloths and linen vestments of the liturgy are quite as they should be when they are made of a good white linen, when their shape and dimensions are correct and proper, when they are adapted to their purpose and to the persons who wear them. They have then a character of great simplicity, they are restful to the eye, and they satisfy the reason. And they achieve this result without great effort or minute toil, and without useless expense. They are then what they ought to be, and *all that they ought to be;* they are *irreproachable.* Isn't that enough ?

Now, we are confident that the liturgical and artistic principles are understood ; what is wanted is logical practice. We grant that it is in harmony with the festal spirit to allow on festal vestments a certain moderate, simple and honest ornament ; but we think it is time to protest against the general invasion of commonplace decoration, whereby the length of the material is diminished and sometimes the beautiful linen surface entirely replaced.

The decoration of church linen takes the forms generally of lace, of which we shall speak presently, and of embroidery. White embroidery (English embroidery, Richelieu, satin or feather-stitch), embroidery on bunting, and embroidery in coloured thread on the material itself, all these suffer deplorably in their shape when they are washed and ironed (fig. 7). Furthermore, those designs in red and blue produce from a distance a bad tint as of wine lees ; while if seen from near to, they are rather glaring and startling. They are very popular in certain countries, notably in Belgium. ² Plain red embroidery upon the white linen sometimes gives good results, if the design is strong and clear. But, as a matter of fact, one rarely meets with such embroidery. And there is this

---

² We read in *L'Ouvroir liturgique:* "Our sacristies (of Belgium) are swamped with red and blue embroideries, both garish and unsightly." And again : "We advise the abandonment of this eternal red-blue, which some people seem to think essential to Gothic embroidery." It would be at once more definite and more *logical* to advise the total abandonment also of the *eternal* red which, for reasons of gain and Gothic, is extolled as an additional beauty for albs and surplices. The fact is that both these garments are beautiful without this red embroidery.

to be noted also, that the thread used, being generally a red, or rather a bold carmine, does not harmonize well with many of the silk stuffs and trimmings employed in the vestments.

As for embroidery in white on white, there is very little of it. It is in fact an artistic mistake ; for, after all, *visibility* is one of the chief qualities of decoration. It ought to be possible to distinguish, even at a distance, we do not say all the details, but the main lines of the design. Now in the case of these white embroideries, on an alb for instance, what happens is nearly always this, that we strain and weary our eyes and we see nothing. What then is the good of this petty ornament on our linen vestments ?

THE CARE OF CHURCH LINEN.—It is obvious that church linen should be kept clean and in good condition. If we change our own personal linen frequently and get it washed and ironed, we owe the same duty and even more strictly to albs, surplices, rochets, amices, and above all to corporals, palls, purificators and altar cloths. They have a right to exact and careful treatment, to frequent and zealous attention.

FIG. 7. A TYPICALLY UGLY PALL
The floral decoration and the monogram are embroidered in reddish thread. Observe the wretched effect of the crumpled lace

We think it useful to utter a word of warning against certain ingredients used in modern washing, ingredients which accelerate and facilitate the work, but help to damage the material. Let us endeavour to be content with hot water, and when poured on the linen let it meet there nothing but a layer of soda or a layer of ash. Some linen, as for instance the purificators, cannot be cleansed of its stains unless it is *boiled* in the water, with a little potash added. After that the work may be completed with soap, deft hands, rain water, and as much sun as possible ; for the sun not content with drying, will whiten and purify. These simple instructions will suffice for the clerical readers to whom this book is addressed. We should trust the specialists in this matter, as for instance certain communities of nuns and certain devout persons, who acquit themselves of this task with a particular attention and love. And we might give the same advice with regard to repairs, for it is no inconsiderable gift to be able to sew, or hem, or darn well.

All church linen, whether cloths or vestments, should be ironed. If albs or surplices become crumpled, an ironing every now and then between the washings puts them in good condition again. The corporal ought to be starched ; it ought not to be as limp as a piece of wet rag, so that the priest when he comes to collect the particles of the host with the paten cannot hold it up with the other hand. A slight stiffness in the material makes this task easier. The pall, if it is only a folded corporal, or if it is made of two pieces of linen sewn together without any stiff substance inside, ought to be starched in order to give it the required rigidity. The altar cloth could be starched slightly. As for the remaining cloths, stiffness makes them unsuitable for their purposes, and if we stiffen the linen vestments (alb, etc.) they lose their pliancy, flow and grace. Sometimes they are so starched as to produce great humps on him who wears them, an effect which is always ugly and often ridiculous.

A certain dose of starch is necessary for the accordion pleat. Dom Anselm Veys is in agreement with the best tradition and the best taste when he answers the question : "Is it any longer a surplice if there are no pleats ?" and we may apply his words not only to the surplice but also to alb, rochet and cotta. "Speaking historically," he says, "pleating is an innovation, introduced here and there about the year 1500 and spreading, without becoming general, from the seventeenth to the nineteenth century." Most ancient documents show albs and surplices which are full, long, and flowing. It is therefore more liturgical, that is to say more traditional, not to pleat. This custom seems to have been introduced through a certain finicking spirit and an anxiety for a cleanliness which is more apparent than real. It was supposed that the surplice which is folded back in its pleats keeps cleaner, while the fact is that the pleats prevent the equal distribution of the dust, which accumulates on their edges. From the aesthetic point of view, pleats presuppose starch and stiffness and are artificial and therefore ugly. The only beautiful pleats are those which produce a flowing and natural draping. . . As to the word "surplice" it has nothing to do with pleat, but signifies a linen choir garment worn *over* a *skin tunic* (*super-pelli-ceum*) . . . .[3] In brief, this pleating does not suit either our surplices or our albs. It may be urged in its favour that garments which are so treated can be folded up into a small space, like bundles of laths, and so we solve the problem of room. But we must be on our guard against this practical spirit, which if it has its way will sometimes ruin all sense

[3] *L'Ouvroir liturgique*, No. 11, 1925. It may be noted that the derivation here criticised is more plausible in French : "surplice" is *surplis* and "pleats" is *plis*.

of what is good and beautiful. And isn't it just as practical to hang them up in a cupboard with double doors, or with a curtain that runs easily on a rod ? or even to fold them simply and put them away in a drawer ? If that be done they will not have those fussy pleats which are inflicted on them by a too rigorous treatment ; they will keep their natural character and they will be adapted to their work, which is to clothe the priest or the cleric respectably.

LACE.—It is quite certain that before the fifteenth century, in spite of some innovations in the vestments of the Church, a predominant consideration was given to beauty of proportions, to the form and intimate nature of things, to truth and substance. In more concrete terms, those ages confined themselves to good proportions, to beautiful lines and to substantial materials, and lace was entirely unknown. And to-day also the liturgy and rubricists, while not unfamiliar with lace, require only linen cloths and vestments of linen. Such then is the voice of the Church, identical throughout the centuries ; and such is the tradition of the liturgy.

The true history of the subject which now occupies us is quite clear. The Renaissance brought with it a very considerable change in ideas and taste, and destroying many ancient things substituted for them much that was new and deplorable. Consider for instance the revolution in taste. The new taste patronized on the one hand pomp and pretentiousness, and on the other prettiness and supposed charm. To this latter category belongs lace. It was in fact a pretty thing which won the favour of the rich and became an indispensable accessory of various articles of feminine dress, and of various parts of the masculine wardrobe also. And then, and quite soon, it began to decorate the vestments of the liturgy. We are not revealing any secret if we say that the clergy of that epoch were often contaminated by the spirit of the world which was then at its full height. Great lords and great ladies doted on lace ; and why should the clergy be out of the fashion ? It remains to us now as a symbol, as a sign significative of the frivolity of mind, manners and taste of that period. We desire a more solid Christian and ecclesiastical life, and its vital complement a simpler, worthier and stronger religious art than that which characterized those days, and therefore we very naturally desire to eliminate lace from vestments and church linen. At the same time we are very ready to allow its use in domestic life, for graceful mantilla, for dress and linen, for table cloths and curtains. But, because it is rather a frivolous material, we have a right to ask that it should not invade the costume which we wear in church. Sound

ideas on such subjects are natural to us priests, or at least they ought to
be. A sane consideration, free from routine and superficial motives (as
that we have been accustomed to it from childhood, or have worn it
often, or know that it pleases our folk)—such consideration will tell us
that linen cloths and vestments gain in every way if they return to that
noble simplicity which excludes triviality and affectation.

The price of lace is such as nearly always to react unfavourably on
the church linen, that is to say that if we dispensed with lace we might
have linen of a better quality, we might have more of it, and we might be
able to change it more frequently. A Carmelite father has very justly
said : "We may lay it down as a general rule that all ornamentation
which is not necessary is therefore excessive, because it will always be
to the detriment of the vestment itself."[4] And his words apply also to
church linen. Yet people go taking away the good honest linen cloth
from alb or surplice, depriving them of their proper length and whiteness, and substituting intricate and useless lace, which by reason of its
apertures produces only vague transparencies and indeterminate greys !

Of course the character of lace varies very much according to its kind.
There is handmade lace, made with needle, crochet, or bobbin (guipure,
torchon, Cluny lace, etc.), and there is an immense deal of machine-
made lace. This latter is sometimes unspeakably ugly ; yet the machine
can produce quite interesting and pretty results and very successful
imitations of the best work. Much handmade lace needs a certain
arithmetical facility rather than any true artistic knowledge, and it
gives us designs repeated over and over again with an intolerable dull-
ness and vulgarity. The best lace is generally the result of efforts many
times renewed, and of a talent which for all its admirable accuracy is an
extremely narrow one. Such work may be undeniably delicate and
pretty so that it flatters our senses and often our vanity also ; its
minute interlacing and reticulation whether in thread or in silk may be
extravagantly and infinitely multiplied ; its tiny designs may sometimes
be charming, but generally are loosely shaped or misshapen, or on the
contrary hard, angular and almost thorny, clinging to all that they
meet. But, however good the lace may be, we prefer the vestments and
linen of the church to be without it. And this not from any mere anti-
quarianism, nor in deference to any style or to the rules of any school,
but simply from reasons of art, that is to say of *liturgical* art. And by
this we mean that artistic tradition which has its roots in the past, yet

4 R. P. Albert de l'Enfant Jésus : *Quelques règles pour la confection des princi-
paux ornements liturgiques de l'autel et de ses ministres* (conclusion).

is ever progressing and advancing to greater perfection. This tradition when it encounters any ornament—and lace is no more than an ornament—which is out of harmony with the dignity and solemnity of the liturgy, seeks ever to bring us back with reason and intelligence to the simplicity of the past.

But let us hasten to add that there are no rules in these matters. Although we have alleged liturgical, aesthetic and economic reasons against lace, yet we have not said that all lace without distinction is to be banned. Many kinds of lace have been and are being produced, some of which are superb and others a miracle of delicate work. We may mention the laces of England, Spain, Flanders and Sicily ; those also of Alençon, Florence, Milan and Venice. These laces and a few others add a special beauty and distinction to the rochets of prelates. In many churches the other members of the clergy, and the men and boys who serve at the altar, wear vestments of linen which are without lace and perfectly simple. We humbly submit to competent authority this suggestion for an appropriate distinction.

THE CORPORAL, on which rests the Body of Christ (hence its name, from *corpus*), is the most important item of church linen. It was originally a real altar cloth and used to be spread out on the altar by the deacons. A Roman *ordo* which was used on Carolingian territory tells us that it "ought to be of pure linen because our Saviour's body was wrapped in a white winding-sheet" and that it "ought to be big enough to cover the whole surface of the altar."[5] But these large dimensions were not the general rule. Yet this sacred cloth was quite large, and it is only since the Renaissance that it has been reduced to the little square of linen which the priest or deacon places upon the top altar-cloth. A corporal of good dimensions as nowadays understood is one that extends from the tabernacle or canon to the outer edge of the altar. It may be smaller than this rule would involve, if the altar be very deep.

The important thing is that it should be big enough to hold the chalice, paten, host, other hosts whether in or out of a ciborium, and the ciborium cover when this has to be opened. We all know that this cloth has to be folded: *Corporale plicatum, quod ex lino tantum esse debet;* and it is folded symmetrically so as to form nine practically equal squares. A very small cross in red thread, in marking-stitch for instance, and as flat as possible, indicates the side which should be towards

[5] Mgr. Batiffol : *Leçons sur la Messe*, p. 83, note 3.

B

the celebrant. A good deal of ingenuity has been expended on designing
and publishing minute crosses of a definitely Gothic style, which, it is
claimed, are very suitable for this important cloth. But this is mere
trifling and finicality. Let us see to it that we have a small cross of the
ordinary shape (*crux immissa*) or another, for corporal, pall and puri-

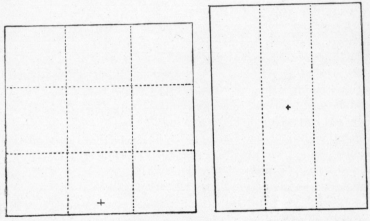

FIGS. 8 & 9.   DESIGNS FOR CORPORAL AND PURIFICATORY
Lace would add nothing but petty frivolity. Without it they are all that
they should be

ficatory, and that will be quite satisfactory (fig. 8 and 9). We speak in
various chapters of ornament which is out of place on these cloths and
of lace which gets in the way of the priest's fingers and becomes horribly
rumpled. Let us add that particles of the host may strike against these
little decorations or stick in the lace.

If one is offered this sort of thing as a present and wants to make the
best of a bad job, I do not see why one may not do what was done by a
priest friend of mine. He was given, for a corporal, a piece of linen with
lace decoration, decoration which in the eyes of the lady who gave it was
most attractive. He made a gift of it to a future bride of his parish, as
an exceptionally fine handkerchief ! He did well ; for after all the intentions of the Church take precedence of the wishes of this or that devout
person.

Dom Anselm Veys in *L'Ouvroir* has a very good note on the corporal,
pall and finger-cloth. "To refrain from ornamenting these three cloths,"
he says, "is from every point of view beyond reproach." But why then
vacillate presently and allow intricate little decorations, even indeed of

cotton lace. If these cloths without such decorations are irreproachable, then let us have the courage not to accept what is open to reproach. The better course is here a very easy course.

THE PALL.—We have mentioned palls elsewhere in this chapter and we have reproduced one which is a typical example— of what a pall ought not to be. Its devastating ugliness is a sufficient condemnation. It is decorated with the conventional monogram, badly drawn flowers, and lace which adds its complement of ugliness to this liturgical object (fig. 7). And how many other very similar horrors are current among us ![6] Another

FIG. 10. A PALL DISPLAYING A
FEARSOME FISH,

which at the least is distracting, and the lace, while regular enough on paper, would crumple badly in reality

pall that we submit to the reader's notice (fig. 10) displays a fearsome fish, which at the very least is a distracting object, and then has round its edges a lace border which behaves very well on paper, but in real life would crumple horribly. The reader will certainly be glad to turn to two other palls, exquisite specimens embroidered in fine silk (figs. 11 and 12). But palls of this quality are expensive. One may indulge in one of them, use it on great feasts, and then wrap it up and put it away. Speaking generally, since a pall has to be washed, it is much simpler to have nothing on it but a small cross of thread. We shall then not notice so readily the distortions that come from washing. The pall with the lamb already has some slight irregularities in the design, which we scarcely notice, so pleasing is the whole effect. But what if this is washed and resewn? I add a pattern which may be of service (fig 13). Keep the proportions, embroider the cross and the border in red thread, and you will then have a pall far better than one with tortured design, or than one overloaded with or denuded of all ornament.

[6] A certain paper suggests embroidering a pall with gold thread, decorating another with festoons and worked figures, lining another with satin in such a way that it may show through openings in the linen. We are told also that the materia of the pall is sometimes arranged like a pillow-case, with buttons and button-holes. From all which petty stratagems and evil devices, *libera nos, Domine!*

Formerly the pall and corporal were one, or rather the pall did not exist. The corporal took its place, for it was big enough to allow of its

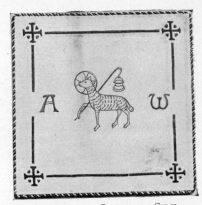

FIGS. 11 & 12.   TWO BEAUTIFUL PALLS, EMBROIDERED IN COLOURED SILK
Thin cording along the edges protects them much better than lace
(*A. E. Grossé, Bruges*)

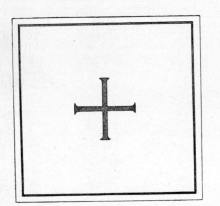

FIG. 13.   A PALL ATTRACTIVE FOR ITS
SIMPLICITY
The cross and border lines being in red
thread.   A smaller cross and no lines
would be better

FIG. 14.   A PICTORIAL PALL
Representing Our Lady and Child in
very good style ; but the subject is
too big for a pall
(*Société liturgique de Nîmes*)

being drawn over the offerings to cover them.   But now we have the separate pall, *parva palla linea*.   That it be small yet big enough for its purpose, and that it be made of linen, that is all that is required by the *Ritus servandus* at the beginning of the Missal.   Sew together two or four

thicknesses of linen to form a rectangle of four equal sides, let it be stiff
and therefore starched, and let it be large enough to be placed in position and removed easily.　You will then have the "little pall made of
linen"; and this is the way things are done in many churches.　In some
countries a light but sufficiently rigid piece of cardboard is always
inserted between the folds of the linen, which is sewn up on the three
other sides ; this form of pall is very convenient to use.　The two fine
palls, figs. 11 and 12, are made in this way.

There is a not unimportant detail.　A *thick* cardboard (*carta grassa*) is
not allowed.[7]　Even with a thin card covered with linen there is this
risk : a drop of the precious Blood may be on the edge of the chalice
and be absorbed by the linen of the pall and penetrate to the cardboard,
which is not washed.　You may doubt the possibility of this occurring ;
but if you admit the possibility and still more if you find it actually
happens, you ought in prudence to be content with linen only, whether
double or quadruple, and that starched; or if you prefer a more rigid
pall, which has its advantages, you may prefer instead of cardboard
to use a piece of celluloid with the corners slightly rounded off ; it is
light and washable.　I only throw this out as a suggestion ; it has been
mentioned in *L'Ouvroir liturgique*, 6 and 13 Nov. 1927.

THE PURIFICATORY is folded twice on itself, giving a triple thickness.
An appropriate width of the folded cloth is the diameter of the cup of
the chalice.　Its length should be twice the height of the chalice plus
the diameter of the cup.　But it is not easy to keep rigorously to this
length, since chalices vary in height.　We have already signalized the
essential qualities of church linen ; one of these qualities, which the
purificatory ought always to have, is absolute flexibility.　So any
starching at all is a mistake, for it interferes with the purpose for which
the celebrant and deacon have to use this cloth.　Nor is it entirely unnecessary to insist on this point.　Figure 9 shows an excellent purificatory.

THE AMICE hardly appears as a liturgical vestment till the eighth
century.　Before that it was an item of clothing, a kerchief which was
used by men and women for reasons of hygiene.　Rabanus Maurus calls
it the *superhumerale* and likens it to the ephod : "*Primum . . indumen-
tum est ephod bad, quod interpretatur superhumerale lineum.*"[8]　But it is
very unlikely that its origin is so remote.　We find it designated by the
word *anagolagium* or *anabolagium*, which seems to be a corruption of
anaboladion, the Greek for a garment of the mantle type, which is

---

[7] Martinucci, *Man. Sacr. Caerem.*, Rome, 1871, *V*, p. 525.
[8] *Bad :* linen or linen cloth—Vigouroux : *Dictionnaire de la Bible*, art. *Lin*.

thrown round the shoulders. That is what the amice was to Amalarius of Metz in the ninth century, for he defines it as a linen cloth "*quo collum undique cingimus.*"

The amice was used also as a covering for the head. A trace of this practice may be found in the liturgy, for the bishop when ordaining a sub-deacon puts the amice on to his head, and the priest when vesting for mass places the amice on his head before adjusting it round his neck and shoulders. In the majority of the old religious orders whose members wear a hood, the amice is put on over the hood, and the head is then covered or uncovered according to the precise directions of the rubrics : "*capite cooperto . . . detecto capite . . . caput cooperit.*" Such priests use the hood and amice where the secular clergy use the biretta.

Up to the middle of the twelfth century the amice remained quite simple and quite white, to receive gradually ornamentation in colour and of gold or pearls, and those *paramenta* or little pieces of embroidery which were sewn on to it. It is certain that this ornamentation was in favour principally during the Gothic period, a period of art which for all its great vitality no longer understood the noble and beautiful simplicity of ancient times. And it is certain also that this ornamentation was of the nature of an appendage and patchwork which overloaded and stiffened the amice. Those in our own times who have followed the Middle Ages in the most minute points have adopted these *parurae* (apparels), or else they use red embroidery. But excepting in the case of religious who wear hoods, this ornamentation is at once inconvenient and invisible. It has indeed been suggested that the rubrics should be revised and that the amice should be worn much as it is worn by monks, just to allow these apparels to be seen. Whatever comes of that, the rubrics make no mention of these apparels, but of a cross only, and they say simply : "*eo vestium collaria circumtegens.*" The secular clergy are faithful to this when they cover their collars right round, inserting the edge of the amice between collar and neck.

ALB.—The alb is evidently one of the most important of the liturgical vestments. It derives in the direct line from the long, white sleeved tunic which was worn by the Greeks and Romans under the Empire. Hegesippus tells us that James the Brother of the Lord was clothed in a linen tunic, and the alb has been known precisely by this name of linen tunic (*tunica linea*); it has also been called *talaris* or *tunica talaris*, because it reached to the feet, and *tunica alba* because of its colour. This long tunic is still with us, a noble vestment, enveloping the priest entirely in its physical whiteness and reminding him of that spiritual purity which should adorn his soul, especially when he is mystically sacrificing the Lamb without spot : *"Dealba me, Domine . . . ut dealbatus in sanguine Agni . . "*

One of the aims of this work is the simplification of the vestments, and the author has already endeavoured in this chapter to show the beauty of unadorned linen garments. Let us be more precise and consider now the beauty of a simple, unadorned alb, which is beautiful for the very reason that it is simple. If an alb is made of a linen of good quality, if it is quite white and newly ironed, if it is neatly arranged on the person according to the directions of the rubrics: *"elevat ante . . . et a lateribus hinc et inde,"*

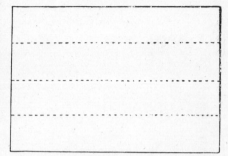

FIG. 15.   DESIGN FOR A FINGER CLOTH, 16 x 20 ins., without lace, and folded in four

instead of being smoothed out at front and sides to the semblance of a great zinc cylinder and with a mass of pleated folds bunched up at the back, then this simple alb will do very well indeed even for a feast-day. It will be a very dignified vestment and one very superior to those albs adorned with networks of flowers, with bobbin or crochet lace, with white or red embroideries. It will be a vestment like to that simple linen vestment, so striking and so pure, with which the Church is clothed in St. John's vision: *"Datum est illi ut cooperiat se byssino splendenti et candido.9* We may add that a very clear contrast is produced if one wears above this simple alb of very restful character, a rich chasuble, whether red, green, or violet-purple. And the contrast is an advantageous one, for it is the union of two qualities which seem mutually exclusive, and yet are good friends : simplicity and richness. But this effect cannot be obtained if we insist on ornament everywhere, on the alb, over the whole surface of the chasuble, on the amice and even on the girdle.

But we must not be narrow-minded in these matters and we must not be supposed to forbid any ornament whatever on albs, even for feast-days. We have already explained our position with regard to that lace which has won such an importance in men's minds and in church linen that sometimes the essential character of a vestment is almost destroyed, or at least considerably impaired. We shall not repeat what has been

9 Apoc. XIX, 8.

said on this point, but refer the reader to pages 15 to 17.

Other kinds of ornament which have great vogue in certain countries are the following : apparels, whether continuous or non-continuous, and embroidery in coloured thread on the material itself of the alb. Let us say a word or two about each of these, and first about the non-

FIG. 16. AP-PARELLED ALB AND LONG STOLE Detail of a tomb-stone of the xivth century

continuous apparel, which is a square or oblong piece of embroidery sewn on to the bottom of the alb, in front and at the back, and also on the wrists. If these apparels are made of rich stuff, such as cloth of gold, or are richly embroidered, the effect is deplorable, for such rigid ornaments prevent the linen from draping properly. It is, however, possible to choose for the apparel a material so flexible that it does not have this effect. As is well known, the Middle Ages made great use of these *paramenta* of which we spoke when dealing with the amice. They ornamented the albs of popes, bishops and priests, and we have many representations of them in the various arts (fig. 16).

The nineteenth century with its zeal, or rather infatuation for the Middle Ages, strove to copy these accessories and many other unnecessary items. Viollet-le-Duc in France, the Baron de Béthune in Belgium, and Pugin in England, were the leaders in this movement. But this rather petty and narrow and imitative art is languishing and dying ; the cold chill of routine and convention has stolen over it, and we prophesy its death at no very distant date. Men are seeking now more and more to preserve the primary and dominant character of things and to discard defective custom and mere antiquarianisms. Now it is quite certain that these non-continuous apparels are only reminiscences of a past age, and that they are not very satisfactory as ornaments ; for they are no more than a corruption or atrophy of the continuous apparel. Already there has been a return to the continuous form in the shape of bands *right round* the wrists and skirt of the alb. Brocade may be used for such long apparels, but not any brocade of complicated colour or striking design. For such complication or assertiveness disturbs the peace of the vest-ment. If we use woven ribbons of thin texture and single colour, then success is assured. Such apparels provide "tranquil zones" and are much more decorative than complicated ornament which so often produces mere discord. They correspond to the red or violet-purple *clavi* (stripes) which stood out so well from the white ground of the ancient tunic, the only difference being that the stripes on the tunic ran vertically from head to foot whereas these run horizontally and round the garment. The alb of figure 18 has a trimming of an ashen blue in very flexible silk ; this band is in harmony with the plush cross of

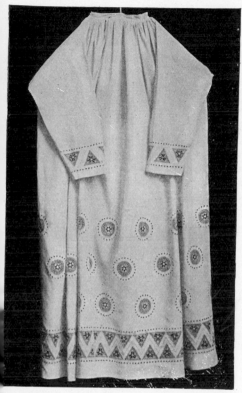

FIG. 17.   AN ALB WITH DELICATE AND WELL-
ARRANGED ORNAMENT

FIG. 18.   A BEAUTIFUL ALB WITH
A CONTINUOUS APPAREL IN SILK

a chasuble which is used with that alb on great feasts. Since it was impossible to find the trimming in a smaller width for the sleeves, these carry no apparels. The alb does not suffer by it, but has enough ornament already in the apparel of its skirt. The important thing is to secure an exact correspondence of colour between the apparels and the cross, or even the material, of the chasuble. An appropriate distinction may be made by having albs with broader apparels for the priest, and narrower ones for deacon and subdeacon.

It is obvious that a linen vestment with apparels must be relieved of these before it is sent to the wash. This means unsewing and sewing again. It means some work, but it need not have to be done often ; for if the apparelled alb is worn only on great feasts and then folded properly and kept in a good place, it may last in quite decent condition for one, or even two years without need of washing.

We have treated of these continuous coloured apparels on albs because they are conformable to aesthetic principles, and because they are an ornament without finicality, complication or pretentiousness.

FIG. 19.   DESIGN FOR EMBROIDERY IN RED THREAD
A very original and delicate composition, but far too complicated

But there are some albs which have not got these master qualities. In the first place there are those which from the waist, or even from the middle of the chest downwards, are composed of lace. The lace is transparent, the black soutane shows through, and the result is that the vestment ought now to be called not the *alba* but the *nigra*. In the second place we have these lace albs lined with red silk. I was told by a certain parish priest that he was vesting once in the sacristy of a church in a big town and found one of these albs laid out for him. He protested gently that he was not a cardinal and had no right to wear this panoply of red. "Oh, that's all right," was the answer, "it's very effective." Such is the consequence of an extravagant use of lace and of an effort after pretentious effects without consideration for the liturgy or for edification. And that is why these pages are a plea for the more extensive use of the alb properly so called, that is to say of the long white tunic (*tunica alba*) entirely free from adventitious ornament. But we do not wish to be pedantic about it. Ornament that is sober and does not usurp the place of the pure linen is quite legitimate ; and so we do not ban the continuous or non-continuous apparel of coloured stuff for the wrists or skirt of the alb. Moreover we should like to make it clear in this place, and we shall repeat it again, that we have no intention of usurping the functions of the Sacred Congregation of Rites. It hardly needs saying and yet we say it to avoid all misunderstanding : All our criticisms and suggestions are made in fullest deference to the authority of that Congregation.

Embroideries in red, made with marking thread, are not apparels added to the alb but decorations of its actual material. We have already said that carmine thread is harsh and does not go well with most silk vestments. But if we adopt it, let the design be clear, sober and mode-

FIG. 20.　RED EMBROIDERY FOR AN ALB
Remarkably strong and clear design

rate. The alb gains nothing by being invaded right up to the waist by poor patterns of mere reddish thread, by floating streamers and inscriptions, by branches and gently twisting flourishes. Fig. 20 shows a composition of great character, a clear and vigorous design, which could be used for the ornamentation of the skirt of an alb and for its wrists (in a smaller size). The effect would be satisfying if it were used, for instance, with a white chasuble having trimmings in gold and carmine red.

THE GIRDLE varies somewhat from country to country. That used generally in France and Belgium is quite white, of small diameter, and terminates in two tassels of moderate dimensions. It is very simple, very easy to use, and costs very little. Other girdles are sold with many tassels, arranged like the tassels of a bishop's or cardinal's hat. There is no need to say that they are very inconvenient. And the same may be said of those alluring contraptions, of a supposed festal character, which are made of white silk and imitation gold, and which terminate in metal trimmings and spangles. Apart from their exceedingly pretentious character, they are far more expensive than simple girdles of white linen thread which have all the necessary qualities. At Rome the girdle is often of the colour of the liturgical season or of the feast. In Spain it is made of white and red cotton thread, or of white and blue.

Photo: Alinari

FIG. 21. POPE SIXTUS IV IN A LONG ROCHET APPOINTING PLATINA HIS LIBRARIAN
By Melozzo da Forli

Some English girdles are very embarrassing on account of their thickness, and especially on account of their exaggerated length. A girdle that is too short is of course useless ; but, on the other hand, there is no point in having your girdle so long that you have to wind it twice round the waist, unless you want it to hang down and trail in a disagreeable and possibly inconvenient fashion. A total length of five yards, apart from the tassels, is sufficient, unless a man be very stout. Having said so much we may pass on, for the girdle is an article of liturgical vesture which is of minor importance. If any proof of this were needed we might point to the fact that there is no legislation about it. It may be of silk or of cotton ; it may be of the same colour as the chasuble you are wearing ; but it is best when made of white thread.

THE ROCHET, SURPLICE AND COTTA are related to the alb, which for-

FIGS. 22 & 23. FROM THE FUNERAL OF ST. FINA, BY DOMENICO GHIRLANDAIO
Note the long surplices which were still in use in Italy in the full tide of the Renaissance

merly down to the middle of the thirteenth century was the garment not only of the priest at the altar, but also of all the clerks. The surplice and rochet were at first as long, or nearly as long, as the alb, and they remained so for several centuries. Since that is an historical fact and has been elucidated by many liturgists, notably by Fr. J. Braun S.J.,[10] there is no point in devoting space to it here. But since some readers, who have no ready access to the specialists, may be interested in the artistic evidence for this fact, we mention a few examples of rochets

[10] *Die liturgische Gewandung im Okzident und Orient*, 1907.

and surplices which reach below the knees. First there is the soft and
pleasing "Ordination of St. Laurence" of Fra Angelico painted in 1449 in
the studio of Nicholas V. Then there is that painting in the Vatican which
represents Sixtus IV (1471-1484) appointing Platina as his librarian

FIG. 24. A FINE,
PLAIN SURPLICE
WITH WIDE SLEEVES
The circular open-
ing for the neck is
the most practical
and best

FIG. 25. SURPLICE
SPOILED BY USE-
LESS EMBROIDERY
AND UNNECESSARY
LACE

FIG. 26. TYPICAL
UGLINESS
The cotta is far too short
and with its accordion
pleats turns this little
boy into a sort of doll

(fig. 21). Then there is the "Funeral of St. Francis" a fresco painted by
Ghirlandaio, in Santa Trinità in Florence. And finally there is the
"Funeral of St. Fina," by the same, at S. Gimignano (figs. 22 and 23).

There are two paintings which are much less well known and are
liturgically very instructive. The first, a work of Stefano Sasseta,
represents Francis of Assisi as a very young man hearing Mass a short
while before he left the world.[11] The priest is represented as wearing an
alb with a small apparel, and a full chasuble ornamented vertically with

[11] This painting, preserved in the Berlin museum, is reproduced in the *Revue
de l'Art chrétien*, May-June, 1910.

a coloured orfrey. The server wears a true surplice, which falls down to
the feet, and which reminds us of the alb, except that there is no girdle

FIG. 27. SIMPLE AND EXCELLENT SURPLICES,
Reaching below the knee, as required by St. Charles Borromeo

round the waist and the sleeves are very full. There is no doubt that
Sasseta has reproduced the vestments that were in use in the Italy of
his day, and this "Mass" was painted before 1450. The second example,

which also displays linen vestments of beautiful dimensions, is a panel from a retable in the cathedral of Leon, carved in the fifteenth century, in which we see clergy and servers in full and long surplices, exactly like those worn by the two acolytes reproduced in fig. 27. And, to repeat, the use of these full vestments continued even after the sixteenth

FIG. 28.   A GOOD SURPLICE
REACHING TO THE KNEES
The stuff is abundant and
flexible. No slit down the front,
no strings, no ribbons. Excellent
circular opening at the neck

FIG. 29.   A SHORT SURPLICE,
Badly decorated with lace and
slit down the front, where it
closes very awkwardly

century. As Dr. Adrian Fortescue pointed out, the illustrations of a pontifical published at Venice in the eighteenth century still show long full surplices without lace. Nevertheless the shortening began at the Renaissance, that period so disastrous for liturgical art. "Since that period they have been considerably shortened in most places, and there may be seen in Italy some that do not go below the waist. These regrettable changes, which are contrary to ancient tradition as well as to the symbolical meaning of the *linea*, have been introduced without the support of any written text and merely with the toleration of authority."[12]

There is every appearance that S. Charles Borromeo had noticed with regret this tendency to shorten rochets and surplices, for he prescribes that they should be long enough to reach to a point about midway between the knee and the foot.[13]

Martinucci, papal Master of Ceremonies, speaks with irony and vigour of certain modern surplices, which in their effort to be pretty have become nothing more than unsuitable ornament : *"Superpelliceum, cujus forma nunc multiplex ad merum ornamentum redactum est . . . cavendum ne forma tum etiam nimia elegantia indecens sit . . . Dissimulare non possumus quod quorumdam superpelliceorum ornamenta potius scenicis representationibus, aut officinis ubi reticula et strophia proponuntur venalia, quam sacras functiones exercenti Clero convenirent."*[14] These remarks are as just as they are severe.   Martinucci knew what he was talking about, and we believe that he had in view that modern cotta which is a corruption of the *superpelliceum* and in the words of Martinucci a *"merum ornamentum."*   In this garment lace, petty embroidery, the stiffest and sometimes the most terribly artificial pleating, are far more important than good linen, though properly that is the true liturgical material. Let us remember that people of intelligence, good sense and good taste, people who have observation and judgment, and are not shackled by habit—that these are humiliated and pained, when they are not amused, by these shortened garments and the accessories which accompany them. And let us reflect also that vanity has often a great share in these trivial decorations. I was once shown by a pious person one of these queer cottas ; it was starched and pleated, it had a fringe of cheap lace, it clung to the body like a glove. "Isn't it charming?" said the good lady, "I made it."

We are not here insisting upon anything like a strict uniformity, and in fact surplices and cottas vary very much according to the country, and according to those differences of temperament and mental outlook which differentiate the nations so

[12] Dom Gréa, abbot, of the Canons Regular of the Immaculate Conception *La Sainte Liturgie*, p. 81.

[13] *"Longe ductum infra genua, atque adeo fere usque ad crura media."*   *Acta eccles. mediol.*

[14] *Manuale Sacrarum Caeremoniarum*, Lib. I, ch. II p. 7 (a).

C

profoundly, and which have so strong an influence on the style and form of liturgical vestments. Rome is very wise, and appreciating this diversity does not impose any one cut or one size for surplice and cotta, any more than she imposes any one style of architecture or church furniture.

In one place we have the cottas described by the great Master of Ceremonies whose words we have just quoted ; in another place (in Germany, France, and various churches in England, etc. . .) we have nothing but simple and noble surplices which reach to the knees or even halfway between knee and foot, exactly as prescribed by S. Charles, as we have seen (fig. 27). In other places again the surplice has no trace of linen in its material ; it has become a tiny garment made entirely of fine tulle and lace. This delicate sort of thing is suitable to women and they can always put it to good use, whether on their persons or in their houses ; but men do not wear lace and transparent material. Why then should the priest, the *man of God*, employ such things ?

But we are not without reasons for consolation. We all know that there is a goodly number of priests who prefer that good yet simple surplice which is commended in such apt terms by a liturgical writer whose knowledge and judgment none will question: "I need hardly point out that artistically the beauty and dignity of this garment are entirely a matter of long, full folds. A long surplice falling in folds, with wide sleeves . . . is an exceedingly handsome garment."[15]

Yet we must have that broadmindedness which is characteristic of our Mother the Church and we must recognize a certain variety of quality in liturgical art, just as such variety is admitted in the three great arts of design. There is, we mean, a place for another sort of beauty, of a more delicate, more exalted, more expensive kind ; and to this we have already referred when we spoke of those rochets adorned with rich and beautiful lace which serve as a very proper and distinctive dress for ecclesiastical dignitaries.

We do not give any measurements for a true surplice made of linen throughout, but they may be deduced easily from the design in fig. 28. That shows a server of, let us say, five feet, wearing a surplice which reaches to the knees. The measurements will naturally vary according to the stature of the people for whom the surplice is made, whether priests or clerks. We have often seen, and in important churches, surplices of even greater length and greater beauty, which were in fact in

[15] Adrian Fortescue : *The Vestments of the Roman Rite*, 1925, p. 10.

conformity with S. Charles' requirements. The reader will observe the wide circular opening at the neck, where the stuff is neatly gathered (figs. 27 and 28), which allows of the surplice being put on and taken off very easily. The slit down the front of the surplice, which is fairly common and generally ugly, is thus avoided. The cotta of fig. 29 is about eleven inches long from the collar to the beginning of the lace ; the surplice of fig. 28 is about twenty-six inches long from the collar to the lower border.

FIG. 30. ANCIENT CHRISTIAN ALTAR, WITH EXCELLENT CLOTH (Rohault de Fleury, *La Messe, vi,* p. 195)

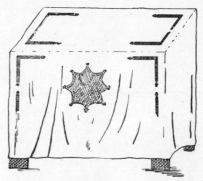

FIG. 31. AN ALTAR OF THE VITH CENTURY, With cloth falling nearly to the ground on the four sides *S. Apollinare in Classe, Ravenna*

ALTAR CLOTH.—Archaeology does not provide us with examples of ancient altars *vested* in cloths. But fig. 30 is a very intelligent recon- struction which reflects the spirit of the early centuries. It is in fact an altar of the early Christian period, with its altar cloth designed in accordance with the present-day requirements of the liturgy. At Ravenna, on mosaics of the sixth century, may be seen two typical altars. One of them (at S. Apollinare in Classe) is covered with a linen cloth, ornamented with gammas and a star, which falls down to the altar feet on all four sides (fig. 31) ; the other (at S. Vitale) is com- pletely surrounded by a dark-coloured material[16] and on top has a linen cloth ornamented with the same designs. The same idea is found ten centuries later on a bas-relief by Mino da Fiesole which represents

[16] The origin of our frontals : P. Batiffol, *Leçons sur la Messe,* 1920, p. 54.

the Mass of S. Gregory (fig. 32).   The enveloping stuff with its many
folds is evidently not linen.   The altar cloth is fringed and falls down a

little all round the *mensa* and
makes one think of those orfreys
which frequently ran along the
top of the antependium in the
Middle Ages.   The modern altar
of fig. 33 is suggested by these
two draped altars.   It is massive,
very ornamental, and covered
with a cloth which falls well
down at the sides and in front
and which might fall even further,
and on all four sides if the altar
is isolated.   An altar of this
character is far superior to those
altars with pillars and sculptures, very poorly covered by
very imperfect cloths.

But the design of the altar
itself does not properly come
within the scope of this book,
which deals only with vesture.
The "vestments" of the altar are
the cloths and the frontal (*antependium*).   Of the latter some
examples are figured in Chapter
X.   The employment of a frontal
naturally diminishes the breadth
of the altar cloth, but not its
fall at either end of the altar.
With or without frontals, the
upper cloth, *mappa superior*,[17]

FIG. 32.   DETAIL OF A BAS-RELIEF, BY
            MINO DA FIESOLE,
Representing the Mass of St. Gregory.
The draped altar is noteworthy

should always cover the altar
and its two ends should fall down
at either side so as nearly to
reach the ground.   This altar

cloth should be of linen, and that is all that the liturgy requires : the

---

[17] We have nothing to say about the two under cloths, or cloth folded in two,
which lie immediately on the altar.

correct thing for us to do is to abide by the rules of the rubrics. If we follow them with docility we shall get a beautiful cloth covering the sacrificial altar in a plain and dignified way. Rome does not vary here in her decrees and very legitimate requirements : *"Servari nequit con-suetudo, ex qua tobalea Altaris usque ad terram non pertingat."* (S.R.C., 9 Junii 1899, No. 4029, ad. 1). It is we who change the true altar design in order to adopt another which sometimes makes obedience to these explicit rules an impossibility ; it is we who add frivolities such as laces more or less delicate and more or less vulgar, or inscriptions in red, neither useful nor necessary : the one and the other representing the triumph of the accessory over the essential. And bad taste seems here in this matter to achieve its masterpieces. I have seen

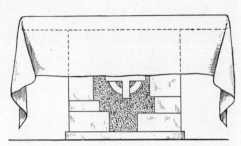

FIG. 33.   AN ORIGINAL MODERN ALTAR OF GOOD DESIGN

It is covered with a plain white altar cloth, freely imitated from the two preceding figures

altar-cloths bordered with enormous lace fringes, on which were depicted the alleged portrait of a saint, a view of a church, symbols and signs of various sorts. The altar was lost to view behind a barrage of lace, and the altar-cloth retained no trace of that flowing white linen which should fall down at either end.

Now although all altar cloths do not present us with such exaggerated and anti-liturgical productions, yet it must be said that their embroideries and dangling lace are in the best shop-window style and calculated merely to arrest the attention of the curious. Doubtless this sort of thing provides occupation for skilful and zealous women, and doubtless too it is inspired by pious motives ; but good taste and the liturgical sense are banished utterly.

But let us take heart ! these things have not got it all their own way ; the simple and pure spirit of the Church is ever alive somewhere. There are cathedrals, seminary chapels, abbeys and parish churches where the altars are covered with cloths of fine linen and without any ornament. They cover the *mensa* completely, but do not come over the front so much as one centimetre ; and they fall down at either end almost to the ground. They have everything they should have, and they are perfect altar cloths (fig. 34). They remind us of the winding sheet that enshrouded the body of our Lord; they are exquisite in taste and they breathe an odour of humility. They are, if we may so ex-

FIG. 34.   A VERY BEAUTIFUL ALTAR, IN WESTMINSTER CATHEDRAL
The crib is there only at Christmas time. Like all the altars of that noble church it has a quite plain cloth in perfect conformity with the requirements of the liturgy

press it, like the perfectly simple yet simply perfect costume of a noble lady.

CLOTH OF CREDENCE TABLE.—If we follow the principles just laid down for altar-cloths we shall get cloths of good character on our credence tables. There is no point in making the cloth come down over the front edge; but a long fall at the sides is in harmony with the similar fall of the altar cloth. The only difference is that there is here no requirement that the ends should reach the ground (figs. 35 and 36).

THE FINGER CLOTH is often made as small and finicking as a lady's handkerchief—a serious fault to which two more bits of folly are added when the tiny finger cloth is starched and then ironed into numerous little pleats. And what is the result ? That the priest makes as little use

FIG 35. A CREDENCE TABLE, Displaying in its arrangements a lack of taste and care

FIG. 36. ANOTHER CREDENCE TABLE, Neatly covered with a fringed cloth. Observe the long finger cloth on the cruets

of this cloth as possible, so as not to punish his fingers. Let us be reasonable ; let us consider the purpose of this finger cloth and then it will be conformable with good sense ; it will be very flexible, and without any wretched tags of lace, it will have fair dimensions, and if those given by Saint Charles Borromeo (33 inches by 26) are found too big, then a cloth of 20 inches by 16, for instance, will by no means be excessive. It has been said that it is best to fold the finger cloth in three ; but why ? It is easier to fold it in four, and one is free to fold it otherwise (fig. 15).

COMMUNION CLOTH.—The same considerations of good taste and simplicity apply to this cloth. I have seen cloths ornamented with all the flowers in creation ; but embroidery is really out of place in a cloth which is intended to catch falling fragments of the sacred Host. A cloth of good linen and entirely unadorned is most in conformity with the spirit of the liturgy.

CHAPTER III

MATERIALS AND COLOURS

MATERIALS.—Some of the ideas which have been set forth in the two preceding chapters will re-appear both here and elsewhere ; they are clearly stated in a quotation which we borrow from a lecture given by Mgr. Battifol : "We moderns are obsessed with the idea that garments must fit closely to the body ; since the Renaissance our chasuble has become a sort of close-fitting jerkin. In antiquity all garments were draped, and the chasuble was originally a draped garment. Since the sixth century the Church has adopted, has so to say sanctified, the use of silk ; but I think our silk stuffs might very well tone down their splendour and what may be called the showiness of their surface. The rich effect of a chasuble should depend principally on the pliancy of its material and the wealth of its folds. You detest buckram, and rightly ; but you must go further, you must dislike cloth of gold. These are the two sworn enemies of simplicity and of draped vestments." We should be inclined to add a third enemy, and call for a ban on watered silks. Happily they are not in common use, but they are still to be found in the shops, and when they are of good quality they are apt to be too stiff. Some satins have much the same defect and are also too readily creased. Their glossiness may please the eye and gratify some tastes, but they may also have a displeasing effect, precisely on account of the uniform brilliance of their surface. Vestments made of white satin are quickly soiled, and if they are in at all frequent use, keep decent for a few years only. Some churches and chapels still tolerate such horrors as fabrics figured with flowers and flowerets in the style of the most vulgar bedroom wallpapers. Closely related to these are other stuffs, vile imitations of ancient fabrics or ugly compositions made up of chalices, hosts, grapes and hearts : all, too often, in the most hideous colours. What a great help it would be to the good cause if the trade had enough disinterestedness and love of ecclesiastical art to banish these vulgar materials from stock ! Their own knowledge, and we may say their consciences, must constrain them to abominate them. What a help it

the disgraceful vulgarity of these so-called liturgical fabrics, and if they offered for sale and taught the public to appreciate such stuffs as figured damasks, with designs that are good and suitable for vestments, and plain silks, either fine-ribbed or self-striped!

UNFIGURED FABRICS.—There are excellent reasons, founded on the taste for simplicity in vestments which animated the clergy up to the eighth century, for preferring these soft unfigured fabrics of one plain colour. They may be got from the ecclesiastical furnisher, and also from shops which have no ecclesiastical connections, but which stock such simple materials. The stuffs we are thinking of have a dull or not very shiny surface, are plain or ribbed, and may be had in many qualities and prices. As long as these stuffs are unfigured they may clearly be used for our vestments. Moreover, these shops often provide a considerable choice of colours: reds, for example, greens, and purples, in

FIG. 37.   DETAIL OF A COPE

The design has no inner congruity or spiritual significance, and is quite unsuited for a vestment. The wall-paper style

a great variety of very beautiful shades. It would be a good thing if our makers of chasubles, copes and other vestments kept in stock as many plain stuffs, or at least series of samples showing several shades of the same colour. That would facilitate choice and would educate the eyes and taste of the public. It must not be forgotten that there is no rule in favour of stuffs with ecclesiastical patterns, or of any particular style of design. Unfigured fabrics are always suitable. This is a great advantage, and the simplicity of such stuffs is a great point in their favour.

We shall not deal at any length with all the various materials that are used in the making of vestments. We have made mention of various silks : plain silks and ribbed silks of various texture. We will now draw attention to velvets and damasks, because both materials, requiring a very special process in the weaving, are of a very distinctive character and appearance.

VELVET is woven like any other fabric by interlacing of warp and weft ; but in order to give the velvety effect an accessory thread, called the pile-thread, is stretched between the threads of the warp, i.e., the threads which lie lengthwise in the loom; [1] when the fabric has been woven, the pile-warp is shaved by means of very sharp blades, which produces the characteristic velvet nap or pile. Plush is a kind of velvet ; its shadows are softer and its high lights more brilliant ; it is to velvet what satin is to silk.

To praise velvet and to recommend it for the making of liturgical vestments is to run counter to some existing prejudices. Nevertheless, we are of opinion that silk velvet may be very suitable, (1) if it is sufficiently pliant and light to drape well, (2) if it is so made as not to crumple, or develop those creases which give an air of old age and neglect to our church vestments. There are velvets which have these decided advantages. If we ask for these and reject all others, then we are likely to obtain satisfactory results. The writer has seen and admired a really beautiful modern red velvet chasuble which combined these qualities, and was both graceful and dignified. Another chasuble, also a very light one, was made of black velvet with a cross of plain straw coloured silk, and likewise produced a very beautiful effect. This refers of course to flexible velvet used as the principal material of a vestment, and not to velvet used for decoration. For this purpose a stiffer velvet is more suitable ; having more substance it cuts out better and makes better appliqué work.

There are various kinds of ornamental velvet. One kind has a very short pile for the background and a longer pile for the pattern, thus producing the effect of arabesques in relief. There are also velvets with gold thread interwoven, velvets woven from silk threads of as many as four or five different colours, and velvets printed in more than one colour. During the Renaissance and later, these fabrics were in frequent use for the more sumptuous vestments, especially in Italy and Spain. At the present day reasons of taste and economy combine to dissuade their use.

CLOTH OF GOLD AND BROCADES.—The stuffs called cloth of gold and cloth of silver are simply fabrics woven of silk and metal threads combined. Brocades are fabrics which are woven by the same process as damasks, and in which metallic threads combined with silk form either

---

[1] *Le velours*, in *Art et Décoration*, Paris, March, 1922, p. 70.

the background or the pattern. Figures, animals, flowers and many

Fig. 38.　Detail of a Chasuble
A rich brocade, but stiff and heavy

other subjects may be used for the pattern. This combination of bright
metallic threads with silk undoubtedly produced sumptuous materials,

which were much in favour with oriental potentates from the tenth century or even earlier. They were much used in the Middle Ages and

Fig. 39.   A Dalmatic in Brocade
The braids and fringes in Japanese gold. Very rich, but as rigid as a tortoise's shell

Fig. 40.   Detail of a Chasuble
Exemplifying the employment of bands of brocade

in the period following the Renaissance. They satisfied the love of display that characterised those times.

It would be well to give up the use of these materials altogether. If they are good of their kind, they are very dear and make painfully stiff and heavy vestments, which have none of the natural grace and beauty of plain silk vestments. And then, after a while, one is apt to be disappointed, because the first brilliancy of these materials wears off. These cloths of gold and brocades, when bought, purport to be made of medium quality gold thread ; but this is in reality only copper thread lightly gilded. I have seen a priest wearing a cope which originally, no doubt, was very re-splendent ; but a few years' use had turned it into a truly shock-ing spectacle, a mere mass of a dirty, yellowish, muddy colour. The utmost use that should be made of brocade is in strips for orfreys ; it must be of really good quality, and it may work out a little less expensive than similar strips of em-broidery or appliqué work (fig. 40). Bro-cades can also be

Fig. 41. Frontal enriched with Bands of Brocade
Everything in this little sanctuary is in just proportion and everything is good

used for rich antependia which are not draped (fig. 41).

DAMASK.—Special mention must be made of damask, which is in very common use. It is a fabric of silk, or of silk and cotton, with a pattern of the same colour woven in mat silk in slight relief. Now, what is this pattern to be like ? Ought it to have a prescribed style, or is it enough if it have something distinctive about it and so be suitable for vest-ments ? This question has recently given rise to several instructive dis-cussions. Many of us will reply that damasked fabrics for use in church should be figured in a style which, if not definitely ecclesiastical, yet suggests something of the kind. But now we are faced with partisans of the modern school, many of whom are excellent Catholics. They de-plore the inferiority of many liturgical objects and beyond a doubt they are justified. But their opinions may be mistaken when it comes to materials for vestments. They tell one in effect that in such and such shops "you will find the most sumptuous and often the most graceful and elegant work that present-day artists can produce for the houses of the rich and the adornment of their women folk" ; and they do not hesitate to suggest that we should "adopt these beautiful figured fabrics, generally inspired in their decoration by God's creatures, the plants and animals, and use them for the embellishment of our sanctuaries and even for the vestments of our priests, making sure of course that the stuffs conform to the definite requirements of the rubrics." [2] If these conditions are fulfilled, does it follow that one should welcome damasks and other fabrics which have been especially designed for ladies' evening-gowns, just because in many of these ultra-modern figured stuffs the artist has drawn his inspiration from "God's creatures, the plants and animals" ? But these plants and animals have not been imagined, conventionalized and woven with a view to the service of God ; they decorate silks intended for a very different, or even for an incompatible, service. The ideas of these designs have indeed been borrowed from the vegetable and animal creation, but they have been conceived, designed and woven to gratify the world of fashion and of pleasure. Nothing has been left untried, no trick of the trade, no refinement, no artifice has been forgotten, that can produce strange combinations, gay, becoming, and charming effects.

We are not decrying all ultra-modern designs, certainly not all modern figured fabrics ; we have elsewhere had occasion to praise the new art, or at least several of its products ; some of these are finely conceived, harmonious, sincere and delightfully original. This art is still in its infancy ; it is possible that it may purify itself and produce work that is securely based on a foundation of fixed principles. In the meantime one is at liberty to remark—it may even be one's duty to do so—that no small number of fanciful and fantastic works have been produced by artists of this school, in which no sense of proportion, no restraint, no rule can be detected. Here is a case wherein we must assert the fullest freedom, and we believe that we have the majority with us. We claim the right to discard fabrics which though they may indeed be "sumptuous and graceful" are none the less devised for very worldly uses and not at all for Catholic worship ; we are right in directing our choice to unfigured fabrics, whose perfect suitability for liturgical vestments we have already emphasized, or at any rate to fabrics

---

[2] Val Reyre, *Les étoffes liturgiques* (*Revue des Jeunes*, June, 1921).

which are figured in sober and restful designs, artistically spaced and recurring with a satisfying rhythm.

Therefore let our artists aim at these qualities in making patterns and designs that are to be woven ; let them not lose sight of the fact that they are designing materials for the sacred vestments and not for fashionable gowns ; and then thanks to them our fabrics will soon show an individual character, be it strongly marked or delicately suggested, that is dignified, solid and devotional. Everything else is secondary.

FIGS. 42 & 43. Material of a good design, combining dignity and harmony, contrasting strongly with the other, which, though used for a chasuble, is suitable only for domestic curtains

The designs may be taken from the vegetable or animal kingdom, or they may be conceived without any reference to pre-existing reality—such as you know is the effort of one school—or they may be according to the new art, or they may reproduce the conventional, stylised forms of antique fabrics.

It must further be noted that although the use of certain monograms and emblems in the design marks out the stuff as definitely ecclesiastical, yet that such emblems do not suffice to make the material beautiful if the above mentioned notes of decorative art be lacking. The reader is invited to make a very practical comparison by examining first the fabric represented in fig. 37 and then that represented in fig. 44. The latter is in the style of the catacombs and was woven a few years ago by M. Biais of Paris to be the material of a full chasuble

FIG. 44. AN ADMIRABLE DAMASK IN THE "CATACOMB" STYLE
(Made by M. Biais, Paris)

FIG. 45. A DAMASK EMBODYING THE SYMBOLS OF THE EVANGELISTS
(Also the property of M. Biais)

intended for a prince of the Church. The designs are well conceived and well spaced on the materials ; the damask of the chasuble in particular is figured in a way that is nothing short of admirable. The technical points are the following : the warp and the weft are of slightly different shades ; the satin background contrasts with the actual pattern which is so woven as to yield the desired effects and to produce half shades where they are required. It is important to notice that the whole scheme of decoration is on a scale that is suitable for a large chasuble and for a

FIG. 46.   A VERY BEAUTIFUL LAMPAS
The ground is white ;   the angels and ornaments are in straw yellow

cope, their ample size allowing of designs that would be too large for, let us say, a tabernacle veil or a ciborium cover.

The reader is now asked to refer, if he can, to the fabrics illustrated in the number of *Arts français* entitled *L'art religieux moderne*. One of these fabrics also is figured in designs derived from the catacombs, but these are too delicate and too finicking for their coarse and heavy scroll work. Another material displays a sorry scheme of lean ears of corn, some upright and some drooping. Another damask is absolutely over-run with ferns, which are bursting to grow and spread themselves, and the poor things can't do so, for sheer lack of space : decidedly one of those examples in which the principle of restful spacing has been lost sight of ; in short, the designers were ignorant of the principles of deco-

rative art. Some half-hearted attempts have been made to push these
stuffs because of their novelty ; but the truth is that they are inferior to
other stuffs that were designed and woven thirty and forty years ago. It
is all very well and only too easy to lump all these latter together and
label them mere imitations. There often are mere imitations among
them, as we have ourselves admitted ; but there are also not a few
examples of well-designed, figured fabrics in the Persian, Byzantine,
Roman and Gothic styles. It is no small achievement to have entered
into the spirit of these Latin and Oriental styles, and by the skilful
delineation of the principal elements in the pattern, and by the good
taste and sense of proportion shown in the spacing, to have secured for
these fabrics an honourable place in their own sphere.

The fabric figured with angels of which we give an illustration (fig. 46),
certainly has these good points : the inspiration is medieval, but both
the general scheme and the detailed treatment have affinities with the
ideas of modern art. The material is white ; the angels, the radiating
ornamentation, the flowers and the fruits are a pale straw-coloured
yellow. This fabric proves that good work can be produced on modern
lines, provided that one does not wholly jettison the past nor the necessary rules of decorative art.

The mention of a white and yellow damask may raise the question
whether materials of the proper liturgical colours may be allowed if they
are figured in gold and yellow. Showy cloth of gold—which is not one of
the proper colours at all—is *tolerated*, and what is it but material woven
entirely of gold thread and yellow silk ? Brocaded materials figured
with a quantity of bunches of flowers, or garlands, or even with an all-
over pattern, are still to be found in use for chasubles, especially in
Italy, where they are quite common. All the more reason to tolerate or
even to permit materials figured in fewer colours, but embellished
within reasonable limits with patterns in gold or in yellow, provided
always that the colour proper to the ecclesiastical season or the particular
feast-day *dominates* the whole : that is the important point. Therefore
let this colour show up well ; best of all let it be the colour of the whole
background ; and then we shall occasionally be able to let our choice
fall on those richer materials which were in very frequent use for more
than ten centuries.

Let us be faithful to the principles which Mgr. Battifol has laid down.
If these principles are clearly understood and faithfully followed, we
shall witness a reawakening of good taste and the introduction of truly
beautiful work into our churches. Nevertheless there are occasions when

the simple and somewhat severe dignity of our liturgical vestments may rightly be replaced by some more striking effect which will rejoice the hearts of the faithful and emphasize the joyful or triumphant character of some great solemnity. Those who have seen copes and chasubles of white or flame-coloured material beautifully figured with gold or golden-yellow and have noted the deep shadows and brilliant high-lights of their many folds, these can understand the part which such two-coloured damasks play, in a way which is both grand and wholly sincere, at Mass, in Processions, and at Vespers and Benediction.

THE COLOURS OF FABRICS.—We often see very ugly colours used for copes, chasubles and other vestments. People call them "liturgical colours," a name which is both false and humiliating. Are we to admit that colours have to be crude or vulgar in order to be suitable for the most sacred garments that exist ? It is possible to find in velvets, in plain silks, and in damask, moss-greens, olive-greens, emerald-greens and others which are worlds apart from certain most displeasing parro-quet greens ; reds of various shades which are much more liturgical than a carmine red ; purples, whether dark purples such as one finds in illu-minated manuscripts, or pale purples, or richer purples made of combi-nations of blue, carmine and vermilion, instead of the crude or indeter-minate violets one too often sees.

The line of demarcation between these shades is not difficult to draw, and it is good to insist on it, so that the reader may in future find it natural to reject those irritating or insipid shades which we have men-tioned above.

We ought to aim at something higher and better, and in this matter it is important to know what really is "better." Not all possible shades of any given colour are suitable for all interiors ; if the stained-glass windows are very clear and the church full of light, soft subdued shades will be those best adapted to the circumstances. On the other hand, if the church is dark, the greens, reds, and purples should be brighter. And to carry this principle to its logical conclusion, the same should apply to the orfreys of the vestments.

There are several sorts of white which are subtly and yet really dis-tinct. Ivory white and silver white are less brilliant than snow white ; and white lightly tinged with golden-yellow has a characteristically warm effect. White stuffs can be bought in these different tints. If the softer hues are decorated with ornament which is subdued in tone, then the vestments will harmonize with a well-lit interior. On the other hand a vivid white with rather bold ornamentation will produce a satisfying and harmonious effect in a dark church ; that is the time for using white satins and other rich materials.

There are also different shades of black, but the variations are slight and of no importance for the present enquiry. It is a good thing to give black vestments a touch of life and warmth by means of strips of gold lace, or embroidery in red, yellow or other colours. Gold and purple, gold and red, or purple and red, connected by bands of gold thread or gold lace, produce a very fine effect if they are skilfully combined. The writer has seen an ample black chasuble, recently made for an archbishop, on which the cross is of a ribbed stuff woven of fine gold thread and red silk. There is nothing else, just the warp and weft of gold and red, and that is the only ornament of this finely draped chasuble ; any addition would be superfluous. The silky lining of the vestment and its accessories is of a rather light red. Here we have an example of an extremely simple black chasuble, enriched and so to say illumined by the rich golds and pale reds.

LININGS.—Linings are not to be neglected as things of no importance. Their importance may be secondary, but it is very real. Too often the makers of vestments line them with dressed materials, and so stiffen the most pliant copes and chasubles. But it is quite easy to get linings of silk and cotton, satinettes of really good quality and beautiful colours, which give some substance to soft materials while falling into folds and draping readily with them.

As to the colours of linings, the two following remarks may give some useful guidance. (1) In choosing the materials for the lining of a vestment, do not lose sight of the colour of the vestment, and remember the theory of complementary colours. (2) Beware of using the same tone or intensity of colour for the lining as for the outer material. A short explanation will make this clear. The dark tone, for example, of a red or purple damask is shown off to advantage if the lining is rather pale ; and, on the other hand, the white of a material is enhanced by means of a lining of a somewhat deep tone. We should aim at well-considered contrasts. A pale-green lining will be suitable with red vestments, a salmon-red with dark-green, a sulphur yellow or a straw-yellow inclining to gold with purple vestments. Again, a yellow or flame coloured material will go well with black vestments. White vestments will be enhanced by linings of a vivid tone : blood-red, brick-red, claret-red, copper-red ; or else slate-blue, royal-blue, ultramarine, electric-blue ; or again by intense greens or purples.

If soft and delicate tones are preferred for the linings of white vestments, sky-blue, pale-yellow, rose-pink and other similar shades may be used, or a white vestment may even be lined with white ; but there is always the risk of producing effects that are too finicking or too insipid. We possess a cope the ornamentation of which is very original and very beautifully executed ; the cope itself is all white and the lining too is white. You have only to picture this vestment worn over a surplice or an alb and you will realize that there is altogether too much white except for a building to which the daylight is only very sparingly admitted, as is indeed the case with the church in which this cope is used. It is not for us to lay down rules, but we may claim that our counsels are based on the theory of complementary colours, as we have said. However, the reader must follow his own judgment in this matter, and

FIG. 47.   EXCELLENT UNLINED CHASUBLES OF VERY MODERATE PRICE
(A. E. Grossé, Bruges)

so long as his taste is grounded on rational principles, he may safely disregard the advice we have given.

   And now we may ask, is it always necessary for a chasuble to have a lining ? By no means. They can be made and have been made without linings, witness the very beautiful ones illustrated in fig. 47. But when a vestment is lined the outer material does not have to bear alone the whole stress of existence, with its crumpling and creasing and rubbing, and the consequence is that lined vestments keep in good condition much longer.

   It will have been observed that we have made mention of a single lining only ; double linings should be banned and we must be prompt to denounce padding of any description, not only the hideous buckram, but any stuff that adds to the expense of a vestment and, what is worse, serves only to make it heavy and ugly. We must be on our guard in this matter, and by a judicious use of finger and thumb make sure that the chasubles, copes and other vestments that are offered to us do not owe their deplorable stiffness to a trick of the trade by which some extra stuff is surreptitiously inserted between the outer fabric and the lining. In many countries narrow chasubles, and even wide ones, are too often padded in this way. If gifts of this description are inflicted on us, there is a remedy which we have used ourself and which we recommend to other victims, which is to send these chasubles to some competent person who will unpick the whole thing, throw away the buckram or other padding, and succeed in making very good vestments out of the remaining materials.

The "Practical Guide" also condemns a double lining ; but it adds : "Nevertheless the use of a very light tissue between the silk fabric and the lining is recommended when these are both exceptionally soft and pliant." [3] This is to open the door to the very aberrations against which we have raised our voice, and unnecessarily. The remedy is quite simple, and the door may be kept shut by not using two flimsy materials at the same time for your outer stuff and your lining. If either of these materials is exceptionally light, then let the other be closely woven enough to give substance to the other.

These remarks do not apply to the stole, nor to the maniple. These accessories have to be crossed or to hang in straight lines, and they need a certain stiffness. A strip of linen or flannel between the silk and the lining will give them a sufficient degree of stiffness.

[3] *Guide pratique pour la confection des ornements gothiques*, p. 11.

CHAPTER IV

THE CHASUBLE FROM THE BEGINNING TO THE NINETEENTH CENTURY

SINCE reproductions are instructive and frequently convincing, we propose in this chapter and in the two following ones to give a certain importance to the illustrations. By means of them we hope to give the

FIG. 48. A CHRISTIAN WEARING A
paenula,
After a fresco of the Catacombs,
vith century

FIG. 49. BISHOP ECCLESIUS
xiith century mosaic, in S. Vitale,
Ravenna. The bishop is wearing a
circular *paenula* which would look quite
different if the material were drawn
up over the arms

reader an exact idea of the forms of the chasuble at different periods. Their essential characteristics only will be indicated, and an effort will be made to sketch in outline the history of their successive transformations. We ask the pardon of any experts who may read these pages; they will be familiar with the subject we are dealing with and will know the chasubles here reproduced.

Photo : Alinari

Fig. 50. St. Apollinaris

vith century, from S. Apollinare in Classe, Ravenna. Long white tunic with *clavi ;*
paenula drawn up over the arms

Paenula and *planeta* were the earliest names for the garment which afterwards came to be called *casula*. The *paenula* was during the first centuries a large piece of material with a central opening through which the head was passed. It fell round the wearer in free and ample folds (fig. 49) ; it was a noble *garment*, not a scanty *decoration*. [1] We find the *paenula* worn by Christians as depicted in the catacombs (fig. 48) and engraved on a fourth century cup. We find it also in the mosaic representations of bishops of Ravenna. Here for instance is St. Apollinaris clad in a long tunic and chasuble (*paenula*) over which is thrown a white pallium (fig. 50). He is in the attitude of prayer and his chasuble being lifted up on his arms appears less ample than does the chasuble of Ecclesius in fig. 49, or that of Maximian in fig. 2. At Rome in the oratory of St. Venantius at the Lateran, in the churches of St. Agnes, St. Mark, Santa Maria in Trastevere, etc., mosaics of the seventh, ninth, and twelfth centuries also show the figures of saints wearing large chasubles ; and from the thirteenth century onwards, the paintings, sculptures, stained glass, seals, and miniatures which represent popes, bishops, abbots, canons and ordinary priests wearing chasubles, always show these as ample garments which really clothe and drape their wearers. Our only difficulty is in making a selection, and we have taken a few examples only from various countries. The admirable St. Firminus of Amiens has been reproduced in Chapter I (fig. 6) ; here, in addition, we give for Spain Don Mauricio, Bishop of Burgos, thirteenth century (fig. 51) : for Italy Bishop Pecci, fifteenth century (fig. 52), a fourteenth century pope (fig. 53), and Pope Martin V portrayed on a most interesting bas-relief, the work of Donatello and Michelozzo, fifteenth century (fig. 54).

As we write these pages we have before us thirty-eight line-drawings of ancient *paenulae* or chasubles, some of them from mosaics, but the majority taken from real chasubles still preserved in churches ; they can be seen at Rome and Florence, Sens and Toulouse, Frankfort and Hildesheim, Metz and Salzburg, Angers, Bayeux, Biville, etc. In these vestments the curve described by the two bottom edges is usually an arc of a circle ; but from the thirteenth century onwards that ceases to be the case and the contour becomes definitely pointed. Except for a few rare cases, first of chasubles still in existence, secondly of chasubles

---

[1] The *Dictionnaire d'archéologie chrétienne et de liturgie* gives a reproduction, from paintings in the catacombs, of two Christians in grotesquely short and narrow *paenulae;* but these frescoes are so roughly executed and the *paenulae* so different from those depicted almost everywhere else that they by no means contradict one's idea of the loose and full garment of the period.

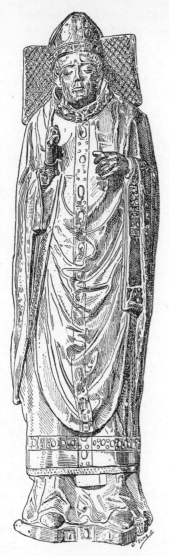

FIG. 51.   DON MAURICIO
BISHOP OF BURGOS
XIIIth century, from the Cathedral of Burgos.   In enamelled
brass

FIG. 52.   TOMBSTONE OF BISHOP PECCI
(1426) by Donatello, Cathedral of Siena.
Observe the full chasuble and natural
folding

painted or sculptured by pre-Gothic craftsmen who as yet paid no
regard either to the positions of the human body or to realism in draperies

—these vestments invariably display a remarkable length and fullness.

FIG. 53. STATUE OF A POPE
XIVth century, St. John Lateran, Rome.
Observe the beautiful folds formed by the
raised arms

They allow for a seam which forms the middle line in front and behind, and calls for a decoration to hide it ; this consists of pieces of material or embroideries in the form, now of the "column" as it has been called, now of the Y-shaped cross which became so common from the twelfth century onwards. On some vestments there was placed at the top of the long vertical strip in front a short horizontal strip which served to strengthen the lower part of the opening of the neck, and no doubt it also suggested the idea of the Tau-shaped cross, the symbol of our redemption ; but with very few exceptions, the Latin cross did not make its appearance on chasubles till the fourteenth century, [2] after which it came into common use, except in Italy and in Spain, where the use of a vertical strip only on the back of the chasuble was adhered to.

Among the full chasubles preserved in the treasuries of our churches we may mention those of St. Willigis, Bishop of Mainz, of St. Godehard of Hildesheim, of Blessed Bernard degli Uberti, and of St. Thomas of Canterbury. We mention also the chasuble of Pope Boniface VIII (which has been shockingly mutilated) and the four chasubles which

[2] *Imitation of Christ*, Bk. IV, Chap. V.

Photo : Alinari

FIG. 54. TOMB OF POPE MARTIN V (†1431)
St. John Lateran, Rome. The Pope is nobly clad in his full chasuble

bear the names respectively of St. Regnobert, St. Loup, St. Peter
Martyr and St. Dominic.   And we are glad to be able to put before
the reader a reproduction of the so-called chasuble of St. Stephen of

FIG. 55. TOMBSTONE OF G. MIRABILI
(†1479), Church of Santa Maria del
Popolo, Rome. Observe the cross
on the front of the chasuble

FIG. 56.   ST. MARTIN
Spanish art of the end of the
XVIth century, from Saragossa.
Note the "Tau" cross

Hungary, a magnificent vestment.   For the rest we would refer him to
the very important collection of engravings in Rohault de Fleury's
great work, where a large number of these chasubles are figured, [3] and
to his seventh volume which contains a chronological table of forty-one
chasubles. The conclusion from this mass of evidence is eloquent in its
simplicity : these witnesses from very different lands and very different

[3] *La Messe*, plates 561 to 614.

PLATE II

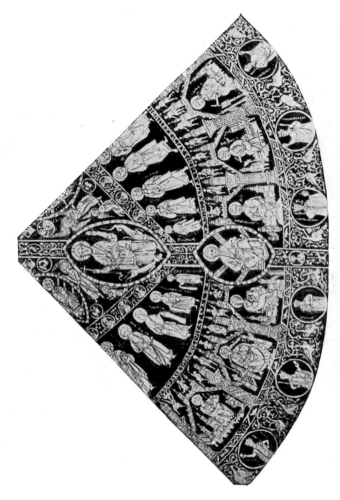

MANTLE OR SO-CALLED CHASUBLE OF ST. STEPHEN OF HUNGARY AND QUEEN GISELA
Observe the well-arranged zones of decoration, and persons, architectural motives,
etc. A noble vestment.

periods one and all testify that the ample chasuble (whose prototype is the ancient *paenula*) has behind it twelve centuries and more of current use—an imposing record, which makes of this vestment something traditional, universal, Catholic.

In Italy as everywhere else, the larger forms were retained until the sixteenth century ; but it is to Italy that we must look for the beginning of transformations, contractions and disfigurements. Even in the time of S. Charles, who was distressed at the shortening of linen vestments and anxious to have them brought back to a seemly length—as we have seen in Chapter II.—the chasuble was supposed to be 51 inches wide ; we have his own word for it. The width subsequently set down by Gavantus is already considerably less, i.e., 34 inches. Benedict XIV [4] tells us that Lindanus *"conqueritur nimium decurtari suo tempore coeptam esse Planetam : Ita enim recisa est et decurtata, atque aliam prope in speciem deformata, ut sicuti illa prisca, unde fluxit et degeneravit, cum ponatur, vix suum tueatur nomen."* [5]

The movement being once begun towards the reduction of a vestment once so noble in its amplitude, its promoters in Italy went so far as to leave a width of 30 inches only. In Belgium, Spain, France, etc., the tailors would seem to have made a point of clipping, docking, and mutilating still further the wretched chasubles which by way of excess of ugliness became almost always stiff, cumbersome, and outrageously commonplace in character. In the sixteenth and seventeenth centuries the Spanish chasuble began to grow wider towards the bottom and very narrow at the shoulders, where the material had formerly fallen freely over the arms. The chasubles also of France or Belgium, with front piece shaped like a fiddle, and rigid, boardlike backs, have not escaped the severest criticism. A certain distinguished writer has remarked rather disrespectfully that our priests, when wearing these strange chasubles, look curiously like big beetles. This vestment has not been generally introduced in England ; but priests who wear it have been compared to the unhappy "sandwich-men" with their boards before and behind.

How were all these disfigurements introduced ? The answer to this question has been given by the learned Abbot Gréa of the Canons Regular in the following sentence: "It was only gradually, without the support of any written text and merely with the toleration of authority,

---

[4] *De Sacrosancto Missae Sacrificio*, Lib. I, Cap. 8.

[5] *Panopl. Sacerdot.*, Lib. IV, Cap. 46, p. 480.

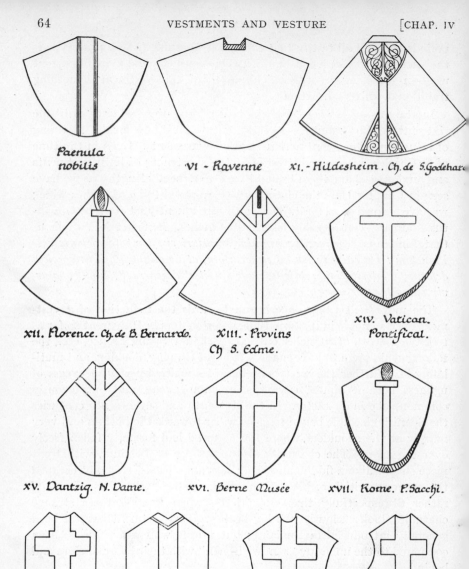

Paenula
nobilis

VI - Ravenne

XI. - Hildesheim . Ch. de S.Godehard

XII. Florence. Ch. de B. Bernardo.

XIII. · Provins
Ch S. Edme.

XIV. Vatican.
Pontifical.

XV. Dantzig. N. Dame.

XVI. Berne Musée

XVII. Rome. P. Sacchi.

France.

Italie

Autriche

Brésil.

Figs. 57 to 69. Thirteen Sketches of Chasubles
(Front or back), from the *paenula nobilis* to the modern fiddle-back

that the material was cut away which used to fall down on either side over the priests arms.'' [6]

And then the chasuble, once so ample and dignified, continued along this path of disfigurement and self-destruction, though the process was

FIG. 70. S. BONIFACE, CONSECRATED BISHOP
From a fresco by Heinrich Maria von Hess, XIXth century

FIG. 71. CHRIST AS KING, PONTIFF AND VICTIM
R. de Cramer in the *Daily Missal*

effected only by degrees, sometimes more or less quickly, sometimes more or less slowly. In many churches there were still in the sixteenth century full chasubles which the possessors could not and would not destroy. There was, in this matter, the fullest freedom, even in the post-reformation period, and all the churches and cathedrals of the Latin rite could keep, use and restore the vestments which they possessed. And so it came about that in some countries the full chasuble maintained itself without any interruption ; even in the eighteenth century there

[6] *La Sainte Liturgie*, p. 94, note.

E

FIG. 72. ST. AVITUS, BISHOP OF VIENNE
Stained glass by Maurice Denis, xxth
century

were such chasubles, and they were in use, at Notre-Dame de Paris, at Saint Denis, at Metz, at Narbonne, at Toul, at Cambrai, and at Arras.[7]

The authentic tradition therefore has been transmitted to us without interruption, thanks to the preservation of the vestments themselves, the use made of them, and the illustrative documents which mosaic-workers, miniaturists, fresco-painters, sculptors, etc., have bequeathed to us. We must in justice add immediately that it is still being maintained, thanks to the artists of our own days who continue this faithful task. For they cannot really do otherwise, knowing as they do the history of costume and having their artistic taste. Like true artists they aim ever at the simplest and best forms, and they seek to discern the great and the true through the mists of transformation and degradation. Therefore, when these artists have to represent a priest, a bishop, or a pope, they clothe him almost always with taste and dignity in the traditional full chasuble. From this select company we shall take a few names only. In the nineteenth century there is

[7] Lebrun, *Explication de la Messe*, 1826, p. 52.

the German painter, Heinrich Maria von Hess, author of the mural painting from which we have taken figure 70 ; in the twentieth century R. de Cramer, whose "Christ, King, Pontiff and Victim" we reproduce (fig. 71) from the well-known *Daily Missal*, published by the Abbey of Saint-André, Bruges ; and Maurice Denis, painter of the glass depicted in fig. 72, showing a sainted bishop in noble vestments. We are specially glad to be able to refer the reader to a fine coloured plate which appears at the beginning of the Vatican *Graduale* (Rome, 1908) which in its centre shows St. Gregory the Great wearing an ample *paenula*, which is obviously of light material and drapes him with delightful ease.

We have several times mentioned St. Charles Borromeo, the promoter of the revision of the liturgical books, defender of the dignity of the sacred vestments and saviour of the Council of Trent. But the transformation of the chasuble began before the first session of that august assembly ; it began even before St. Charles (1538-1584), since the saintly archbishop, concerned at its diminishing size, attempted to stem the process of diminution by a compromise between the old chasuble and the new forms, and laid down 51 inches as the breadth of the vestment. But he did not succeed in arresting the decline, for the chasuble shrank yet more after his death. In brief summary we may say that the changes to which we refer are to be ascribed to the sixteenth century, but still more to the two centuries which followed.

Since the chasuble is no isolated thing, out of relation with historical circumstances, it will be appropriate and useful if we pause to consider the character of the period and of the country which witnessed the accomplishment of these changes in our liturgical vestments. This, as I freely admit, is a digression ; but it is a digression which is necessary for a grasp of the question.

At the period of which we are speaking Italy possessed men of genius endowed with those rich and powerful faculties which were responsible for the Renaissance within her borders, and which while ravaging society produced the arts we know. This historical and artistic period began before them ; but the complete blossoming of those arts is due to them. After the first forty years of the sixteenth century art little by little grew weaker, lost its sincerity, and then degenerated into the conventions of the school and the recipes of the workshop. We have alluded to the effects of the Renaissance on society ; they are manifest to those who are acquainted with the dramatic changes of history. In every country a revolution in talent, in taste and in the arts is always accompanied by a revolution in the manners and feelings of the people. In Italy the Renaissance, which was largely due to the discovery of manuscripts and works of art belonging to pagan antiquity, produced in turn ways of life which also were more or less pagan. The human form became the aim of art, as it had been the aim of Greek and Roman art ; and the very natural and far from supernatural consequence of this was the voluptuousness of people, princes, and clergy. But here it is better to draw a veil. Anyone who cares to refer to the sermons of Savonarola and certain writings of the time will understand the condition of minds and manners in the sixteenth century.

All that excessive culture which is known as the Renaissance, and which as we have seen was really in certain ways a decadence, brought with it a general lack of interest in the Divine Mysteries and in the vestments necessary for their celebration. Men were henceforth too much occupied in seeking their own well-being, too bent upon indulging themselves and their impulses, to accept the very slight discomfort which might be occasioned by ample vestments and abundant material. So the chasuble was hacked about and its dimensions reduced. Originally a genuine garment and intended to serve as such, the chasuble now became a scanty ornament consisting of two flat surfaces. Real simplicity departed and with it both beauty and dignity ; such was the effect of the pursuit of comfort, of merely human aims, of exquisite and sometimes very dubious pleasures.

Among the types of Italian chasuble at the present day are three which derive directly from the chasubles of the sixteenth century. First there is the chasuble whose only decoration is the stiff and meagre one of metallic galloons. Secondly there is the "column" chasuble, embellished with that ornament, which is often too wide and very ornate. Thirdly there is the chasuble which is ornamented over its whole surface with a riot of volutes, acanthus leaves, and flowers in the manner of ancient Roman art. It would be easy to particularise other monotonous schemes and outworn designs : cornucopias, sprigs crossing one another at haphazard, festooned lambrequins (on a chasuble !), etc., sprawling about merely with the object of filling empty spaces. Pray do not plead that such designs are given us as our models by Rome, the high protectress of the arts. They are the work, not of Rome, but of the Roman shopkeeper, of the trader who is content to repeat and multiply such designs in an effortless and loveless way. "But" it will be said "all this is still lit up by some gleam of the Renaissance." That may be so, but it is a much bedimmed gleam of the decadence of the

Renaissance ; it is the degenerate art of the seventeenth and eighteenth centuries, or rather it is a solitary form of art which contents itself with being what it is within its narrow limits ; it is an art which still lives a sort of existence in a very few countries, but which is on its way to a rapid disappearance. The flow of sap is stopped ; the tree is growing withered and stunted ; it will die soon.

People of taste in every country, those who are familiar with the decorative arts and their various developments and have followed their historical evolution and necessary progress—these people are grieved, humiliated and indignant when they meet that style of decoration to which the label of "religious art" is attached. Now this is a serious matter. Are we to hold on obstinately to forms of decoration which were described in our presence by an artist of repute as "degrading" ? We might fairly be accused then of degrading liturgical art, while every other art—architecture, sculpture, painting—is taking a new lease of life and striking out on new lines, often in suitable and perfectly logical directions which are a credit to our churches.

We have just mentioned that routine production which stamps with its own unmistakable stamp a species of ornament that is still produced in Italy ; and not in Italy alone, but also in France, Spain, and elsewhere. Italy has been mentioned in a special way because she gave birth to the Renaissance and communicated its impulse and spirit to the rest of Europe ; and also because we see well exemplified in Italy the very distinctive social conditions of the Renaissance period. It is notorious that Renaissance manners found a home also in France and Spain, and produced there an art similar to that of Italy ; less general however, less persistent, and with differences inherent in the original temperament of the two nations.

Flanders likewise, which in the fifteenth century was with Italy the richest and most prosperous country in Europe—Flanders knew all the pleasures and frivolities of Renaissance fashion, all the pomps of the senses. But faith, inward piety, and Christian feeling had remained strong and living there. The revived paganism of Italy, and certain features of Italian art were, and still are, repugnant to the Flemish spirit.

We beg the reader to allow us to continue this apparent digression and to take an example from the art of building. Italy was impregnated with the classical and basilical styles, styles which were almost inevitably neither known nor loved in Flanders. The architecture whose name of *Gothic* or *barbarous* comes from Italy, was never much appreciated in that country. It was implanted there mostly by Franciscans and Cistercians from France ; and the Cathedral of Milan, one of the few buildings of the peninsula purely Gothic in spirit, is attributed to German architects. Germany indeed had profoundly assimilated Gothic architecture, which is there represented, as in France, England and Spain, by hundreds of very beautiful cathedrals and important churches. It was the same in Flanders, where even in the middle of the sixteenth century the arts remained Gothic and were appreciated by clergy and people alike. Classical and academical importations scarcely reached Flanders except through Rubens ; and in despite of his display of audacious nudes and triumphant sensualities, Rubens was a good Catholic and went to Mass every morning. In the first half of the seventeenth century, when he surpassed in power all the artists of his day, the religious art of Flanders, in so far as it was religious, fell to a low level, and with it naturally the noble forms of vestments also. But the nation lived upon the works of its past, held fast to their fundamental and indelible qualities, and was prepared for a return to excellent liturgical tradition. Of this it has given proof in the nineteenth and twentieth centuries. It is to Brussels, Antwerp, Ghent, and above all Bruges, that the various countries of Europe and the two Americas have had recourse in order to get very beautiful vestments of superior execution and an undeniable decorative character ; this will be evident presently.

After its terrible Revolution France, the *"Regnum Galliae Regnum Mariae,"* was reborn from the blood of its martyrs. Presently a thrill of joy passed through the French people, capable now of appreciating at their proper value the noble achievements of the Middle Ages. They were seized with admiration for the cathedrals built by the Ages of Faith ; and in particular they admired their splendid façades, with their rows of bishops well-sculptured and well-vested, as if prepared to celebrate the sacred Mysteries. This new spirit, so different from the neglect or hostility of the past, was very favourable to tradition. And added to it was that love of the Church which is innate in the French clergy and had now been revived. In view of these things we can readily understand how the return to the Roman liturgy was facilitated, in spite of the temporary obstacles raised by Gallicanism. Then, somewhat later, the great churches felt themselves as it were called upon to take up once again a kind of vestments surely more in harmony with their own style and altogether more appropriate than the degenerate vestments of so-called French form.

If Germany and England suffered, with the loss of the full faith, that also of the Great Sacrifice, of external worship, of liturgical rites and vestments, these two kindred nations could not lose their individual temperament and predilections. In the case of the first, the calm, reflective spirit, directed towards learning and abstract theory—in the case of the second, the regard for everything which makes for peace, respect and dignity—helped to bring back in the nineteenth century the usages everywhere in honour before the Reformation. Neither in Germany nor in England did people care for mean and stinted form, poverty of decoration, or its opposites, pomp and parade. So that there was no hesitation in returning to ancient forms, and to ancient ornament, sometimes sober and austere, sometimes rich, yet without the exaggerated display of the centuries immediately preceding. For the last eighty years quiet effort in this liturgical direction has gone on steadily in Germany and England.

CHAPTER V

THE CHASUBLE (2) : THE GOTHIC REVIVAL AND AFTER

ALREADY, at the end of the first chapter, we alluded to the contemporary liturgical revival, and we have glanced at it again in the last few pages. We must now show, by adducing testimonies, facts, and examples, what was its character in the days of its infancy and early youth. We do not attempt to chronicle the difficulties and checks which it met in its course, for that would take us beyond the scope of this book, which claims to give no more than a simple, positive record of the activity and achievements of the liturgical spirit expressing itself in liturgical art.

The reader will already have appreciated the character and purpose of the chasuble, and he will have grasped its most striking quality. And what is this ? In the good chasuble it is its fulness and excellence as a genuine garment ; in the other chasuble it is its lack of such fulness and the consequences of that defect, skimpiness and sketchiness, and failure to vest the priest decently.

We have seen in the last chapter at what period of European history the chasuble came to be reduced in dimensions, and we are going to witness its gradual return to beautiful proportions, in the period of time which begins about the year 1840. That period saw the powerful " Gothic Revival," which was inspired in part by an ecclesiastical and religious revival. Barry, Pugin, and Gilbert Scott in England, Viollet-le-Duc in France, Béthune in Belgium, Cuypers in Holland : these were protagonists in the movement and did a very great deal for the liturgical renascence. For they were not merely builders or restorers of ecclesiastical monuments, they were the intelligent admirers of church vestments ; and they were better able than many others to appreciate their true form and proportions. Several of them have even left us useful studies in this subject, notably Pugin,[1] Gilbert Scott,[2] and

[1] *Glossary of Ecclesiastical Ornament and Costume*, 1844.

[2] *Discursus on the History of the Chasuble*, in *An Essay on the History of Architecture*, 1881.

Viollet-le-Duc. ³   These writers, it is true, belong to a period that is
now past, but we should not therefore treat them slightingly.   We
should remember the times in which they lived, and we should not
forget that, if we have now any appreciation of Gothic architecture
and the vestments which accord with it, it is due in large measure to
these leaders of the Gothic Revival.

While the countries which we have mentioned were witnessing their
Gothic Revival, Germany and Austria contributed to the movement,
by solid research and by a taste for ancient vestments.   As one example,
we may allude to the writings of Dr. Bock, which represent a very
considerable contribution to the revival in religious art, especially
in the sphere of vesture. ⁴

Quite frequently in America also has the evil style of vestments
been held in horror, and we have recently heard from the editor of
an important review that the best churches in the United States have
imported from England and Germany, during the last thirty years,
a good number of the finer specimens of chasubles, restored to something
of their original proportions and beauty.

In Italy also there were scholars who set themselves the task of
expounding those monuments which the Gothic genius had planted,
though very sparingly, in that country.   But that renascence of the
spirit which manifested itself so clearly elsewhere did not become
prominent in Italy, and it failed entirely to affect the clergy or the makers
of vestments.   Italy was not prepared to accept a Gothic revival,
a fact for which we have already given some explanation.   We may
add that in that country the ancient classical civilisation is by no means
dead.   Its monuments lie around on every side, and it has exercised,
and does still exercise, a very considerable influence.   Of this fact we
had an interesting instance at the Paris "Exposition des Arts
Décoratifs" (1925), where, among the twenty or so nations that had
their special pavilions, all were of a very modern character, except
Italy's, which was built in the ancient Roman style.

We shall be accused, doubtless, of digression, but we wished once
more to emphasize the fact that from the point of view of the arts,
not excluding the ecclesiastical arts, Italian feeling and Italian taste

---

³ Various articles in *Dictionnaire du Mobilier*, 1858-1875.

⁴ The author treats of liturgical vesture in his *Geschichte der liturgischen Gewänder
des Mittelalters*, Bonn, 1849-1871.   The illustrations to that book are rather defective,
but it was the best that could be done then.   However, they reproduce numerous
documents, and several of them are not to be found except in this work.

remain antique, and for this very reason differ very considerably from the spirit and taste of other nations.

Apart from certain isolated phenomena, such as those which we shall mention presently, Italy held fast to that liturgical vesture which was introduced in the period of decadence. The chief merit of liturgical vesture in the first centuries of the Christian era, that is to say, its beauty of ample folds and chaste simplicity—this was no more. Instead of cherishing the substance, men devoted themselves to the accessory, that is to say, to an ornamentation which had some little classical spirit, but which had become vulgarized by the habit of insipid imitation. There was no more creative work, nothing but the products of the manufactory.

In the other countries of Europe liturgical vesture had suffered the same degradation. Churches were short of money, and the clergy, having no aesthetic education, were attracted by the meretricious charms of the manufactured products, and thought themselves happy that they could, at a small expense, satisfy the taste, or rather the want of taste, of the devout laity. Then came the time of "la bonne souffrance," when men began to suffer at seeing vestments of mean and vulgar character (figs. 73 and 74) used at the altar. And, when the hour struck for the return of a certain artistic and religious culture, then in many a place men were ready to welcome with gratitude full chasubles, and other vestments of a style and shape less unworthy of the God of infinite beauty. And then it was that a future champion of the cause of Rome was preparing himself, by study and in the silence of the cloister, for the rôle which Providence had assigned to him. Dom Guéranger—for we refer to him—is one who in any matter which concerns the Church is above suspicion of disloyalty. It was boldly said of him by the Bishop of Le Mans, Monseigneur D'Outremont, that "from his lips the Church gathered her dogmatic definitions."[5] He was the "restorer in France of the Roman Liturgy," and was denominated by Monseigneur Bertaux "Liturgical Doctor." Well, this first abbot of Solesmes and loyal son of the Church was never more loyal than when he made it his business to restore and defend the better vesture of the Middle Ages. He did not hesitate to go back to that period when vestments were of ample form and great dignity, and full of liturgical significance. He had raised the monastery of Solesmes from its ruins and founded priories besides ; he was without pecuniary resources ; but if ever there were a man of

[5] In allusion to Dom Guéranger's treatises on the Pope and on the Immaculate Conception.

FIGS. 73 & 74. TWO "BOARD" CHASUBLES IN THE COMMERCIAL STYLE
The one with the column, the other with the cross

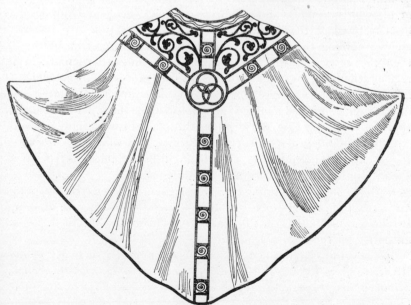

FIG. 75. A FULL AND FLEXIBLE CHASUBLE WITH CHARMING ORNAMENT
(A. E. Grossé, Bruges)

faith, Dom Guéranger was one. At the price of many sacrifices he revived in his abbey the use of the full chasuble. Others copied him and his chasubles. Ancient vestments were, so to say, discovered, studied and imitated. Better still, with inspiration from such models, original work was produced. The sacred fire was enkindled on all sides throughout France, and in the very life time of the Abbot of Solesmes you might have seen bishops of thoroughly ultramontane views, bishops who on ordinary days wore the tiny so-called "Roman" chasubles, arrayed on festivals in noble *paenulae*, and so pontificating in their splendid cathedrals. And on all sides there was but one opinion and one judgment, on the part of the clergy and laity alike, that the bishops (and we might add archbishops and cardinals also) had never been so well clad nor ever looked so noble as when robed in these ample chasubles. The writer of these lines will not easily forget that period and the experience it brought to him. It was his youth's first lesson in liturgical art.

It might be questioned whether Dom Guéranger himself lived to see the revival of the full vestment in the cathedrals of France. But, however that may be, there is no doubt that he desired it vehemently, as may easily be deduced from his acts, and as is explicitly indicated in his words : "We confidently repeat, that when our churches have been restored on the lines of their original inspiration, or constructed anew according to the architectural rules of the Ages of Faith, that then the vestments which we use in them must participate in this regeneration, and lose at last those ugly and grotesque forms which the nineteenth century, improving even on the scanty and stunted styles of the eighteenth, has managed to impose upon them. I am confident that we shall then see the gradual disappearance of those chasubles with fronts stiffened with unyielding buckram, which, to use the all too accurate description of the distinguished English artist, Welby Pugin, are like nothing so much as fiddle-backs."[6]

In Dom Guéranger's times also, Monseigneur de Dreux-Brézé obtained authority from the Holy See for all the priests of the diocese of Moulins (France) to use full vestments ; and Pére Lacordaire obtained the same authority for the French Dominicans.

Special studies published in various periodicals, such as : *Annales Archéologiques, Revue de l'Art chrétien, Zeitschrift für christliche Kunst, Stimmen aus Maria-Laach*, etc., and the researches of scholars such as Grimouard de Saint-Laurent, C. de Linas, V. Gay, C. and G. Rohault

---

[6] *Les Institutions liturgiques*, Vol. II, Ch. XIV, p. 629.

de Fleury, etc., gave constant accession of strength to the cause of good ecclesiastical vesture. And above all, in our own time, the writings of Father Joseph Braun, S.J., have provided and will continue to provide invaluable support for the same case. They display an erudition which is the fruit of a whole life consecrated to the study of liturgical vesture, and they supply numerous reproductions which have a great evidential value.7

FIG. 76.   CARDINAL WISEMAN'S CHASUBLE
St. Edmund's College, Ware

Moreover, the technique of materials, the cut of vestments, the methods of manufacture, in fine all that concerned vestments was well studied and examined ; and, as we may testify, thousands of chasubles were produced, some of a middle shape, others of full dimensions, for hundreds of churches. London, Paris, Lyons, Cologne, Munich, Vienna, Bruges, etc., vied with one another in artistic activity and excellence. Bruges in particular excelled in this matter, thanks to the firm of L. Grossé, Senr. The master made a point of giving his staff a long training. They had, moreover, the constant advice and encouragement of L. de Farcy—an expert if ever there was one—who stimulated their efforts by putting generous orders with them.8 We owe to this Flemish firm the most beautiful

7 *Die priesterlichen Gewänder des Abenlandes*, 1897. *Die liturgische Gewandung im Okzident und Orient*, 1907. *Handbuch der Paramentik*, 1912. *Praktische Paramentenkunde*, 1924, etc.

8 L. de Farcy is the author of a good number of very careful studies on the priestly vestments, and in particular of an important folio work : *La Broderie du XIe siècle jusqu'à nos jours.*

chasubles, copes, mitres, etc., that the religious world saw in the
nineteenth century.

England deserves a place apart in the history of liturgical vesture.
When the Church in England experienced the renewed vitality of the
"Second Spring" the clergy, looking about them for examples of ecclesi-
astical art, could not look for them in the religious arts of the three

FIGS. 77 & 78. CHASUBLES OF THE GOTHIC REVIVAL
Not of full size, but of pleasing cut and ornamentation
(L. Grossé, London)

preceding centuries, for the simple reason that in England no such
arts existed. The old churches and cathedrals of England were in the
hands of an heretical body, and ecclesiastical art as applied to vestments
was simply dead.   Nor could they be influenced by the liturgical costume
of other countries, for they were not familiar with it, except with a
few copes and chasubles which had been imported with difficulty
from France, and which were used by stealth at the beginning of the
nineteenth century. Ugly, worn and soiled, they disappeared with
the penal days, when suffering and fear gave place to hope and joy.
Then the desire was general for the vestments which were used in
all the churches before the Reformation, and there was an instinctive
and loving movement in this direction. We have evidence of it at New
Oscott in 1838,[9] and many times afterwards. The great Cardinal
Wiseman—one of the first to set the example—never officiated
except in an ample chasuble, proportioned to his great stature. His

[9] Bishop Ullathorne tells us in his *Autobiography* (I, p. 142) that at the opening
of the chapel at New Oscott, the more ample form of vestments was introduced.

chasubles are preserved with jealous care at S. Edmund's College, Old Hall (fig. 76).

Pugin, one of the leaders of the Gothic revival, was then studying and building.   With a talent, which, considering the time in which he lived, was genius, and with a heart ravished by the beauty of good vestments, he sought them in particular for the numerous churches which he built, and he created for England certain types of chasubles, based upon the ancient standards.   They were not the ancient *paenulae nobiles*, but they were of pleasing size, and their ornamentation was in good taste (figs. 77 and 78).   They were appreciated widely and adopted in nearly all the churches and cathedrals of the country.   They still exist ; but many sisters of theirs, younger and of slightly more ample form, have to some extent replaced the original types.

The key to this liturgical revival in England was indicated in 1924 by Father Edmund Lester, S.J., in the *Tablet* (April 26th).   He first quotes from another Catholic paper as follows :

"A correspondent of 'Pastoralia' wrote in October, 1899, that it is a fact, which ought to be known, that in the first Provincial Council following the re-establishment of the Hierarchy, the use of Gothic vestments was enjoined.   When the decrees were sent to Rome for approbation, the term 'Gothic' puzzled the Roman authorities.   They did not know what Gothic meant.   It was presumed something to do with the Gothic or Mozarabic rite.   The word 'Gothic' was, therefore, struck out, and 'Roman' inserted.   Some of the bishops then sent a representative to Rome with a set of Gothic vestments.   When the authorities saw them they said : 'But these are Roman Vestments,' and approved of them.

"The term 'Roman' vestments can, therefore, be said to apply to the description of vestments, e.g., chasuble, stole, maniple, burse, veil, etc., and not to the *cut* or form.   France uses Roman vestments, but cuts them like sandwich-boards ; and Spain also uses Roman vestments, but cuts them like fiddle-backs.   The Gothic or medieval form, therefore, I hold, is the most dignified and appropriate for Gothic churches."

On this passage Father Lester comments :

"One point here worth noticing is that seeing the Gothic cut vestments *are* Roman the Decree of the First Provincial Council holds, i.e., that the Catholic Church in England is 'enjoined' to use this cut or shape.   Of course, let there be liberty, and we should not recommend the Gothic-Roman cut in the Oratory.   No doubt, the Gothic cut is nearer to the vestments of the first centuries. Rome deals with rites, not cuts, and seeing the Gothic cut *is* Roman there seems to be every reason for the revival, especially as it is so linked up with pre-Reformation Catholicity."

FIG. 79. A PUGIN CHASUBLE AT USHAW
A vigorous design in the Gothic style and very
well ornamented

Here certainly is a passage which is very encouraging for all those who use full or fullish chasubles, which are thus found to be Gothic *and* Roman. So the use of such vestments has been approved, and no decree proposes to abolish them ; just as no decree seeks to interfere one jot with the highly individual ceremonies of the various non-Roman, but thoroughly Catholic liturgies. There is no point, therefore, in besieging the Sacred Congregation of Rites with questions that traverse this same ground over and over again.

So Gothic chasubles are Roman chasubles, and your docked and clipped chasuble has no right to claim the exclusive use of that name.

Let us listen for a moment to the emphatic words of Dr. Adrian Fortescue, one of the best liturgists of our time, who though dead yet speaks to us in his books.

"Dismiss from your minds that it is a question of *Roman* shape. . . . It is not a question of *place*, but of *period of time*. These modern shapes are not specially Roman ; they came in at the same time nearly everywhere. And the older shape was used at Rome just as much as everywhere else. Rome is full of pictures and monuments which show that popes wore the same large vestments as everywhere else in the West, till Baroque taste swept over Rome too. Let us be as Roman as possible always. But in artistic matters let us look to Rome's good artistic periods. It would be absurd to defend mangled plainsong and operatic music as Roman. It is just as absurd to claim the name of the ancient city for only one period of her long artistic development. Skimped chasubles, gold braid, and lace are not Roman ; they are eighteenth century bad taste."[10]

We may say, therefore, that while the Gothic Revival lasted, and in that other revival of spirit and taste which succeeded to it, the full chasuble found its way, little by little, into most of the dioceses of Europe. Sometimes an indult was obtained, and sometimes it was introduced without special indult, but "in perfect good faith and relying upon the actual state of affairs and in accord with the rubrics, the New Code, and examples in high places." These examples were given at Rome itself, where full vestments have been used in several churches, especially in the last forty years. The Archbishop of Utrecht was in Rome in 1867 and observed, even at that date, that the Redemptorists were using chasubles made according to the dimensions given by St. Charles Borromeo (51 ins. wide), and that Pius IX wore even wider ones. Pius X also used quite wide chasubles ; he frequently presented such chasubles to churches ; and in the visitation of the Roman churches, which was made in 1904 in his name, the use of such chasubles was recommended.[11]

All who were interested in the liturgy, all those who yearned for better things for the House of God, rejoiced to see such action in the highest ranks of the Church. They followed the lead thus given, and helped the

[10] *The Vestments of the Roman Rite*, London, 1925, p. 22.

[11] Canon Callewaert, President of the Seminary of Bruges : *Collationes Brugenses*, 1926, p. 185. The Editor of the Ushaw Magazine informs me that he once assisted at a High Mass sung by Cardinal Rampolla in Rome at which very ample vestments, with a Y cross on the Chasuble, were worn.

F

good cause with their knowledge, labour, and money. New life thus
began to flow in the veins of this art of liturgical vesture. With perfect
justice and all confidence, dioceses, communities and private persons
began to present these liturgical vestments not only to their churches,
but also to bishops and even to the Holy Father himself. Since their
preference was given in a marked manner to copes, we may be permitted
to record here one instance among many others. In the year 1877,
Monseigneur Pie, Bishop of Poitiers, and afterwards Cardinal, offered
Pope Pius IX in the name of his diocese, a superb cope. It had been
conceived and designed by Père de la Croix, S.J., whose archæological
learning was a guarantee against petty trivialities. The body of the
cope was decorated with a symmetrical repetition of the cross of St.
Radegund and the fleur-de-lis. On the hood, on all the lower border
of the vestment, and on the vertical orfreys down the front edges,
Père de la Croix had arranged very beautiful designs, inspired by
Merovingian art, and twenty-six heads of saints in fine embroidery.
The composition and designing must have taken fully a hundred hours ;
the needle-work, if done by one person, would perhaps have required
a thousand hours.

In 1924 I saw, in the Husson workrooms at Paris, another vestment,
more original, lighter, and more artistic still. It was a rather full chasuble
of a very pure Celtic character and extremely charming in feeling,
design and colour. There were no figures on it ; its beauty lay in its
shape, its very graceful curves, its majestic cross, and its Celtic inscrip-
tion, very firm and ornamental, which ran across the whole width of
the vestment. A son of France, of noble birth and great learning, had
himself supplied the design and directed the execution, and he intended
to take it himself as a gift to Pope Pius XI.

A short time afterwards, at the very beginning of 1925, the same
Sovereign Pontiff blessed a great number of vestments which had been
inspired by antique models. In fact, the Holy Year received quite a
liturgical stamp from the Exhibition of sacred art which was held in
the Roman "Cenacle" on the 2nd, 3rd, and 4th of January, and at
which were seen hundreds of full chasubles, dalmatics and copes, etc.
All these vestments were then taken to the Consistorial Hall in the
Vatican, so that the Holy Father might see them. Some of them had
been offered by "Les Amis de l'Art Liturgique," by the Benedictine
nuns of Rue Monsieur (Paris), by Mme la Comtesse de Gramond d'Aster,
etc. Eighteen chasubles of the full shape came from Holland ; fifty
others, equally full, were given by ladies of Milan.

We should not be surprised at this beautiful manifestation. If the shops of Italy, like many others, still clung to those miserable shapes and that pompous decoration which habit alone could make acceptable, Rome, the guardian of liturgical beauty, was looking beyond the last three centuries to that ideal costume of which she was, so to speak, the trustee ; and Rome understood the matter so well that the Pontifical Commission wished to have no other vestments than those inspired by this ideal. All the chasubles that figured in this exhibition were of full or fullish form. They were of light or flexible material, with the consequence that they draped well and fell in good folds. They offered moreover a very interesting, and at the same time, a very satisfying variety in their use of the cross, of bands and of orfreys.

But we should never finish if we attempted to give a complete account of the progress of the full vestment in our days. We shall not even attempt to record the outstanding events, such as the support given to the movement by learned liturgists and by bishops and cardinals. We may add, however, that in 1922 an Italian cardinal celebrated the Sacred Mysteries in the Basilica of San Clemente clad in a full chasuble ; that the "Sacerdos magnus" of Belgium, Cardinal Mercier, had a whole series of full chasubles made at Bruges for his seminary in the University of Louvain ; and that other princes of the Church have in these last few years done likewise and procured themselves noble vestments wherewith to pontificate in their splendid cathedrals, or say Mass in their private chapels.

To this we need hardly add that many parishes have followed these examples. A short while ago we were reading, in a review, of the Belgian churches destroyed in the War, themselves and their vestments. The writer told us that new churches were springing up on the soil of Belgium to replace the old ; and that these churches, in place of the narrow, skimpy chasubles of old, were being provided with chasubles that were full, simple, and light. In those three words are expressed the master qualities of the true vestment.

CHAPTER VI

THE CHASUBLE (3): THE LITURGICAL REVIVAL OF THE TWENTIETH CENTURY

WITH the help of the explanations given in the last two chapters and better still, with the help of the drawings and photographs therein reproduced, the reader has followed the evolution of the chasuble from the first centuries down to the present day. He will have observed that liturgical art, after a long period of prosperity, fell into a period of decline, and that this in course of time was succeeded by a period of revival. This revival, which has taken place in our own days, has been marked by much earnest desire and powerful effort, and has produced many fruitful results, determined by the needs, the knowledge and the deep feelings of our age, that is to say by our mental outlook. This sequence of elaboration, relative perfection, decadence and revival is not a new phenomenon. Every art, beginning with the most ancient, has arisen, developed, ripened and then decayed ; to be succeeded by a new, or at the very least, a much transformed art.

Although this fact is known and admitted by the immense majority of thoughtful and observant people, yet it is set down here because there are those who are sometimes far from comfortable when there is a renewal in the matter of ecclesiastical art. One might reasonably complain of such an attitude. Does not our faith itself gladly admit the fact of a considerable development, which makes its doctrines better known and better appreciated ? And the law of nature itself is revealed each spring in the renewal and fresh growth of plant and tree. The life of a tree knows no long immobility ; were it to arrest its growth it would soon wither and die.

Yet liturgical art has marked time and has become commonplace and vulgar, through the *sterility* of routine, through the *fertility* of money, through the *falsity* of appearance, and through the *finality* of the useful. [1] But it could not wholly die. We are witnessing a Third Spring, more powerful than the Second, which is bringing an inevitable

[1] *The Philosophy of Art*, being *Art et Scholastique*, by J. Maritain, translated by the Rev. John O'Connor, S.T.P., 1923, p. 53.

revival in religious art. The artisan of the manufactory shall be replaced by the master artist who alone has feeling for beauty, understands the task entrusted to him, manages it intelligently, loves his work and loves even the toil it gives him. We desire that our eucharistic vestments should bear the stamp of mind.

We should be unworthy of our task if we remained captive to inveterate and faulty habits, since there is a necessary process of evolution in every sphere. We should be accused by innumerable voices of being accomplices of obscurantism, if we determined to disregard ideas and methods which could be profitable to liturgical costume. Of course, we are not here preaching either certain theories subversive of aesthetical principles, or certain ultra-modern styles, born of arbitrariness and fantasy. Human conceptions and human manifestations will always have an infinite variety ; but, when religious art is in question, they are submitted to appropriate conditions and laws. A man may ignore these conditions and transgress these laws ; but a sane evolution recalls us to the one and the other, takes note in a practical spirit of all the good there is in the new productions, and revives, if they are suitable, the best productions of the past. And so we have an evolution forwards, and sometimes backwards also ! To allow oneself to be guided by the first is to be intelligent and docile ; to accept the second requires courage and humility, especially in the case of artists who desire, and quite reasonably, to be men of their own age.

Just as study, comparison, science, and in one word truth, have ousted very faulty editions of the liturgical chant, which have been replaced or will in time be replaced by the Vatican edition, so also a deeper understanding of the essential characters of ecclesiastical costume, and the discovery of modern decoration, oblige us to abandon all unworthy imitations, to take our inspiration from the best models of good periods, and to rejuvenate what we take, not merely with the help of better methods of procedure, but by means of those methods of the intellectual order which are the possession of our present age. We cannot refuse to admit the logical consequence that a revival in thought and in art entails a renewal in the sphere of liturgical vesture. As we have said, it has already begun ; and it is making good progress on all sides, particularly in Christian Rome, ever ancient and ever new. The Exhibition to which we have referred in Chapter V is a manifest sign. The vestments and accessories collected then in the Cenacle Convent at Rome were very numerous, but we felt ourselves desiring a greater variety in materials and ornamentation, such materials and

ornament, that is, as would have better expressed the atmosphere of
Christian antiquity which was desired by the Pontifical Commission.
But, apart from this criticism, practically all the examples of liturgical
vesture gave proof of a just understanding, and often of originality.
All the vestments were of ample cut ; their flexible materials guaranteed
good draping ; most of the stoles and maniples were designed according
to excellent models ; all the hoods and orfreys of the copes were of
discreet dimensions ; embroidery was used sparingly, while on the
other hand many of the crosses and orfreys were made of bands of a
woven material, either polychrome or monochrome.   All this gave us
a type of vestment inspired by a spirit that had freed itself from the
mediocrities of the past ; better methods had been accepted and put
into practice ; there was evidence of communion with the new movement
in art.

Let us profit by the important lesson thus given us ; and let me repeat
once more that we shall get vestments of superior quality when the
shapes are noble, when the proportion and arrangement of the motifs
form an harmonious rhythm, and when the variety of colour marks
and precises these values.   You may be guided only by that principle—
so often wrongly interpreted—that "nothing is too rich for the service
of God," so that you lavish money on sumptuous materials, complicated
ornament, gold embroideries, and produce nothing but the pretentious
and the inappropriate.   I have before me dozens of exact reproductions
of chasubles and copes which manifest no initiative, or desire for it,
and no real effort.   Their ornamentation is nothing but an imitation
of out of date models, executed in raised gold and silk bullion ; and,
of course, the prices are in keeping with this misguided extravagance.
From twenty to eighty pounds is asked for each vestment, although
you may, for merely eight or ten pounds, get a cope or a chasuble of excellent design and execution.

Reproductions and explanatory notes will presently explain what
we have said.   The various items of costume which are reproduced
in this chapter were made between 1910 and 1925.   None of them is of
an unpleasantly archeological style, and those which have an archaic
character are yet definitely marked with the impress of our age and of
the countries in which they were made.   The examples are borrowed
from Belgium, France, Germany, and England ; and many others are
given throughout the book.   The chasubles are reproduced—let us
emphasize this point—less to provide models for exact reproduction than
to suggest new ideas, new designs, new vestments.   If some copies of

excellent works are perfectly legitimate, when made with a jealous exactitude, yet the *viae certae et determinatae* of art, its sure and settled ways, are not the beaten tracks of imitation. It is the artist's business on every occasion to apply the laws of his art, to discover a new way

FIG. 81.   RED CHASUBLE, OF A SIMPLE AND CLEAR
ORNAMENTATION
(A. E. Grossé, Bruges)

of using his material according to his good sense, his perspicacity and the leisure of his soul. This is the golden rule.

The reader will observe different stages in the art of decoration. From vestments of very simple ornamentation and technique we pass to chasubles which present designs that are entirely embroidered. A prominent place is given to vestments decorated with appliqué work,[2] because this is a very economic method, and the result is often

---

[2] This method is briefly described in Chapter XVII.

marked by a distinctness and strength superior to the effects obtained by embroidery. However, many such pieces of appliqué work may be set off by true embroidery.

If bands and ribbons of silk or velvet are applied and used for orfreys, they may stand out against the main material without the least border and make very good vestments. That is the first step in the degrees of ornamentation. The chasuble reproduced here (fig. 81), is a good example of this ; the bands have no bordering, but are decorated with small crosses arranged as on a pallium. That is a very simple chasuble and in perfect good taste ; you can get one like it for about eight pounds.

Sometimes galloons outline the appliqué bands, as is shown in fig. 82. The two crosses, in front and behind, are in copper-red plush ; they are bordered with gold and stand out extremely well on the damask field. The vestment is one of great beauty, due to the simplicity of the crosses and to the superb material, decorated with the monogram XP, palms, circles enclosing the fish and basket of loaves, the lamb and the vessel of milk. [3] It might be deduced from what has just been said that the bands which here form the crosses, being of a strong colour, do not require the galloons that border them ; but these define them to advantage, and add to the vestment a note of richness and completion which gives pleasure. When pale-coloured bands are applied to white chasubles or white copes, a border of a dark-coloured galloon is extremely useful for distinguishing the pale tints and for adding boldness and vigour to the vestment. As to gold ornament on white material, the effect is often delicate, but also often insufficiently decorative. On the other hand galloons of pale silk, or galloons of gold, are the proper border for coloured bands (green, red, purple), when these have the same, or practically the same, intensity of colour as the principal material of the vestment. These galloons then connect and at the same time separate somewhat the two tints ; they enhance, that is to say, they make effective, the intensity of the two stuffs thus juxtaposed. If no attention be paid to these rules, which are supposed to be familiar to the makers of vestments, the colours annihilate each other, or at least their effect is reduced to the point of insignificance. I have seen bands of violet velvet, without border, on a black chasuble, tunic and dalmatic ; the failure of this ornamentation was manifest, for at a short distance away the vestments appeared to be entirely black. A light-yellow galloon or a gold braid, at the joint of the bands and the stuff, would have mended the whole ; the violet velvet bands would

[3] See Chapter III, p. 47, and Fig. 44.

then have become visible and vigorous.   Another example is a chasuble
made for His Eminence, Cardinal Bourne (fig. 83). It is rich, but very
sober.   The olive-green damask is adorned with two crosses, in front
and behind, made of velvet which is likewise green ; but these stand out

FIG. 82.   CHASUBLE OF WHITE DAMASK WITH A PLUSH CROSS IN
COPPER RED
(Biais, Paris)

very well because the character and effect of the velvet differ notably
from those of the damask, and especially because the velvet is bordered
with a fine gold galloon.   The small crosses, of the superb gold stuff,
are appliqué work, and are outlined with fire-coloured silk.   From the
arms of the large cross hang chains embroidered on the material and
terminated by heraldic roses in gold.   All this has about it a touch of
Byzantine art, but obviously interpreted in a modern sense.

Decorative galloons, woven and of a moderate width, are often utilised to make the crosses of chasubles and the orfreys of other vestments.   The reader will not have forgotten that great use was made of

FIG. 83.   VERY BEAUTIFUL CHASUBLE IN AN OLIVE-GREEN DAMASK, MADE FOR
HIS EMINENCE CARDINAL BOURNE
The crosses and rosettes are appliqué work
(A. E. Grossé, Bruges)

them, for various items of liturgical vesture, in the examples exhibited
at Rome in 1925.   Although it is a delicate matter to lay down a rule
about such a thing, we may enunciate this one : galloons produce a

satisfactory effect only when two conditions are fulfilled, that the designs be not very varied, and that the colours be not multiplied. Yet these two rules are often broken. One may be attracted at the first view of such galloons and realize later, to one's disappointment, that they

FIG. 84.   WHITE SILK CHASUBLE, UNLINED, WITH A CROSS OF A
WOVEN GALLOON
(A. E. Grossé, Bruges)

produce a disagreeable medley. With two, or at the most, three colours, and some conventional or natural design repeated symmetrically, one may obtain clearer and stronger effects. Here is an example which cannot, in black and white, convey complete the feeling of art and distinction which is given by the reality (fig. 84). The chasuble is made of a cream-white silk, fine-ribbed ; on the woven cross, of which the ground is likewise cream-white, there is a series of brick-red designs. This is an unlined vestment, completely free from pretentiousness, which yet leaves nothing to be desired. It costs only seven pounds.

FIG. 85.   VERY UNCOMMON DECORATION
After that on a Chasuble of St. Thomas of Canterbury,
now at Sens
(A. E. Grossé, Bruges)

The woven galloons, which appear on the chasuble reproduced in fig. 85, effect a very interesting decoration. Their arrangement evinces not only a very sound sense of ornamentation, but also a praiseworthy courage, guided by a return to the medieval. This type of ornamentation is, in fact, inspired by the ornamentation of a chasuble of St. Thomas of Canterbury.   But the Bruges artist has selected galloons with strong decorative designs, has obtained with them more open angles, has

changed the proportions, and so has produced a better vestment
than St. Thomas's. Its price is moderate : some ten pounds.

Let us go one step higher in our decorative ascent and consider a
chasuble which will not fail to trouble those who judge according to

FIG. 86. CHASUBLE OF RED AND YELLOW LAMPAS, OF VERY RICH EFFECT
The flames in gold on velvet bands. Made for Westminster Cathedral
(A. E. Grossé, Bruges)

trite designs and motifs. It is original without a doubt, but it is also
decorative and powerfully decorative (fig. 87). Let us relate how it
was conceived and designed, for we knew the artist and his method of
procedure in the matter ; if the reader will follow, it will be a useful
lesson for him. The artist received three precise directions only :
the chasuble was to serve for feasts of Our Lady ; it should be sufficiently
splendid ; and it should not cost much, somewhere about fifteen pounds.
The designer worked at his task as a labour of love, so that he worked
truly *gratis pro Deo et Maria sanctissima*. Silk embroideries, well-

made and expensive, these were out of the question. Ornament in high relief and effective trimmings, these he loathed. To begin with he did nothing whatever with his hands, but he worked hard with his head. He considered how and with what materials he might produce

FIG. 87. AN ORIGINAL AND VERY EFFECTIVE CHASUBLE
The cross of an ashen-blue plush ; the centre medallion and squares of
dark red satin. Rock-crystal ornamentation
(A. E. Grossé, Bruges)

a somewhat striking, yet utterly sincere effect ; he considered with the help of his knowledge of decorative themes, of colour and of gold, how he might realise contrast without violence, how he might arrange the motifs, while respecting the main lines of the vestment. He then put together his sketches of the elements which were to be employed on the vestment ; he made a water-colour painting in life size, that is in the size of the actual chasuble, and sent the whole to the firm of A. E. Grossé,

of Bruges. On a beautiful white damask were extended two crosses of
an ashen blue, intersected lengthwise and bordered by galloons of an
intense red with bezants and quatrefoils of a gold yellow, which also
make pendants that are regarded as hanging from the arms of the cross.
At the extremity of these galloons are squares of brown-red satin.
Brown-red also is the field of the medallion on which is a well-set M,
surmounted by an indented crown. Finally a note of splendour is
obtained by means of small stones which sparkle in a good artificial
light, or in bright sunlight. A piping of real gold thread emphasizes the
rows of these transparent hemispheres. And now consider this chasuble,
and you will realise that the mere labour of conception, composition
and design represents the work of hours, or rather of days. And, finally,
let the reader judge this noble religious vestment as he will, but let
him believe us, since we have seen it. It is original, it is festal, it is
well-executed. A professor who saw it in our company said to us :
"The Easter chasuble in our seminary cost eight times as much. It
is decorated with a quantity of very beautiful compositions, skilfully
executed in fine embroidery. But its effect is far from equalling the
effect of this chasuble."

While we pass thus to the consideration of embroidery, the criticism
just reported should not make us unfavourable towards a practice
which has been held in honour for centuries. However, some distinctions
must be made, and the task is not a difficult one. A considerable
number of vestments, antependia and other articles, preserved in the
treasuries of churches or in museums, demonstrate quite fully that
"needle painting" produced marvels from the twelfth to the sixteenth
century, likewise heavy, pompous and tasteless works in the seventeenth
and eighteenth centuries. Everything depends upon the technical
knowledge and skill of the embroiderer, but primarily upon the design,
character, proportions and propriety of the figures and decorative
compositions which are rendered in silk. For instance, the chasuble
of fig. 88 presents us with embroidered ornament which in appearance
is rather stiff, but which is well arranged, of a calm and exact feeling,
and of an extremely rare artistic taste. Note especially the beautiful
central medallion, with its anchor of salvation, supported by two fishes
which symbolize the faithful. In fine, this vestment well represents
German feeling, to be more precise, the feeling of a special school of
art influenced by the art of Beuron.

The reader will now remark a wholly different taste and style, a
perfect dignity and perfect ease, in a chasuble made by M. Poussielgue-

Rusand, of Paris (fig. 90).   It is made of a violet velvet, a species of
velvet which is specially suitable for vestments, since it is light and
gives a pleasing drapery.   Some kinds of velvet are strong and unyielding,
so that they take and preserve very ugly folds.   This is a great defect,

FIG. 88.   CHASUBLE WITH SOMEWHAT SEVERE ORNA-
MENTATION, BUT OF A VERY ARTISTIC FEELING
Observe the beautiful medallion with its anchor of
salvation and fishes representing the faithful. German
art

and we should remember it in our purchases.   The ears of corn, the
vine and its bunches of grapes, very beautiful symbols which have often
been represented in a pitiable fashion and repeated to satiety, are not
on this chasuble conceived in that inferior manner ; on the contrary
they form admirable compositions, in the modern style, but in a decorative modern style which indicates an artist of good quality.   His work
is a work of art ; you may divine that with the help of the printed

G

photograph, although it cannot give any idea of the beauty of the golds and of the colours. The ears of corn and the monogram are in gold, the leaves of the vine in green, and the grapes in white. The cross seems too broad in the reproduction ; but it is not so in reality, because the chasuble is very ample, and secondly because the ground material is visible throughout, between the vine branches and the ears of corn. In many similar cases the artist has run up against a difficulty and failed to surmount it, when the lines which mark clearly the limits of the orfreys have been suppressed. This is the case in a chasuble reproduced in *L'Ouvroir Liturgique*, January 13th and 20th, 1924, fig. 1. But this vestment is a failure, not only because of its *curled* borders, turned in the manner of certain petunias, but also because of the flowerets and branches arranged without any consistency and without any border lines to support them. This luxuriant vegetation, spreading itself at large over the ground of white satin, indicates the sort of thing we get when we follow instinct alone and lack any real training in, or knowledge of, the art of decorative composition. If the artist responsible for the Poussielgue-Rusand chasuble has been successful, it is because he had first-class knowledge. But it is none the less true that there is a difficulty to be faced in dealing with this problem. And so we affirm that well-outlined orfreys are usually preferable to orfreys which are not plainly outlined. The lines of the orfreys provide a clear and precise demarcation, and may be said to lay down rules which are required by the very structure of the cross. They prevent the artist, who would ornament the orfreys, from developing his decorative motifs in too fantastic a fashion. And, finally, they help the faithful to distinguish, even from a distance, the form of the sign of our Redemption.

FIG. 89.   A DUTCH PRIEST
His chasuble remarkable for its precision and grace
(*Het Gildebook*, March, 1923, p. 182)

Another chasuble that will doubtless attract the reader's attention

FIG. 90.   CHASUBLE OF VIOLET VELVET
Decorated with ears of corn and vine branches ; a masterpiece
of good arrangement.   The decoration is all embroidered
(Poussielgue-Rusand, Paris)

certainly attains the highest degree of decorative art as applied to
liturgical costume. It shows fine point embroidery representing personages and scenes (fig. 92). This work is very expensive, and generally

speaking it has neither the strength nor the simplicity necessary for being well seen from a distance. But it has other qualities, and these very noteworthy ones. They are, in the case we are considering, the delicacy and grace of the compositions, the suavity and harmony of

FIG. 91. BEAUTIFUL PALE RED CHASUBLE OF EXCELLENT DIMENSIONS
(Which the size of the page has compelled us to cut down at each side.) The central cross in dark red velvet ; the other ornaments rather slender but well arranged and, being in gold, they stand out well on the red stuff
(*The Art of the Book,* 1914, p. 77)

the colours, and the perfection of the technique. Observe the medallion on the front of the chasuble, representing the Last Supper, the orfreys decorated with angel musicians, the palms distributed over the orfreys and on the stuff of the vestment. The aim has been to give abundant eucharistic instruction by means of scenes and symbols. So we have the Sacrifice of Calvary embroidered on the back of the chasuble, and in the little medallions we have the Tree of Life, the Seven Ears of Pharoah's dream, the Vine of the Promised Land, the mystic Wine-press, the Brazen Serpent, etc. Such symbolism can be understood only by those who are familiar with the Bible. And such small compositions are practically lost in a big church. The case is different in a small church or chapel, where such an admirable chasuble ought to have very great charm and be doctrinally very instructive, especially as it is completed by a cope on which are embroidered the Adoration of the

FIG. 92. AN ADMIRABLE CHASUBLE
Without the strength of the others in its decoration,
but distinguished by delicacy, grace and perfect
technique
(A. E. Grossé, Bruges)

Lamb in Paradise, the miracle of the Marriage Feast of Cana, the sacrifice of Abel, etc.

The ornamentation of the vestments which I have dealt with might not be accepted without dispute; but at any rate it has its good qualities. Sometimes there is great simplicity, sometimes relative simplicity ; and we have encountered well-disciplined compositions, technical knowledge, and clear effects, whether strong or delicate. It is obvious that other examples might have been chosen, reproduced, analysed ; and that, besides the firms mentioned, there are others which make vestments of severe beauty and with well-balanced and well-executed ornament. Archæological styles no longer obsess the artists who make vestments. Without perhaps distinguishing the spirit which directs them, they work with that good feeling which was characteristic of the good periods.

CHAPTER VII

LITURGICAL VESTURE AND MODERN ART

IT is only right that we should say something regarding the latest developments of the decorative art and their suitability for liturgical vesture. Our times have witnessed many revolutionary experiments in the region of artistic expression and the results of these experiments have often been of an extraordinary character. But we should make a mistake if we rejected all modern art without discrimination. For contemporary art is in fact almost infinitely various, according to the artist's temperament, according to his education, and according to his relations with artistic groups and with the traditions of a particular country. Its ways of expression vary from forms which are round, soft, and delicate, and from colours which are tender, sweet, and caressing to the eye, to hard, angular, square, jagged and pointed forms, and to all the ugliest and most startling combinations of muddy and cadaverous or sharp and violent colours, so that we are reminded of the hurly-burly of a jazz band.

A few brief observations may be of use to those who have no experience of these manifestations of beauty or ugliness, of simplicity or complexity, of originality or eccentricity. Liturgical vestments are naturally differentiated according to the sacred Orders, and according to the particular use for which they are destined. And we may reasonably suppose that these main differences are stable and permanent. But, as to all the rest, it may be repeated once more with advantage, that there is necessarily much variety according to epoch, nationality, temperament and education. We have already seen that the religious arts are in process of freeing themselves from feeble imitations of the Gothic style, or the Renaissance style, or the nondescript style which many have adopted as being pious in character and supposedly ecclesiastical. Liturgical artists, being worthy of their name of artists, cannot live any more in that vitiated and tepid atmosphere which has been breathed and rejected so many times before ; they would all think and work in a renewed and fresh atmosphere. They desire to return to the classical ways, and also to welcome and adapt the methods of modern art. A movement towards classical standards does not mean any copying of the antique styles, still less of the Romanesque, Gothic, or any other style. For all these, being things of the past. cannot express our own age. So the movement is rather a return to the fundamental ideas or principles which guided the old masters ; and among these directive principles are restraint, dignity, purification of reality, abstraction, severity—or at least that austere simplicity which does not exclude grace. It is a reaction against impressionism and romanticism, against that religious sentimentalism which has been and still is expressed to such ugly effect. Or, if the reader prefer it, it is just true art.

But one would naturally like to know, when applying to them for a set of vestments, what these modern artists are going to do in the matter of their ornamentation. This is their procedure. They take their inspiration directly from nature, interpret and modify according to the needs of the case the elements which nature offers them, and so produce vestments like that chasuble ornamented with vine branches and ears of corn which we have already admired (fig. 90). Or else they have recourse to geometrical ornaments, whether alone or combined with human forms, animals, plants, or the works of man—and all according to the imagination, native talent and receptivity of the individual artist. But their art is subjected to certain laws of arrangement, connection and proportion, and also to the laws which regulate colours, their gradation, harmony and contrast. What is the aim of these artists ? To produce what satisfies mind and eye. But this pleasure is not produced save by the just balance of the principal parts, by the correct choice and use of the elements, by the clarity of the ideas that one would express, by the harmony of the colours, whether these are isolated, juxtaposed, or superimposed. Look once again at the various illustrations of the previous chapter, not excepting those that display very simple vestments, and you will discover these qualities of order, proportion and serenity.

But, in the ultra-modern art, there is a spirit that is not prepared to conform to precise principles and conditions in the matter of colour and design, or of the interdependence and logical relation of parts ; its law is mere arbitrariness. As a natural result, the works produced are distinguished for eccentricities, discords and violent collisions, and for a wild turmoil of effects, though these things were not the artist's aim. But this result, though not intended, is attained ; and the artist seems content and satisfied.

The means used consist, for example, in the translating everything that crosses your mind, including the human form, [1] into rectangular, obtuse-angled, or acute-angled figures, but particularly into the last named, and in forcing and compressing all the possible motifs of ornamentation into other angular forms.   Some of these systematical productions were exhibited at the Paris "Exposition," of which we

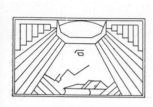  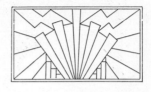

FIG. 93.   THE OX OF ST.   FIG. 94.   THE ANGEL OF   FIG. 95.   GROUP OF
          LUKE   ST. MATTHEW   ANGULAR MOTIVES

Details for a missal cover in the latest style. The ox is grotesque and the angel rather unsuitable. A square head is no more acceptable than an oval square.

have previously spoken.   The best critics of the new art have justly scourged such works, and have told us that " the Parisian public, whose good taste is well known, shrugged its shoulders at this Central African cubism."

The pity is that certain positive and earnest spirits add a sort of electricity to the air around them, although that is already sufficiently charged.   The war and the post-war period have been responsible for a painful unsettling of men's minds.   What they need is a soothing, calming influence ; and a sober art will provide part of this sedative. But, however this may be, it is quite certain that neither cubism, nor quadrangulism, nor systematic and extravagant triangulism is suitable for sacred vestments.   The church is the place for attentive prayer, for tempered joy, for the pacification of the soul ; but the works in question scarcely do anything but distract, excite and dissipate the mind.

What has just been said is not an argument against the use of polygonal designs.   The ancient artists and many of the modern have used

[1] The magazine *Colour* has published an illustration of this in a design wherein numerous personages are represented by regular and irregular polygons, with quadrangular heads, triangular eyes and mouths, clothes represented by broken lines, to the exclusion of all curves. Amusing and grotesque !

them ; but without exclusiveness, and without ever losing sight of the proper qualities of liturgical costume, especially the quality of dignity.

A very few examples of ultra-modern decoration are submitted for the reader's consideration. If I am not very much mistaken he will not admire their broken, angular designs and distorted forms. I could wish that it was possible to put before him a cope or chasuble ornamented with orfreys made according to these patterns, for that would enable him to form a truer judgment on the modern style. But I must ask him to take my word for it that the same effect of angularity and fragmentariness is conveyed by the finished vestment. Now in every really excellent work of art the main lines are simple and a mere look can grasp the whole. But in vestments ornamented with these patterns there are no grand lines, there is no main structure, there is no organised whole. There should be an organic form and an organic unity; but in these compositions we have no organised form or unity. The whole is composed of fragments juxtaposed or superimposed, and

FIG. 96.   THRONE FOR EXPOSITION OF THE BLESSED SACRAMENT, VIEWED AT AN ANGLE (From *L'Artisan liturgique*).   A heavy structure of wood and tapestry

the result is a disturbing complexity which destroys the intrinsic value of the vestments.

Moreover these artists do not fail to give us some awkward compositions, as for instance the designs on a tunic and dalmatic that are not reproduced here. What, we ask, is represented by certain ornamental plaques, attached to the end of sticks, which start from the hem of one of these vestments, without any sort of connection with the sur-

FIG. 97.   DETAIL FROM FIG. 96 : GROUP OF DISJOINTED FRAGMENTS

roundings ?   One is tempted to suppose that they are *flabella* (fans). But, if so, why are they figured on a vestment ?   And what is this on an orfrey ?   Is it a vine leaf and some grapes ?   Or perhaps rather a bee furnished with long, spiral antennae ?   Ought we really to go so far that the sacred vestments encourage elaborate speculation and appeal chiefly to the sagacity of the observer ?

There is a law of art which governs the ornamentation of liturgical vestments, the symbolism and many other things : viz., that a modification should be either towards significance or towards beauty ; it should elucidate and accentuate what is represented.   Now, in the vestments of which we have been speaking, this law is not kept.   The transformation of the plant-forms operates in the direction of attenuation and obscurity ; it hinders clear and easy vision ; it confuses and obfuscates by that disunitedness which compels us to run from one detail to another in order to discover whether it is really the eucharistic vine that the artist has been representing.   In short, must we not say that the artist's invention, in quest of difficulties, his intellectual qualities, and his knowledge—all of which are evident in these compositions—have achieved a manifold failure ?

The material, at least, presents us with clear designs.   We have seen the two kings, David and Saul, represented in gold on a red ground ; a biblical material, and therefore very appropriate for the liturgy. Saul seemed entirely at his ease on his invisible throne ; the royal Psalmist far less comfortable, being reduced, himself and his harp, to a geometrical figure.   The Middle Ages would very probably have set both personages within that perfect frame, a circle.   But our artist wanted novelty ; and, when all has been said, we can appreciate the freedom which his composition may very justly claim.

We have seen another vestment in this modern style, a white cope, that seemed to us very successful. The eye falls restfully on the decorative parts, which are clearly expressed and which moreover stand out well from the white ground of a beautiful medieval damask, directly inspired by an antique oriental material. It is the "cope of squares" ; they occupy the preponderant place and they draw our attention far more than the crosses. But alas ! we have again to make what will seem a severe criticism ; the ornament is far too reminiscent of those rows of tiles which decorate certain bathrooms ; and even the false joints have not been forgotten. We would do well to leave this sort of ornament to the workmen who specialise in the arrangement of terra-cotta or marble squares. Our flexible vestments do not take well to ornaments which suggest rigid materials ; they demand compositions which are in harmony with silk and velvet, and in harmony above all with their sacred character.

However, upon the whole, the vestments in question are far better, from several points of view, than many other vestments which parade a superficially artistic appearance, as for instance a hackneyed imitation of Gothic or Renaissance ornament, and repetitions which prove the ineffectiveness or the absence of any genuine and valiant effort. What manifold effort, on the other hand, went to the making of the vestments we have just been considering. And audacity, originality, vigour ; these are written all over them. But also, the frigidities of angularism, crudity, complexity, and extravagance.

If the new art be guided by that faculty which discerns and eliminates extravagance, vexatious complexity, startling and fantastic effects; if taste for order, serenity and discretion be respected, as was the case when the arts attained their full expansion, at different historical periods, then we shall have an artistic "modernism," in the best sense of that word, which will be welcomed and used in our churches. In many places steps have been taken towards this end. In others the good work has still to be done ; but there is no doubt that it will be done.

CHAPTER VIII

FULL CHASUBLES LAWFUL, TRADITIONAL AND BEAUTIFUL

To some of my readers, no doubt, the full chasubles which we have been considering and admiring will be unfamiliar and will seem very strange. Having been accustomed all their lives to the narrow chasuble, they will be disposed to wonder whether the other has full ecclesiastical authority. And, indeed, the matter has been more than once debated in recent times, for we find the Sacred Congregation of Rites issuing a letter on the subject in 1863, and a decree only a few years ago, in 1925. We do not propose in this chapter to enter fully into the question, nor do we promise the reader any authoritative judgment. We believe that we are right in saying that there is no positive and precise law about the shape and fullness of chasubles, and we shall appeal chiefly to the liturgy and to the tradition of the Church.

But the decree of 1925, to which we have just alluded, gave rise to a very considerable amount of discussion at the time of its appearance, and we feel that we ought to say something about it. The question put to the Sacred Congregation was as follows : "Is it lawful, in the matter of vestments, to depart from the received usage of the Church and to introduce another fashion and another (though ancient) shape?" The reply of the Sacred Congregation was: "It is not lawful to do so without consulting the Holy See, according to the letter of 1863." The letter of 1863 is too long to cite here, but we may summarise it as follows: "Vestments have recently been introduced which conform to medieval use, but are at variance with the use of the last three centuries. An abrupt and considerable change in the style of vestments should not be made without consulting the Holy See, because such changes trouble the faithful. The Holy See would be glad to have the views of the bishops."

This decree and letter have received various and opposite interpretations, some arguing that they condemn the full chasuble, others that such a condemnation is far from their intention. We ourselves, being of this latter opinion, are glad to be able to cite for our view such wise and well-founded interpretations as are given by the *Nouvelle*

Revue Théologique (April, 1926), the *Revue Apologétique* (15th May, 1926), the *Collationes Brugenses* (1926), and the *American Ecclesiastical Review* (August, 1926). We would mention also a very brief yet very solid article by P. Bayart in *La Vie et les Arts liturgiques* (April, 1926), and the fuller article by R. B. Pierret in the same review (July, 1926). That we are able to cite these valuable studies simplifies our task. But since there are many of our readers who will not have access to the articles just mentioned, it will be better if we insert a few notes on the matter.

The decree says that the "received usage of the Church" (*usus in Ecclesia receptus*), should not be departed from. What is the "received usage" here referred to ? According to some of the interpreters, there would appear to be precise laws regulating the length and width of chasubles, the character of the materials, the arrangement of orfreys and galloons. But the Sacred Congregation does not so conceive the matter. It is far too wise to indulge in excessive precision, to desire uniform patterns for the churches of the whole world, to shackle the artistic genius and to force the liturgical arts alone to become fossilised. It is not Rome that is narrow and rigid ; but there are always commentators somewhere who are ready to exaggerate Rome's intentions, and from its prudent rules to deduce precepts and peremptory laws. The phrase "the received usage of the church," is a phrase of such loose definition that at least one commentator can argue that it does not reter to the universal Church, but only to the particular local church. "It certainly does not mean the usage of the *universal* Church, because apart from the full chasuble, there are at least three other forms in use in our time in the Latin Church, namely the Roman, the French and the Spanish." [1] In fact there is no general law prescribing any particular form for the Latin chasuble ; and besides the forms mentioned by the writer just cited, we might adduce the Belgian, Polish and Brazilian chasubles also. Moreover, the full chasubles exist in their thousands in cathedrals, churches and chapels ; and they were in use in many churches, at least for certain occasions, down to the end of the eighteenth century. In many churches there are now no other chasubles but full or fullish ones. Let us give a concrete instance to illustrate the situation. In a certain English diocese, for a good number of years, use has been made of chasubles made according to certain models anterior to Protestantism, and which still exist ; their form is " practically identical with the form prescribed by St. Charles Borromeo in 1572." Here then we have "a traditional form of vestments which

[1] Canon Callewaert in *Collationes Brugenses*, p. 183.

constitutes the *usus in* (*hac locali*) *Ecclesia receptus,*" and further
"an uninterrupted tradition from pre-reformation times," as is said
by an esteemed writer in *The Oscotian*, 1928, p. 58. And elsewhere
there exist other forms different from the Italian form which yet
constitute "types of vestments in approved use in the Church," as is
justly observed again by the same writer (p. 56). How are they
approved ? By the very usage made of them for a long period ; which
is to say by tacit approbation. But for exactly the same reasons, the
chasubles of other dioceses, which are "practically identical with the
form prescribed by St. Charles," and even those which are a little more
ample, enjoy the *"usus receptus."* This usage, which has been uninterrupted in certain churches, has, as we have said elsewhere, been taken
up anew during the last sixty or eighty years in many churches where
it had been interrupted—exactly as people endeavoured in the first
half of the nineteenth century to adopt the so-called chasuble of St.
Charles. In both cases there is undoubtedly a truly immemorial custom
(*consuetudo immemorabilis*), but especially in the case of the more
ample chasuble, which is many centuries anterior to the saintly archbishop.

As has been remarked already, in a previous chapter, for every
good vestment there are certain essential qualities of a superior sort.
And there are moreover certain conditions strictly requisite for the
vestment that is intended to be a chasuble of the Latin Rite. The
chasuble is made of stuff which hangs down in front and behind ;
it must have an opening for the head ; it has not got the sleeves that the
tunic or dalmatic should have, and it is not open in front like the cope.
As regards the varying qualities or defects of chasubles, it is absolutely
inevitable to have such variation : because we shall never have all our
chasubles measured and cut and made at Rome by the same maker ;
because there will always be a certain latitude allowed ; because special
permissions have been and will be granted ; and finally, because tastes
vary inevitably, according to times and countries, according to liturgical
knowledge or ignorance, and even according to the particular makers
and designers. All this has been said before, but it is necessary to insist
upon these divergences, which have always existed and will always
and everywhere exist still.

And so we may distinguish with precision four sorts of chasubles
used in the Church. There is the atrophied chasuble still well-known
in France, Spain, Belgium, Ireland and elsewhere ; there is the so-
called Roman chasuble, reaching just to the junction of shoulder and

arm ; there is the medium-sized chasuble which reaches as far as the
elbow, and conforms to the dimensions laid down by St. Charles ;
and lastly there is the full chasuble reaching as far as the wrist. Each
of these chasubles in its turn may have its special characteristics more
or less accentuated, according to particular circumstances, traditions,
countries, dioceses, and so on.

If we take account also of other received usages, we shall see no less
clearly that the *"usus in Ecclesia receptus"* does not signify that rigid
uniformity which is so congenial to certain minds. For instance, in Italy
the chasuble has its cross in front ; in France it is on the back ; in Spain
the chasuble has no cross at all ; and the author of the *Imitation* tells
us that there is a cross both in front and behind. It must have been
so, at least in his time and in his country ; and we may remark that it
is nearly always so with the full chasuble, which has, in fact, two
crosses with raised arms that join on the shoulders. Here then we
have striking differences, quite as striking as any differences in the
length and breadth of the vestments.

The Letter of 1863 deprecates innovations which may astonish
the faithful and disturb their minds. In that we see the prudence of
our Mother and Mistress, the Church, ever solicitous for good, even
in matters of small moment. But do full chasubles astonish and disturb
the faithful ? On the contrary, it is the opinion of Canon Callewaert
—and his opinion is shared by a considerable number of cardinals,
bishops and priests—that, when they see the Divine Mysteries celebrated
by priests arrayed in a dignified manner, in full chasubles, our people
have great joy and great edification.

"I believe," writes the canon, "that the use of the wider, Gothic
chasuble, even with the forked cross passing over each shoulder, cannot
nowadays disturb anybody or cause any sort of astonishment among
the faithful. For this chasuble is now known in practically every
country, and not only is used without causing disquietude, but even
wins admiration and praise . . . some cardinals, many bishops, and
innumerable priests use full chasubles, with the applause of the faithful.
They are, moreover, admitted as lawful by practically all authors, and
are commended by them on historical, æsthetic and liturgical grounds.
And they are praised by liturgical periodicals, even by the Roman
Ephemerides liturgicae, and in all liturgical and eucharistic exhibitions,
by all lovers of religious art, and are declared especially suitable for
the greater dignity of worship." (*Art. cit.* p. 184, 185.)

These are weighty considerations which their lordships the bishops will not fail to represent at Rome. They were invited to do so *"verbis amantissimis"* (in most cordial terms) ; and, as we hope, by means of indults and numerous approbations the full chasuble will come into ever wider and wider use. This development is inevitable and will be accompanied by one very happy consequence ; namely, that we shall have in future no more of that surprise or puzzlement, which is felt not only by connoisseurs, but by all the intelligent faithful, when they observe that the personages figured in works of art of very various periods and styles are vested nobly in the ample chasubles of former days ; whereas the bishops and priests of our own time are rigged out in skimpy and tawdry garments, sometimes of extreme extravagance and pretentiousness, often also of the worst taste and lowest quality, in vestments indeed which they can neither understand nor love.

All priests are conversant with the liturgical rules which should be observed. The Codex of Canon Law (Canon 1296 §3), lays it down that we should observe "the prescriptions of the liturgy, ecclesiastical tradition, and the laws of sacred art." *Serventur prescripta liturgica.* What guidance do we get from the liturgy ? On this point we shall be content to quote from a Master of Ceremonies, Père Maranget. This is what he says :

"No official and authentic liturgical text determines the form of the ornaments with precise definiteness. But there are rubrics which fully justify the use of chasubles of Gothic shape. The Rubrics of the Mass, which prescribe that the ministers shall hold up the celebrant's chasuble at the incensing of the altar and at other parts of the Mass, are incomprehensible and pointless when the chasuble is of the modern, skimpy sort. Moreover, in the *Ceremonial of Bishops* we read : 'The Bishop is vested in his chasuble, which is arranged and gathered up carefully on either side on his arms.' (Book II, chap. viii, No. 19). This rubric alone is sufficient to justify the full chasuble, for it is to such a chasuble only that it can apply. In the ceremony of ordination the bishop puts the chasuble on the shoulders of him whom he is ordaining, and the prayer which he says while he is performing this action explains the symbolism of the chasuble. 'Receive this priestly vestment which signifies charity ; God is able to increase in you charity and perfect works.' The old chasuble alone, in its amplitude, fully justifies the significance thus attached to this vestment by the Church." In covering the whole body it very well expresses that perfect, generous, and universal charity in which the priest's soul should be vested. But if its form

H

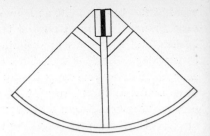

FIG. 98. CHASUBLE OF ST. GODEHARD, HILDESHEIM, XITH CENTURY
This conical form is characteristic of chasubles of the XIth, XIIth and XIIIth centuries

FIG. 99. CHASUBLE OF ST. EDMUND OF CANTERBURY, NOW AT PROVINS
It belongs to the XIIIth century which did no more than copy the cut of chasubles used in the two preceding centuries

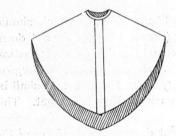

FIG. 100. A FOURTEENTH CENTURY FORM
Showing an evolution in the cut

FIG. 101. A SIXTEENTH CENTURY CHASUBLE IN THE MUSEUM AT BERNE
It has practically the dimensions required by St. Charles Borromeo

FIG. 102. MADE IN 1928 FOR A SEMINARY

FIG. 103. MADE IN 1928 FOR A CARDINAL

Two excellent chasubles in the form now most used ; same fullness as 98 and 99 but not their conical form

be skimpy and meagre, and it only half covers him, does it not then symbolize a narrow and restricted charity, which covers only a moiety of sins ?   Is it not then rather a caricature of the greatest of the virtues ?

We have spoken already (in Chapter V) about the names "Roman" and "Gothic" as applied to chasubles ; and we have seen that the appellation "Roman" has been applied, even in Rome itself, to chasubles of the form commonly called "Gothic."   The Codex of Canon Law speaks of the vestments, but does not say anything about any Roman form (Can. 811, § 1).   Nor is there any such epithet employed in the Decree of December 9th, 1925, concerning the liturgical vestments. And, as a matter of fact, if we were to ask whether the adjective Roman is correctly used in this context, we should have to reply in the negative. For the vestments used in Rome and in all Italy are more correctly termed "Italian," because they are of a *national* type, exactly like the French and Spanish vestments.   But these varieties of cut and shape did not emerge until the Renaissance, and did not become stereotyped until the seventeenth and eighteenth centuries.   Previously, as we have more than once seen, there was nothing but full or fullish chasubles; the world was content with the *liturgical* and *Catholic* chasuble.

But, since this use of the word "Roman" applied to vestments has given rise to some unfortunate misunderstandings and unfavourable judgments, we venture to suggest that it would be better if we spoke rather of the "small" chasuble.   That appellation would do very well for the French, Spanish, Polish, Brazilian and other chasubles ; and we should not, by applying the name "Roman" to an ugly and debased form, afflict the souls of those who glory in being children of the Catholic, Apostolic and *Roman* Church.

The appellation "Gothic" is quite of another sort.   It signifies the artistic styles characteristic of the thirteenth, fourteenth and fifteenth centuries.   But the word is often employed in a vague fashion which lends itself to confusion, or even to error, whether we are concerned with the so-called Pugin chasubles, or with those modern chasubles which are supposed to be inspired by chasubles of the Gothic period.   Let us see what the " blessed word " means in the two cases, in order to assist exactitude in notions and terms.

The so-called Pugin chasubles began to be used in England precisely in 1838.   It has been seen in Chapter V how the Church in its revival desired to recover the forms of vestments current before the sixteenth century ; even in these matters of taste and liturgy she wished to throw a bridge across the abyss of Protestantism and join the nineteenth

century to the Ages of Faith. But at that time timidity, or at least
prudence, was in control ; they did not dare to restore at once the true
ample forms, and two types of medium amplitude were adopted everywhere and are still in use in many churches. These two varieties are
exactly depicted in figures 77 and 78 of Chapter V. But vestments of
this cut never existed in the thirteenth century, the period of the
Gothic prime. These chasubles appeared in the fourteenth century
and were fairly common in the fifteenth and even in the sixteenth. It
is impossible to regard them as truly typical of the Gothic era. They
are graceful in form, but they do not drape much and they drape badly.
As we look at them, we feel that the makers have been very sparing
of their stuff.

The term "Gothic ornaments" has crossed the Channel and has been
very inappropriately applied, in Belgium, France and elsewhere, to
chasubles of a more ample form.   It is regrettable that this appellation
should be maintained, not only in the manufacturers' catalogues, but
also in articles and in books. Consider, for instance, that excellent
work, most useful to those who devote themselves to the making of
vestments, the *Guide pratique pour la confection des ornements gothiques*.
We recommend it to our readers on many grounds, but we do not commend its title. The two words *ornements gothiques* are inexact ; we do
not want to array ourselves in *ornaments* or *decorations*, but in *liturgical
vestments*. If these two words had been used in the title, then the title
would have expressed what the book gives us, and gives us so well.
The word *liturgical* has obviously a wider connotation than the word
Gothic, and in fact the work contains excellent designs that possess
no Gothic character. So it would have been a far more appropriate
title.

In reviewing the work which has just been mentioned, writers have
refined upon the title, saying, "This is a Gothic book" ; and that what
we need now is a treatise on the "ornaments based on Gothic principles,"
etc. But vague conceptions, a false terminology, and a sort of "Gothic"
obsession do not advance the liturgical cause ; quite the contrary.
They are calculated to disgust those very people who love *good* Gothic
and *all* other artistic styles, not excluding modern art, which, generally
speaking, borrows not at all from the recognised styles and yet, none
the less, has produced works of great beauty.

Let us pursue our enquiry and advance the precise opinion that there
is no such thing as a Gothic chasuble, if we take cut as our determinant.
And really, the cut is the important matter, for ornamentation is

obviously of very secondary importance. The thirteenth century did not produce a special form of its own ; it borrowed the form of the eleventh and twelfth centuries, well known by the chasubles of Maintz, Metz, Bayeux, Florence, Hildesheim and Sens. It was during the three succeeding centuries that people departed from the received type. That type is once more put before the reader in figures 98 and 99. The differences became very numerous, if we judge by the chasubles which still exist and by those of which we have illustrations preserved by many authors. Except in two or three cases no very extraordinary forms were produced ; but there were distinct variations in the cut, and others in the shoulder lines and the fullness of the material, even so early as the end of the thirteenth century. To sum up, the so-called Gothic forms were manifold, and there was never any *one* Gothic form.

Before passing on let us recall the fact that the rage in the seventeenth and eighteenth centuries for diminishing the full, or fullish chasubles was so great that many of these chasubles were horribly mutilated, as for example the chasuble of Boniface VIII, which must have been superb, judging by the portion that remains. It would therefore be a mistake to infer the narrow form by reference to certain ancient chasubles still surviving ; for a good number owe that form to subsequent vandalism.

Besides the appellation "Gothic" one hears also of Dominican, Benedictine, and Belgian chasubles, and there are probably others. But since these appellations imply limitations and restrictions, and since they enclose the chasuble within too narrow moulds, we could beg that such adjectives should henceforth be abandoned. As to the term "Belgian" quite recently, and for the first time, applied to ample chasubles, it may be said to be the worst conceivable appellation, since the Belgian chasuble is in reality just as narrow as the French chasuble.[2] It is true that full or fullish chasubles have been made in Belgium, but quite as many have been made in England, Germany, Holland, France, etc. The Roman exhibition mentioned in chapters V and VI contained only full or fullish chasubles, and, if I am not mistaken, not one of them was made in Belgium. They were made in Italy, France and Holland ; and their makers did not consider any national usages ; they sought only to produce vestments with the flexibility, good draping and dignity which characterised the ancient and most of the medieval chasubles,

---

[2] The difference between the two consists in this : The Belgian Chasuble has a circular opening for the head, while the opening of the French Chasuble, like the Italian, forms in front an acute angle.

but without any sort of effort to produce ancient or Gothic chasubles. They made good chasubles ; that was and is the important thing.

As regards the shape, whether of the upper edges, running along the arms and shoulders, or of the lower edges, which may be so cut as to

FIG. 104.   A CHASUBLE OF A DELICATE AND WELL-CONCEIVED DECORATIVE COM-
POSITION
(After a chasuble by M. Biais, Paris).   It is one of those chasubles which are neither
antique nor Gothic, but which aim only at being good and beautiful vestments.   It
is the only thing that matters

form a perfect semi-circle, or an oval, or a pointed arch,[3] this is a secondary matter, and there is no reason why we should confine ourselves to an absolutely identical shape.   Here again Dr. Adrian Fortescue has a note inspired by a broad and sure judgment : ". . . Nor do we want to restore any one period of the past, as you would in a scene of a pageant. . . . It is first a question of artistic beauty, though historic associations count also.   And beauty demands a return to a tradition of larger, ampler shapes.   No artist in the world doubts that. . . . It is quite possible, observing all laws, to restore such a type of vestment

[3] The pointed arch is not the characteristic mark of the Gothic style that it has been supposed to be.   Pointed arches occur in the East, from the earliest times, and are to be found in many Romanesque buildings.

FIG. 105.   A PRIEST EXCELLENTLY VESTED
He is wearing the chasuble of figure 104, a beautiful alb
without lace, and a long stole. Proportion and effect just
right

now (not necessarily Gothic ; on the contrary . . .). There is no rule
of *absolute uniformity* in vestments, any more than in other points of

ecclesiastical art. We do not build all our churches on one plan, nor
make all our chalices on one model." (*Op. cit.*, p. 23).

In fact, under the influence of a stronger instinct, a more vivid
liturgical sense, and more exact knowledge, some types of vestment,
slightly different, have been in "received use" for nearly a century,
independently of the two types of the English "Gothic Revival," and
yet simultaneously with them. Here is an example (fig. 104), and others
have been reproduced in Chapter VI.

Let us sum up and repeat our conclusion, which is, that the terms
"small" chasuble, "medium-sized" chasuble, and "full" chasuble
would simplify the whole matter and would be clear to all.

Questions of detail or decoration are not ignored, but these things are
put in their proper place, subordinate to the outstanding and principal
character of the vestments. One might wish, in the case of some of these
modern chasubles, a style of ornamentation more in harmony with the
churches which they are destined to serve. One might also desire a
decoration or a simplicity that would exclude any rigid definiteness of
style. If that were achieved, then these chasubles would suit Gothic
churches, or Romanesque churches, or churches in the "new style,"
or the Roman and Byzantine basilicas ; in one word, they would suit
all Catholic churches.

CHAPTER IX

THE main purpose of this book is not to give patterns of all the various liturgical vestments in use and to comment on them ; this has been done in other works. [1] The only reason for giving some shapes of chasubles and accessories is that priests require, not so much a multiplicity of measurements and details, as some plain outlines and brief general notions which will help them in working out and in explaining the orders they wish to give. The measurements given in this chapter will have to be modified if the priest in question is very short or exceptionally tall. It is much the most satisfactory way, if means allow of it, to have one's chasubles and even one's stoles made to measure. I have seen at the altar a very tall priest vested in a mean chasuble which barely covered his back, an astonishing, not to say ridiculous sight, except for those who can take no notice of such things.

The dimensions of the Italian chasuble, which I have got from one of the principal makers of vestments in Rome, are 29 inches by 44 ; but even in Rome there are slight variations in size.

The narrow chasubles still used in France, Belgium, Ireland, and elsewhere are two or three inches narrower than the Italian ones, and generally shorter as well. They are all much of a shape, except that the Irish chasuble tends to be narrower at the top whereas the Polish chasubles are wider across the shoulders, and the Brazilian ones exaggerate the Spanish shape, which has been described elsewhere.

As for "wide-shaped" chasubles, we have quoted, in the preceding chapter, the comments of a competent judge, Canon Callewaert, on their use in a large number of churches. If the *usus in ecclesiis receptus* is well established there is no need to fall back on mediocre or poor shapes just for fear, one might say, of the beautiful. Figures 106 and 107 show two chasubles, one of them abominably vulgar, the other ostentatiously tapering in form. They may be called "Gothic," and

---

[1] The *Guide Pratique* has dealt with every kind of vestment. *L'Ouvroir Liturgique* has given some very accurate illustrations, *L'Artisan Liturgique* has printed some rather fanciful and inadequate designs.

are so called ; as a matter of fact they are simply fanciful or even downright bad shapes. And there are other neutral forms of recent date which we need not inflict on the reader. They are not likely to win much appreciation or acceptance.

The same may be said of the conical chasubles shown in figures 98

FIG. 106.   HORRIBLY HEAVY SHAPE
AND VULGAR ORNAMENT

FIG. 107.   BAD SHAPE WITH PRETEN-
TIOUS ORNAMENT

and 99 of the preceding chapter. These vestments fall in very beautiful folds, but they are most inconvenient, as we had occasion to observe while watching a priest at the altar who was vested in a chasuble shaped exactly like St. Thomas of Canterbury's ; it was painful to see him entangled in a vestment which he had to keep on hitching up at the sides by means of strenuous movements of his hands and arms. The shoulder lines in chasubles of this shape are so steeply sloped that if they met at the neck they would form an acute angle. Fig. 108 shows one half of the back of a chasuble ; if both halves were shown the line corresponding to D E would form an obtuse angle with it, thus obviating the difficulty caused by the conical shape. The line C D represents a length of 28 inches, so that the lower edge at D reaches to the wrist ; the line may be raised to H or even to M, but shapes cut along D E give very good results.

The length of this chasuble from A to B is 46 inches, which is a good size for a priest of an average height, say 5 feet 9 inches. If the chasuble is too long the alb does not show below it. The curved line CK at the top is for the front of the opening. [2] The line KG is for the front of the vestment, which is shorter than the back ; this lets the two ends of the stole be seen if the stole is long and worn in the right position.

The total length of one half of the stole, including the fringe, is

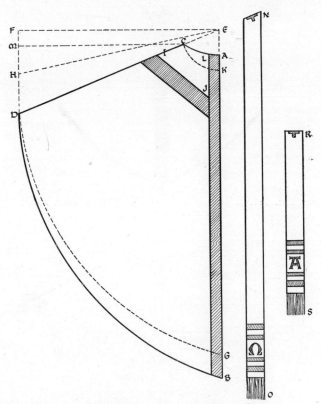

FIGS. 108, 109, 110.   PATTERNS OF A HALF-CHASUBLE, STOLE AND MANIPLE
All three well-proportioned

52 inches (from N to O) ; the maniple is 24 inches long from R to S. Each of these ornaments is three inches wide. The plate gives the two accessories side by side with the chasuble and shows the relative dimensions.

Fig. 111 is given merely as an example of a chasuble ornamented in a graceful and original manner with pendants and rock crystals which

[2] A slit in front requiring a button or other fastener is a new invention and an unnecessary complication. If the opening is big enough to go over the head, all is well. If a little of the alb shows round the neck, so much the better.

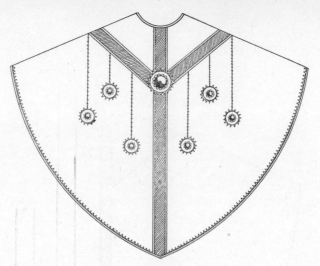

FIG. 111.   BACK OF A CHASUBLE ENDING IN A POINT
Observe the rock-crystals

FIG. 112.   CHASUBLE ENDING IN A VERY WIDE ELLIPSE AND
DECORATED WITH A "LATIN" CROSS
Made in 1928 for a seminary ; in black velvet with gold-yellow
cross and braids flame-red

are inexpensive. This vestment terminates in a point, whereas the chasuble shown in fig. 112 is cut on a wide ellipse. According to the attitude and movements of the priest, the two arms of the "Latin" cross sometimes drop a little, but that is no reason for excluding this form of cross. To have it on some vestments and the cross with arms sloping upwards on others gives a pleasing variety. However, as a fact, wide chasubles are not often ornamented with a Latin cross. One also sees the single vertical orfrey, or column, both front and back, which is characteristic of Italian chasubles in the Middle Ages and at the present day. Rome is never likely to forbid either the Latin cross or the cross with arms sloping upwards. The latter form of cross adorns many of the ancient chasubles and the majority of the modern full chasubles. Lateral orfreys go very well on the upper halves of these vestments.

The *Guide pratique* is right in maintaining that the lines which go from the vertical orfrey to the shoulders should be *straight* lines, though an attempt has been made recently to prove that they would look better curved or forming an irregular octagon.[3] Ingenious sketches have been published and a number of measurements given for a chasuble of which the orfreys would form an octagon. These geometrical calculations are unattractive and the result obtained is very little different from that produced by the straight arms of the cross, to which the objection is raised that they make an ugly angle when they slip down the arms. But this drop is very slight and can easily be avoided. If the orfreys reach exactly to the shoulder joint, they will not slip down. That being so, and considering the extra work involved in cutting out and applying curved or octagonal orfreys, it is likely that straight-armed crosses will continue to be put on to wide chasubles. This has been the practice, up to the present time, of the best firms, and it has not prevented their producing very beautiful vestments. But there is no compulsion in the matter, and those who prefer the other shape can refer to the two articles that have just been quoted.

The three accessories, the stole, the veil for the chalice, and the burse shown in figures 113, 114 and 115, go with the chasuble shown in figure 112. The design on them, a tau surmounted by a circle containing a cross, is ingenious and in keeping with the design on the chasuble. The veil is supposed to be 22 inches square, which allows of its hanging down equally on all four sides of a not very tall chalice. If a smaller veil is preferred, it can be cut down by an inch or two. The burse is 9 inches square. The stole is slightly narrowed from the bottom upwards.

[3] *L'Ouvroir Liturgique*, 1925, No. 13 ; and 1926, No. 16.

We now come to the question of the convenience in use of full chasubles, and first to an objection that is often raised against them ; for people will raise objections even to the very best of things.   This is the sort of thing one hears : "You call full chasubles convenient ! Why, one is

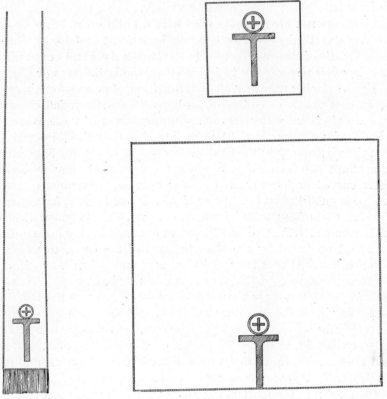

FIGS. 113, 114, 115.   STOLE, BURSE AND CHALICE VEIL
Accessories of the preceding chasuble (fig. 112)

for ever hitching the stuff up right and left, which is most distracting. I don't call that very practical." And more to the same effect. Our reply is that the inconvenience, if it exists, is very slight.   There are other excellent and meritorious acts which are even more troublesome in the effort they demand, or in the call they make on our care and attention. But if we are determined to think of nothing but comfort, and to devote all our efforts to the avoidance of trouble, where are we going to end ? This is the way in which the standard of taste and feeling for liturgical values is lowered.   And, in any case, the effort involved amounts to no more than a slight jerk of the fore-arm, so as to keep the edge of the chasuble above the wrists ; and the thing can be done even more easily with the hand. It must not be imagined that comfort depends solely on the width of vestments ; it depends first

FIG. 116. PAENULA NOBILISSIMA
A vestment which expresses that amplitude of charity which it is supposed to symbolise. The effect of such a chasuble is shown in fig. 117 and Plate III

and foremost on the material being light and supple. If the two sides of a full but flexible chasuble are once well raised, they easily keep in place, because the priest at the altar never has his arms hanging by his side. The habit is quickly formed and becomes no trouble at all. The trouble, if any, is more likely to be in the minds of priests endowed with a feeling for the liturgy, who find themselves wearing narrow chasubles and are conscious that they have not got to lift up the sides of vestments which thousands of pontiffs and priests have lifted up. What they have done, we can do ; let us do it cheerfully and skilfully and all will be well.

The preceding remarks are applicable to chasubles which come below the wrists. The very great width of the *paenula nobilissima* (fig. 116) would cause no real difficulty for the reasons we have given, and the very name of this chasuble makes us think how nobly it would clothe a pontiff or a priest. The artist has drawn a white chasuble, ornamented with a tau and a XP, which would be made of coloured material cut out and applied. This vestment could be made in colour and have the same ornament, which could then be in yellow. The shape of the cross and monogram is certainly antique, but now as ever they symbolise the Christ who " dieth no more." The designer was inspired by liturgical and æsthetic ideals and aimed only at producing a vestment that should be simple and dignified, flexible and light, and consequently easily gathered up on the arms. An idea of the effect can be got from fig. 117 and Plate III, which show priests vested in chasubles with beautiful wide folds, and as full as the *paenula nobilissima*.

But most of the full chasubles which are shown in the illustrations of this book are not of the size of the vestment we have just been discussing, and those shown in figures 111 and 112 come down only to the wrist ; there is therefore no difficulty about wearing them. The material will not need hitching up more than once or twice at the most ; many priests do not even do this and nothing untoward happens. Some timid persons may object that the material reaching right down the arm may touch the host or interfere with the manipulation of the pall and chalice. This fear is groundless and I have never heard of any such accident, though I know many priests who use none but full chasubles. There is no real danger from them ; but there is a real danger from the customary short and stiff maniple, which often touches the corporal with edge or fringe and is seriously inconvenient. And so there is now a demand for longer maniples. But note this fact, that the short and stiff maniple is own brother to the stiff and narrow chasuble, which hangs from the shoulders like more or less decorative sandwich boards, and is perpetually getting out of the perpendicular unless the priest is very careful. The full chasuble is no more dangerous than one of these. A priest told me not long ago that one day, when he was turning round to face the people, part of his short chasuble got on to the altar and knocked over the pall ; he made an instinctive movement, and the chasuble knocked over the chalice. Very fortunately this occurred at the *Orate Fratres* and before the Consecration. But such accidents are practically impossible if one is vested in a natural manner with a chasuble that adapts itself to the various attitudes and motions that the rubrics require. 4

Cupboards with coat hangers fixed on to wooden pedestals, or hanging

---

4 Dom. Veys strikes the right note in a short article entitled *Ampleur et Commodité* (*L'Ouvroir Liturgique*, Nos. 19-20, 1926).

PLATE III.

A PRIEST LITURGICALLY WELL-DRESSED

Full chasuble, simple and beautiful alb, long stole and long maniple. Observe the altar cloth also. Designed and drawn by Dom Sylvester Fryer

from metal rods, are often used, not only for copes but for chasubles. Copes may very well hang on cope-stands, but the proper place for

FIG. 117.   THE COMMUNION OF ST. JEROME, BY DOMENICHINO
The chasuble is quite as wide as in fig. 116. It falls into beautiful folds and
does not inconvenience the priest

chasubles, dalmatics and tunics is in drawers, where they may lie flat ; the accessories and the veil of the book-stand can then be put on top of them. We all know that the dressers on which these vestments are laid out ready for mass afford plenty of room for drawers or shelves, one above the other, and if these are labelled it is easy to lay one's hands on any vestment one needs.

I

The common practice is to turn the chasuble inside out before putting
it in the drawer and to turn it back again when putting it out for the

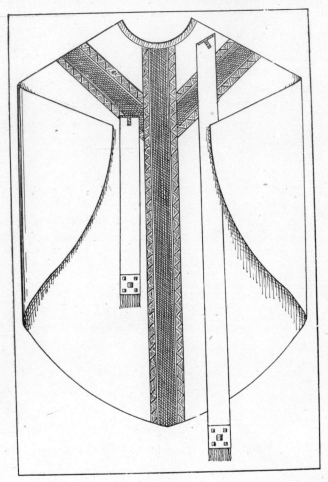

FIG. 118. A FULL CHASUBLE TAKES UP NO MORE SPACE IN A
DRAWER THAN A NARROW CHASUBLE

priest to vest ; this practice is very detrimental to the vestments,
because it causes friction which, in course of time, wears out not only
the braid and other ornaments, but the actual material. It is an established practice that might with advantage be given up.

The drawers or shelves in which the chasubles are laid should be lined with some woollen material—serge or flannel—and if the chasubles are especially fine, pieces of the same material should be laid between them.   Ordinary chasubles in frequent use are placed one on top of the other with nothing between ; and they are taken out and put straight away on to the dresser.   This may be covered with stuff permanently fixed on to the wood, or, if pieces of stuff that can be removed each day are preferred, it is a good plan to fix them by means of metal button-holes, that are made to fit over buttons screwed along the back of the dresser ; otherwise the cover slips off too easily together with the chasubles.   When the masses are over, these covers can be folded up and put away out of the dust.   In some Churches, in order to save time, the vestments are laid directly on the top of the dresser ; but it is certainly better to lay them on some kind of woven material.

The drawers should be long enough for the chasubles to be laid out at their full length, but they may be much narrower than the vestments ; then the two sides are folded over, care being taken not to crease them (fig. 118), and in this way full chasubles do not take up more space than narrow ones.   It is a wise precaution to open the drawers wide from time to time, when the atmosphere is warm and dry, so as to air them well and prevent their getting damp.

CHAPTER X

STOLE AND MANIPLE, DALMATIC AND TUNIC, COPE, HUMERAL VEIL,
BURSE AND CHALICE VEIL

THE stole is derived from the *orarium*, or from the *lorum*, a kind of scarf worn by certain Roman dignitaries as an outward sign of their being engaged on some official duty. In the same way the deacon's stole, the stole of the priest at the altar, and the pastoral stole of the parish priest are the insignia proper to the deacon, the celebrant, and the parish priest. It is therefore right and proper that this liturgical ornament should be so worn as to be visible ; but to make a great display of it would border on the pedantic. We are now referring to the *pastoral* stole which is often rather aggressive with its tinsel, its embossed gold embroidery, its complicated decorations, and, in some countries, the exaggerated width of the lower part. A good stole never ends in a trapezium, or in a huge spade; it is of the same width throughout, or widens very slightly from the top to the bottom.

FIG. 119. SKETCH SHOWING THE LOWER PART OF A CHASUBLE
A beautiful plain alb and a stole of correct length

Sometimes it widens, and that *very little*, only towards the two ends. The pastoral and the sacramental stole are long enough if they reach the knees; to be worn with a chasuble, the stole must be even longer, so as to come below it. The sketch in figure 119 shows the normal proportions. Supposing the chasuble, for a priest of average height, is 40 inches long in front, then a stole which measures 54 inches from its centre cross to each extremity would be approximately correct, and would show sufficiently below the chasuble. These figures must not be regarded as anything more than suggestions, and there is no rule or official decision in the matter. The length and width of stoles

and maniples, like many more important things, will naturally vary
from country to country, and ought even to vary with the stature of
their various wearers.

PASTORAL STOLES

FIGS. 120. Horrible shape and mincing ornament.   121. Branch ornament.
122. Appliqué work.   123. Stole in the new style ; more suitable for a necktie

The excellent *Guide pratique*, which has previously been referred to,
says that " the essential ornamentation of a stole consists of three
crosses . . ." (p. 70). This is, indeed, the general opinion, but it is a
mistake. Only *one* cross is essential, the one at the top of the stole, and
with this exception, no rule has been laid down for the ornamentation
of this accessory. There is therefore nothing to prevent the ends of the

stole, as also those of the maniple, from being ornamented with full-length figures, heads, monograms, emblems, crosses, or purely decorative designs.   The stole may also be embroidered from top to bottom, so as to form one continuous orfrey.   We give two examples (figs. 124 and 125), which show how stoles were ornamented in the thirteenth

Figs. 124, 125.   Ends of Two Rich Stoles
From statues of Chartres Cathedral

century.   If these designs were carefully copied in appliqué work or in embroidery, that would undoubtedly give us magnificent stoles ; but very beautiful ones can be had that are not so richly decorated and are, consequently, much less expensive.   The stole shown in fig. 127 is a good example from this point of view ; it matches the maniple which goes with it (fig. 126), and which is inspired by the one worn by St. Clement in a fresco in the crypt of San Clemente at Rome.   There may seem to be an exaggerated simplicity about this stole and maniple ; but purity of line, beauty of form, and a clear, well-proportioned cross are often more to be prized than overmuch decoration.

To repeat what we have said already, *one* cross only is required, in the middle of the stole.   When the priest is vesting for Mass he kisses the stole at this cross and then puts the stole round his neck, that is to say, on the collar of his tunic (soutane, etc.).   But that collar being covered by the amice, in effect he places the stole on top of the amice. The stole should not be thrown so far over the shoulders that it hangs half-way down the back, for then it will not come down much below the waist in front and will be entirely invisible. And why wear this symbol of office if you insist on hiding it? If you look at the recumbent figures on ancient tombs, or at the stately statues of bishops over the doors of our old cathedrals, you will see that they wear very long stoles, which not only come down below their chasubles and dalmatics, but often reach to the bottom of the alb.

Stoles and maniples need not have fringes, but look rather meagre and skimped without them; silk tasselling, or long flexible fringes, give to these ornaments a finish which is pleasing to the eye (fig. 130). The beautiful stole shown in this illustration is a conclusive argument in favour of the trimming we are recommending. Compare this stole with the one that is shown in figure 123 and you will immediately be struck by the difference. Such stoles as this "modern" one afford a painful contrast with the beautiful traditional shapes. This stole in particular, with its angular extremities, ornamented with fat grapes and half-starved ears of corn, might satisfy a maker of neckties, but not a liturgical artist. It is one example among many of the results obtained by seeking after symbolism at any price and by believing oneself endowed with a creative genius for designing ornaments in the modern style.

A rather silly custom has crept in in many churches and more chapels. All the top part of the stole is covered, for fully half its width, with a longish strip of muslin, tulle, or cambric, edged with the inevitable little lace-edging, which no doubt will be outlined to-morrow with gold thread, on to which by the third day a tiny little fringe will be tacked; and so on. If one asks the reason of this tucker on the stole, one is told that it prevents the stole getting soiled when it is put round the neck; which reply is neither accurate nor reasonable. That the stole should

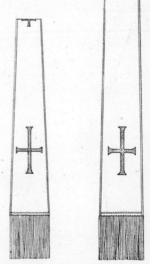

Figs. 126, 127. Maniple and Stole
Very beautiful in their simplicity
The maniple inspired by a fresco
in San Clemente, Rome

occasionally touch the neck is practically inevitable, but "occasionally" is not the same thing as
habitually ; and, as a matter of
fact, the stole is not put round the
neck but on top of the amice,
as we have just explained. If the
priest is not wearing an amice, but
has a pastoral stole or a sacramental stole cut as is shown in figs.
127 and 128, such a stole is placed,
and easily stays in position, on the
collar of the cassock or the top of
the surplice; if the priest is a regular
and wears a hood, he puts the stole
under the hood. So that little
argument won't hold water ; it is a
mere pretext for sewing on one of
these fancy bits of millinery, which
will only have to be unpicked,
washed, ironed, and stitched on
again ; and that is how much useful
time is wasted. We do hope that
parish priests and chaplains of
communities will listen to us when
we beg of them to put an end to
these futilities and this waste of
time ; otherwise they will soon find
nursery tuckers of muslin and lace
being put round the necks of their
chasubles, because, forsooth, they
get a little soiled by being constantly put on over one's head. And
things won't stop there ; maniples,
burses and chalice-veils will all

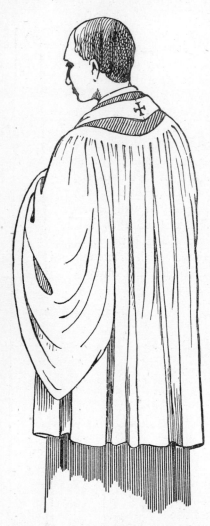

FIG. 128. PRIEST WEARING A FINE
LINEN SURPLICE AND A WELL-FITTING
STOLE

have to have these miserable
protectors, for they too get soiled
in the long run, because they are
handled.

The MANIPLE (*mappula, fano*) was originally a cloth carried in the
hand or over the arm, and used to wipe one's face. It has undergone

Fig. 129. Stole overrun by out-
of-date Ornament
Mere filling up

Fig. 130. Good Stole, with sober
Silk Decoration in old rose
Colour

transformations similar to those through which the stole has passed,
and from being a cloth with a specific use
it has become a symbolical vestment.
Sculptures dating from the Middle Ages, and
a few ancient maniples that are extant,
show, as is well known, that at that period
the maniple was a long strip of stuff, either

FIG. 131. A BAD MANIPLE FROM EVERY
POINT OF VIEW
Too short and widened to the shape of a
spade ; the fastening is defective

FIG. 132. A VERY GOOD MANIPLE
From the cross at the top to the
bottom of the fringe is 24 inches.
The fastening is an elastic loop and
the two parts are joined at the
point A

plain or embroidered, nearly always fringed at either end, and worn over the forearm or wrist, from which it hung down on both sides.

The maniple of St. Thomas of Canterbury, which has been preserved at Pontigny, is longer and more practical than ours, which are so short, that at certain ritual movements they brush the corporal and may touch the sacred Host. A moment's consideration will show that this danger is avoided by the use of a maniple long enough to fall below the table of the altar when the priest has his hands joined or raised. The *total* length of the maniple of St. Hugh of Grenoble (thirteenth century) is 58 inches. This great length is not really inconvenient, but it is not necessary ; we suggest 48 inches as a good length for the full maniple, including the fringe (fig. 132). A very beautiful statue of St. Remigius (or of St. Sixtus), in the transept of the Cathedral of Rheims, has a maniple of which each half would be equal in length to the extended arm and hand.

We have already alluded to the ornamentation of the maniple, which should match that of the stole ; they should also agree in shape ; if the stole is widened out at the ends, the maniple also should widen out slightly from top to bottom (figs. 126 and 127).

The fixing of the maniple in place has been considered a difficult problem. A little flap sewed on the top of the maniple and pinned on to the alb is in common use in France and Belgium, but this method is most unsatisfactory ; the alb becomes full of small holes and tears in the wash, and, moreover, pins get lost easily. Another plan is to join up the edges of the maniple, leaving a kind of large ring to fit round the arm ; the difficulty is that it may fit some arms, but that other bigger ones put a strain on it and then the thread breaks and the stitches come unsewn. In Spain a loop of cord is fixed behind the cross and a thick linen ring is slipped up the loop, joining its sides and pressing upon the fore-arm. The defect of this device is that it is difficult to work it without the help of a sacristan or server. It has been suggested, by way of an improvement, that a button might be sewn on to one of the inner sides of the maniple and a small loop on the other ; but the device is still worse than the others. We have had experience of several unsatisfactory devices in France, in Spain and in England ; but there is one excellent plan that we can thoroughly recommend ; let a loop of fairly wide elastic be sewn to the maniple just under the cross and let the two sides of the maniple be sewn together at a point about half way down their length ; the place is marked by the letter A in the fig. 132. By this means the ornamental vestment is easily kept in position and hangs vertically as it should do.

Fig. 133.   A Coptic Deacon wearing a long and Flexible Tunic of
the VIth Century
Ornamented with vertical bands and medallions.   Drawn by Dom
Sylvester Fryer

DALMATICS AND TUNICS.—The dalmatic is a garment which came originally from Dalmatia and was introduced into Roman society during the reign of Diocletian. It partially supplanted the toga, which was less convenient to wear. The tunic is a shorter and plainer dalmatic. Both vestments preserve traces of the *clavi* or stripes which one sees on the tunics of the early Christians. The stripes which were originally quite plain, soon became joined at the bottom, or sometimes at the top, by orfreys, as a large number of sculptures and paintings goes to prove. A very interesting Coptic dalmatic, reconstructed by C. Rohault de Fleury, [1] shows stripes of embroidery going down to just below the knees and embroidered discs lower down and on the shoulders. Although this manual is in no sense an archæological treatise, we print a most interesting picture (fig. 133), in which the artist has introduced this dalmatic ; it shows how deacons were vested in Egypt in the sixth century. The vestment is simple in shape and the ornamentation shows both good taste and originality.

Owing to notions of symmetry which are often quite out of place, the tunic of the sub-deacon and the dalmatic of the deacon are nearly always of the same shape and size and are ornamented alike, although the deacon ranks higher than the sub-deacon and has quite different functions to fulfil at the altar. It is really more logical that the two vestments should differ to some extent ; for instance, the dalmatic might be longer and more richly decorated than the tunic, and the tunic might be shorter and have longer sleeves, as is laid down in the *Ceremonial of Bishops*. And when we say *sleeves*, we mean true sleeves, as is the custom in Rome, not horrible flapping squares of stuff such as are in use in some countries. In the decoration of these two vestments bands or orfreys sewn on from top to bottom are reminiscent of the *clavi*, whereas narrow parallel galloons connected by other transverse galloons make a very poor ornamentation. The difference between the dalmatic and the tunic is roughly indicated in the two diagrams, figs. 134 and 135. The reader will notice that the shoulder line is slightly sloped ; this is done for aesthetic reasons, and the point is both simple and important ; if the sleeves are so cut as to correspond to the horizontal dotted line of the diagram, the result is ugly folds which pull the orfreys out of the vertical and drag the lower part of the vestment forward or backward ; at least this happens with dalmatics and tunics

---

[1] *La Messe*, Vol. V, p. 78. There is a tunic of the same character in the British Museum, reproduced in *Catalogue of Christian Antiquities*, by V. M. Dalton, p. 168.

that are at all stiff. Now they are stiff, and, what is more, they are heavy, when they are made of cloth of gold or of silver, when their orfreys are too heavily decorated, and especially when the decorations are allowed to extend all over the vestment.

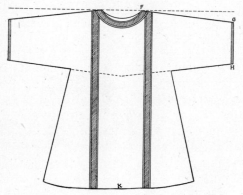

Let us now explain how the dalmatic shown in fig. 136 is made ; it will not take long to study, and the reader will then be in a position to compare it with the two diagrams given above. The first thing that will strike him will no doubt be the very beautiful inter-laced ornamentation in the Celtic style. It is very interesting and very beauti-ful, as we do not hesitate to maintain ; but the cloth of gold and the wide bands of embroidery preclude any draping. Moreover, the medallions of the saints do not go well with the inter-laced work. If just the head and shoulders of these saints had been depicted, with perhaps their names added, the medallions would have been simplified, and yet quite recognisable ; but

FIGS. 134, 135. DIAGRAMS SHOWING A DALMATIC AND TUNIC THAT DIFFER FROM EACH OTHER, AS INDICATED BY THE CEREMONIAL OF BISHOPS The dalmatic is longer, has wider sleeves and an orfrey joining the vertical bands

depicted as they are on a background of buildings or of land-scape, they remind one of modern minatures. It would have been wiser in this instance, as in many others, to aim at attaining the maxi-mum of expression with the minimum of means. This is a very important principle in certain of the arts, and not least in the decorative arts as applied to vestments. Let us remember this and let us not exact of artists in embroidery, any more than of artists in decorative painting, in mosaic, or in stained-glass, designs which are too complicated and too detailed, which, as they are well aware, are not suitable for the particular medium. And again, the very fact that the sleeves of a dalmatic should not be open along their length has led to the lower edges of the sleeves of this one being joined together by means of the

FIG. 136. A MODERN DALMATIC
Made by the Dun Emer Guild, Dublin

kind of bows of ribbon that one used to see not so very long ago on the heads of little girls. They were all very well in that position ; but they are wholly out of place on a vestment. Do not let us stoop to tactics of this kind, but rather insist on sleeves that really are sleeves and such as rightly belong to dalmatics and tunics, and show some regard for the history of these garments.

THE COPE is the *pluviale* of the Romans, who used it, as the name indicates, to keep off the rain. They also called it *paenula*, and in point of fact it is often difficult to make out what was the difference between

the cope and the *paenula* proper (the latter *planeta* and *casula*), since
the garment depicted in frescos and mosaics and supposed to be the

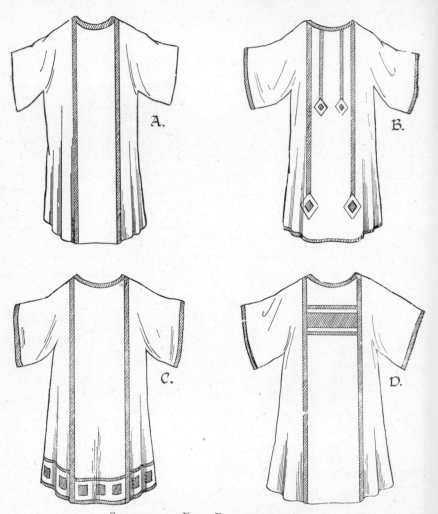

SKETCHES OF FOUR DALMATICS OR TUNICS

FIGS. 137. A. Simple *clavi*.   138. B. *clavi* ending in lozenges.   139. C. *clavi* and an
orfrey at the bottom.   140. D. An orfrey near the top

original of the cope is not open in front, but covers the whole figure
exactly as does the *paenula*. But the cope was sometimes worn open
in front as early as the sixth century. The proof of this—and the only

clear one—is the garment worn by the Jewish priest depicted in the scene of Christ before Pilate, fig. 141, in the mosaic of Sant' Apollinare Nuovo at Ravenna.

A hood was sometimes added to the cope, but by no means invariably. During the Middle Ages, the hood, which had originally been used to cover the head, shrank into being a small triangular appendage ; this was the origin of the present hood, which for several centuries remained small, but later on grew very much wider and longer and also began to be fixed on below an orfrey, which resulted in its coming much too low down. The three designs shown in figs. 142, 143 and 144 illustrate what we have said.

As can readily be imagined, the cope retained for many centuries many of the beautiful characteristics of the chasuble. But we all know into what forms it has sometimes evolved. In many places, the cope, made of imitation cloth of gold, all stiff and heavy, has become a kind of sentry-box in which the unhappy priest is confined. We are all familiar with those half metallic over-ornamented vestments under whose weight many a parish priest, already wearied by the duties of his ministry, groans on Sundays and feast-days.

Another type of cope is represented by the very commonplace and so-called cheap vestment that figures in illustrated catalogues and is extolled in descriptive notes as "best quality damask," "charming combination of colours," "perfect elegance," and so forth. Let us put the catalogue on one side and consider the actual vestments, and we

FIG. 141. A JEWISH PRIEST WEARING A COPE
A sixth century mosaic in S. Apollinare Nuovo, Ravenna

shall find that the material has often been dressed so as to give it an air of superior quality ; the orfrey or its equivalent is exaggerately wide, to give an air of grandeur ; and the hood is adorned with some small floral design or pattern of rays which is the really tempting detail. And so we have what the catalogue calls "a really rich cope," or else, one "of a very good appearance," which is in actual fact a wretched affair. The only idea behind either the one or the other is the desire to sell off the goods. And this is how the good taste of priests and donors is perverted, and the whole standard of taste in church ornament lowered.

We shall no doubt be met with the objection that we are injuring trade and diminishing the scanty earnings of the seamstress. To which we make the following reply, in two parts :

(1) It is an excellent thing to promote work, provided that it is good work. But we want church work to be taken seriously, and we do not want directors of workshops who raise no objection to scamped work and inane designs (fig. 145). We want artists who will give the workers perfect patterns from which to do the cutting-out, designs that are simple but well worked out, or original compositions animated by a genuine feeling for decorative art. This serves to educate the workers

Figs. 142, 143, 144.   Sketches Illustrating the Development of the Cope in Three Stages
From the true hood through the conventional hood to the comic hood

who can work just as well on a good design as on a bad one ; in fact they feel a special interest in producing really beautiful vestments, and their wages are no less secure.

But the fact must be boldly stated ; the real artists turn their talents to secular uses and very rarely apply them to the production of beautiful vestments. The catalogues we receive from England, Ireland, France and Italy afford ample proof of this humiliating state of affairs. When they are carefully examined it becomes apparent that what they aim at is the showiness that impresses an untrained eye, or the false parade of richness, which, it is imagined, is what will pay the shop best. No value at all is attached to the harmony of the lines, the suppleness and natural draping of the vestment which give the liturgical gestures that impress of dignity and simplicity which is justly admired in so many paintings and sculptures. And why ? Because the importance of these qualities is not recognised.

(2) Secondly, we wish to forewarn the clergy so that they may recognise vulgarities when they see them and not waste their money

on spurious richness. And we want them when they buy to know that it is possible to procure really interesting vestments that are original without being eccentric, and are not so dear as those shown in advertisements. The following illustrations will, we hope, prove our point.

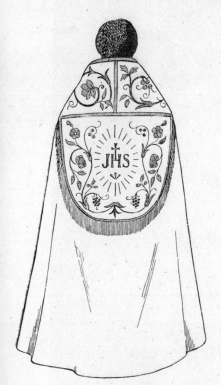

FIG. 145. A COPE
Afflicted with far too broad a band around the top and with a hood of exaggerated dimensions and commonplace ornament

FIG. 146. A GOOD COPE, LYING WELL ON THE SHOULDERS
The hood is simple and decorative. The price half that of the previous one

Only two horribly ugly copes have been inflicted on the reader (figs. 144 and 145). The descriptive notes attached explain them sufficiently. Compare figs. 146 and 147 with them and you will readily grasp the enormous difference.

Fig 147. It will be noticed that the band across the shoulders and down the front, which is ornamented with gold galloon, is of modest dimensions, and that the hood does not come down below the waist.

Moreover, instead of a scheme of decoration consisting of rays issuing
from a central monogram—the mechanical kind of design that the

FIG. 147.   A COPE OF LAMPAS, FLEXIBLE AND DRAPING WELL
Ornaments in velvet with rock crystals.   Made by the nuns of Filey
Convent

manufacturers produce—there is only a large red-velvet cross set off
by gems.   The squares of velvet set between the arms of the cross and
along the band form a simple and effective decoration, much more

effective than a conglomeration of branches and buds. Another point, against which objections are not usually raised, is that the cost of this ornamentation is one-third that of the devices which adorn the cope in fig. 145.

FIG. 148. A WHITE SATIN COPE WITH VERY BEAUTIFUL APPLIED WORK
OF A BYZANTINE CHARACTER
Also by the Filey nuns

An unusual cope is shown in figure 275. The colours reduce themselves to three : white for the stuff, old-rose for the grounds of the orfreys, and on this rose ground quatrefoils of black velvet assisted by their complement of gold. Three things there are which militate with quiet effectiveness in favour of this cope: (1) The fine material and the lining being light, the cope is light. A bishop tried on this cope in the presence of some priests—I was one of them—and expressed his pleasure in spontaneous appreciation : " What a charming vestment ! It is a

mere feather-weight.   What a contrast to some of our usual copes
which tire one out, they are so objectionably heavy." And it was
remarked, after the consecration of a church, how another bishop
wearing this cope—which swung delightfully from him—acquitted
himself of the long ceremonies with wonderful ease.   (2) It is a restful
pleasure to see a hood ornamented with a broad branch from which

Fig. 149.   A Beautiful Cope, very light and flexible
Notice the position of the hood.   Drawn by Dom Sylvester Fryer.

grow conventional leaves, and not with that eternal central design
surrounded by its trifling banalities.   (3) The price of this cope is eight
pounds.

Two more fine copes are reproduced in figures 148 and 149.   The
first shows beautiful Byzantine ornaments in applied work on white
satin ; the second illustrates the correct position of the hood, as we
shall now endeavour to explain.

We have been describing various copes in which the front bands
or orfreys are carried over the shoulders and continue along the back
above the hood, this being the customary form in some countries.
But it is an established fact that the hood, from which our present false
hood is derived, was attached to the upper edge of the hood and hung

down from that top edge. And it is no less certain that if the hood is not placed in the position which the true hood used to occupy, but is attached to the lower edge of an intermediate orfrey, it often hangs too low down. Many churches pay attention to this point and always have the hood attached to the top edge of the cope. For an example

FIG. 150. A SHAPED HOOD, WITH GOOD DECORATION

see fig. 149, which shows a very fine cope draped in a plain and dignified manner. A comparison of this vestment with the one shown in fig. 145 will remove all doubts on the subject. It will be observed that in the latter cope the hood, which hangs too low and assumes grandiose dimensions, merely succeeds in producing a comic effect— a not uncommon result when we aim at the grandiose.

We have previously had occasion to remark that the inspiration derived from what is best in ancient vestments is always fruitful, but that it is a dangerous thing to affect divers uses just because of their archaeological interest. This remark is very much in place here, in connection with the attempted revival of a genuine, though ornamented hood. It is a matter, of course, that Rome should decide, and it is not our business to allow or forbid this return to ancient usage ; but we may be permitted to indicate a logical view of the matter. The ancient hood was a true hood, a covering and a protection for the head ; is there room nowadays for an ornamented variety of this true hood ? It would seem not. For the secular clergy have no need of it, since they already have the biretta ; and the regular has another hood, attached to his habit, which he uses as the secular uses the biretta ; give him a hood on his cope and he will have two hoods. The fact is that this is a good case for the application of common sense. Let us refrain from providing an appurtenance which has no justification in use, and be content with the conventional hood ; but let this be no mere little pouch, nor a big sort of apron coming down to the knees, but a well-proportioned piece of work of moderate size.

We have given several examples of copes with the orfrey continuous right round the neck and the hood hanging from its lower edge ; and several examples also of the other style of cope in which the hood is attached to the top edge without any intervening orfrey, as already explained. In the latter case the hood is generally shaped somewhat in order to make it fit well round the neck. The former cope is obviously of simpler design, but it is apt to come up too high on the neck, so that the head has the appearance of emerging from a sort of funnel. Moreover it constricts the shoulders disagreeably, because it has a cloth or metal clasp half-way up the chest ; whereas the cope with a hood cut out to fit the neck and a clasp in its proper place, that is to say, quite at the top of the chest, is sensible, practical and comfortable. The neck of this cope is, after all, very like the neck of a tippet or cloak ; and what is the *pluviale* but a cloak ennobled by the liturgy ?

HUMERAL VEIL.—The name itself denotes the purpose of this veil, namely, to cover the shoulders, and to do so in the way one expects of a beautiful scarf. It should therefore hang in easy folds, and to insure this, should fall quite naturally over the shoulders of the priest or sub-deacon. It follows that it should be light and flexible, and that anything stiff or heavy is in direct contradiction to the characteristic beauty of a veil. If the veil has the rigidity of a metal plaque and is adorned with florid gold or silk ornaments, surrounding a central medallion, too often seen crooked, it loses all grace and simplicity. Ornamentation on the two ends of the veil encourages these aberrations,

and is also very inconvenient for holding the monstrance. Fig. 151
exhibits all these defects ; fig. 152 has all the characteristics of a really

FIG. 151. HUMERAL VEIL WITH EXPENSIVE AND VULGAR ORNAMENT

FIG. 152. A SIMPLE AND BEAUTIFUL DAMASK VEIL WHICH DRAPES
NATURALLY

good veil. The *Guide Pratique* suggests that two pockets should be
made, of the same material as the lining, near the ends of the veil,
into which the priest can slip his hands—which is one more sin against

simplicity and one more contraption to be avoided. As regards the fastening, ribbons are not very practical and are awkward for the priest to manipulate ; he has to pause while he ties a knot. A little chain is easily fixed on to a hook, and many priests find this a good way of keeping the veil in place. This applies to the veil used at Benediction, and not to that of the sub-deacon, which does not need a fastening.

CHALICE VEIL AND BURSE.—The reader will not be surprised to find us encouraging the idea, which is gaining credit among the clergy, of having chalice veils made large enough to cover the sacred vessels completely and all round, at the back and sides as well as in front, and

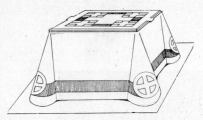

FIG. 153. BURSE AND CHALICE VEIL
Faulty in their ornamentation. The
veil also stiff and artificial in its folds

FIG. 154. A VEIL WHICH FALLS
NATURALLY
Smoothed out in front. The crosses
correctly placed

hanging in easy folds from the pall to the table of the altar. Fig. 153 shows a veil which fulfils these conditions, but also displays three defects, which it is as well to point out, as this veil has been highly commended. There is no adequate reason for having a cross on the veil or on the burse ; but if it is to be there it would be better to have it in a good position, on the centre of the burse and at the front of the veil, rather that in eight unimportant corners where some other decoration would do. This veil gives the impression that the crosses have been multiplied because the designer did not know what emblem to use. It shows poverty of imagination always to fall back on the sign of our Redemption as soon as any difficulty arises. Secondly, the burse is drawn the same size as the pall, but the pall should be somewhat smaller than the burse ; for if the latter does not project a little, there is a risk, in removing it, of upsetting the pall, the paten, and the Host. Lastly, the design on the burse suggests an empty frame which has lost its picture. There is no precise rule for the decoration of these two accessories. We may use monograms, emblems, etc., and put them if we wish at the four corners of the veil ; or we may abstain entirely from such ornament. The faults of the design shown in fig, 153 are corrected in figs. 154 and 155. We leave it to the reader to examine and compare the three and so form his own judgment.

Everyone is familiar with our undersized veils which are stretched tight over the chalice and shaped to the form of a truncated pyramid. If larger veils are used, they can be allowed to fall in graceful folds on three sides ; but this does not imply that they should not be straightened out slightly in front, so that the cross or other emblem placed there may be visible. But a careful or orderly person will do this naturally.

FIG. 155.   AN OPEN BURSE
The sides joined by two loops, which is the better method

The burse is made of two pieces of cardboard covered with some material and sewn together along one side, so that it will open and close in the manner of a book. At least that is one way of making it and a good way. Another way is to connect the two pieces, not only at the end, but also at the two sides, but these only loosely with gussets, which allow of it opening sufficiently to receive the corporal. The same effect is achieved, in a third method, by means of two loops which connect the pieces at the sides. See fig. 155. Of the three forms of burse the last seems to us the best. We may be allowed to insist that the burse, since it is intended to receive a square cloth (the corporal), should itself be square ; there is really no excuse for the oblong forms which one sometimes meets.

CHAPTER XI

FRONTALS AND OTHER HANGINGS

THE FRONTAL.—The General Rubrics of the missal are precise on the subject of the ornaments of the altar. They say, for instance, *Altare in quo sacrosanctum Missae sacrificium celebrandum est . . . pallio ornetur coloris, quoad fieri potest, diei festo vel officio convenientis.* "Let the altar on which the most holy sacrifice of the mass is to be celebrated . . . be ornamented with a pall of the colour (as far as possible) proper to the day or to the office." We may note three distinct points in this rubric : (1) The altar of sacrifice should have that ornament which is now called an antependium or frontal, names which denote a hanging placed in front of the altar. (2) The colour of this ornament must agree with the colour proper to the feast or to the season of the Church's year. In this way it speaks through the eyes to the heart and the mind ; it varies its teaching with the liturgy ; and it is one, by its colour, with the vestments of the celebrant and the ministers. This is an instance of the unity in variety so dear to liturgical art and to the heart of the Church. (3) The rubrics do not lay down an absolute rule ; but say with the proverbial prudence of Rome : *pallio ornetur, quoad fieri potest,* that is, "as far as possible." But where is the impossibility ? Is there any great difficulty in having frontals, at least for all the Sundays of the year and the Holidays of Obligation ? "If anyone fights shy of the idea of hiding the sculptures of the altar from the sight of the congregation, let him consider that for one authentic and really artistic bas-relief there are hundreds in which ostentatious ugliness and bad taste vie with one another ; and that such frauds are better hid when one calls upon God. Those altars are few which, when their ritual ornament has been removed, reveal to archaeologists, to artists, and to lovers of art, beautifully balanced sacred scenes in which they will acknowledge a permanent homage offered by human thought to the divine Love." [1]

[1] H. d'Hennezel, *Les parements d'autel* (*La vie et les arts liturgiques*, Sept., 1913, p. 24).

The use of the frontal is often only a question of liturgical zeal, of a desire to do what is best, and, in the first instance, forethought when one is having an altar made. The architect must be given precise instructions in order that he may so design the altar as to facilitate the observance of the rubrics. The following example can surely be followed. In a certain basilica in which precious marbles and golden mosaics display their splendours in honour of their Lord, there is a typical altar, a block of Cornish granite, a mighty and solid block.

FIG. 156.   WHITE FRONTAL
Interwoven monogram and cross in appliqué work or embroidery.   Coloured strips at either end

A sumptuous altar, or a work of art, would have cost much money; such a one was not desired ; but what the liturgy prescribes was desired : a frontal. That is very good, and shows not pretentiousness, but moderation and intelligence. Plain or only slightly ornamented frontals cover the front of the altar on ordinary days, and finer ones on the greater feasts of the Church.

This example leads us to dwell once more on an important subject ; the fact, namely, that economy often coincides with sound liturgical taste. It is quite possible to have a simple and inexpensive altar, a block of stone, or even a neat wood-work frame containing the altar stone, and a frontal to cover it tastefully. It is not essential that the frontal should be embroidered. A piece of silk damask in yellow and white, or red and yellow, or of a single colour, red, or green, or whatever it may be, is all that is required. One may allow oneself the addition of a monogram, or of a fringe along the upper edge or at the lower edge of the frontal ; or one may have two or four vertical bands, hanging like stoles from the upper edge. The monogram and the orfreys are a distinct improvement if they are well-proportioned and rightly adjusted (fig. 156). They are certainly to be preferred to the narrow strips of gold lace, stiff, monotonous and not appreciably decorative, that are stitched on to certain frontals (fig. 158). Let us give another example which is also very practical and instructive. We have already mentioned Dr. Adrian Fortescue, the builder of a very primitive sort of church —four walls and a roof, with no attempt at style. His pecuniary resources were limited, but he was deeply learned in the liturgy, a lover of the arts, and no mean draughtsman. In place of an altar with little pillars and capitals carved in foliage and flowers, he designed one with no carving or moulding ; it was the simple wooden framework to which we have already referred. He himself designed the frontals and a very good canopy which was made by a skilful carpenter to whom it was a

FIG. 157. EXCELLENT IN CONSTRUCTION AND IN ITS GENERAL PLAN
The simplicity of the draped frontal and of the dossal sets off the richness of the canopy
(*Fort Augustus Abbey, Scotland*)

labour of love. This learned priest is no more ; but he has left behind him this little church, a sanctuary compact of sincerity and good sense, a worthy companion to his books on the liturgy. As he was good enough to send us some drawings of his frontals, we print one which may be found useful. It is only a sketch in outline ; but it is accurate, and shows an altar vestment which for all its great simplicity is admirably conceived (fig. 159).

Another altar (fig. 157) forms part of a whole, which in its finish, delicacy and stateliness is very nearly perfect. Look well at it and consider the merits of this altar with its fringed frontal gracefully draped ; examine the canopy which gives a reverent covering to the altar of sacrifice ; and then judge whether the whole composition and its constituent parts are not preferable to many a pretentious altar,

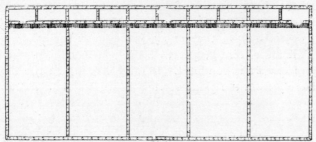

FIG. 158.   FRONTAL SHOWING MEAGRE AND UNINTERESTING
ORNAMENTATION
Compare with figures 156, 157 and 169

FIG. 159.   ALTAR OF A POOR PARISH, BUT WHOLLY INSPIRED BY THE
LITURGY
The pillars belong to a wooden canopy ; the tabernacle has its veil
and the altar is "vested" with a very simple and well-conceived
frontal.   The whole designed by Dr. Adrian Fortescue

which with its ornamental sculptures costs ten or a hundred times
as much.

There are, of course, frontals which are richly decorated and whose
designs are of great beauty ; fig. 160 shows one which we have published

in our *Ancien Trésor de Silos*, and which is entirely covered with patterns that are skilfully designed and artistically embroidered ; but works of this kind entail very considerable expense, while they are unnecessary or even distracting. One does not go to church to examine such things minutely, or to analyse the pretty figures and the whole gamut of colours of an altar frontal, but to be helped in one's prayers by the solemnity of one's surroundings. Besides, looking at the hangings of an altar merely from the point of view of art, we are convinced that if

FIG. 160. FRONTAL FROM THE ABBEY OF SILOS (SPAIN)
The embroidery very delicate, but too elaborate

their decoration is simple, economical and well spaced, they contribute to an atmosphere of peace and religious awe, but wholly fail to do so if they are smothered in a multiplicity of ill-assorted designs, whether in appliqué work or in embroidery.

We have seen from examples that the frontal may be either flat or draped. Let its upper edge be fixed at the top of the altar and *below* the *mensa*. Let the *mensa* project far enough to prevent the celebrant and ministers from touching the frontal with their feet.

CURTAINS for the altar, the sanctuary and the church. Here we have no text from the rubrics to quote as we had for the frontal, but we appeal to the extensive use made of curtains in churches prior to modern times. This is fully attested by history, by ancient inventories, and by some surviving monuments. One cannot cut oneself clean off from the tradition of the past ; to do so would not advance the cause of good taste in liturgical matters, but would rather favour innovations of a possibly dubious orthodoxy and encourage a certain degree of anarchy in religious art.

If therefore we desire to see curtains restored to certain select positions, and in particular employed round the altar, let us make sure that we are actuated by the motives which inspired our forefathers. These motives may be stated briefly as follows : These hangings were a ready means of providing a decoration that was artistic, and, what is more important, one that impressed on the mind and heart of the faithful the reverence that should surround the Catholic altar ; they proclaimed and emphasised its dignity. The *vela in arcu presbyterii*, or on the walls of the sanctuary, performed the same function, and formed, one might say, a guard of honour round the Holy of Holies.

FIG. 161.   FRONTAL ORNAMENTED WITH EMBROIDERED BANDS
The moulding across the front is the communion rail

These are reasons enough to make us wish to restore the hangings of the altar and of the sanctuary.

Gone are the times in which churches were equipped with complete sets of hangings, and in which rich fabrics, covered with designs drawn from the flora and fauna of the East, were hung between the columns of the nave and along the walls of the aisles. We are poorer, and moreover we are anxious not to cut off the worshipper in the aisles from the worshippers in the nave. And as for curtains figured with all sorts of fantastic animals, we are somewhat of the mind of St. Bernard ; two-headed dogs, four-footed beasts with human heads, hunting scenes, battles and so forth, would nowadays conduce only to distraction or to ridicule. Oriental exuberance and magnificence mean less to us than do simpler decoration and more reposeful designs ; and we are justified even from the point of view of art alone.

Fig. 162 illustrates what we have just been saying ; and it shows a great curtain skilfully designed and executed. The reader will note that even in the form of mural painting, curtains are valued by able architects, and that they do succeed in decorating a large surface of wall without having any pattern on them except a border, which is in its right place at the bottom.

L

Let us now turn to real hangings, and the reader will realise how much plain curtains are to be preferred to figured ones, and in how

Fig. 162.   Painted Hangings Making a finely-con-
ceived Mural Decoration
(*Capuchin Church, Barcelona*)

many different ways these curtains may be used.   We shall take our first lesson from a semi-circular apsidal sanctuary, in which sumptuous-ness is combined with exceptional simplicity (fig. 164).   The materials

used for the altar and its accessories do not come within the scope
of our inquiry ; our concern is with the great rose-red silk hanging,
which is outspread, with very little
in the way of draping, over the entire
wall of the apse, being hung from just
below the semi-circular base of the
Sanctuary vaulting. Unquestionably
the use of one plain colour for this
curtain is intentional, and is meant to
emphasise the splendour of the altar.
Nothing very wonderful to have
thought of, perhaps ; but the point is
that thought has been given to combining the parts into a harmonious
whole. Too often, in similar circumstances, the temptation has been
yielded to of using some many-
coloured fabric bright with gold-thread,
without giving due consideration to
the general effect, and the result is
a lack of those happy contrasts which
a little more discretion would have
ensured. We have them here ; the
white altar with its rich and brilliant
gilding stands out against the plain
colour of the hanging, which is
ornamented only with bands of embroidery at the top and at the bottom,
like the painted drapery shown in the
previous illustration. There has been
no servile copying of the antique ; the
inspiration comes from the *vela serica*
that were in common use in the
Middle Ages and earlier times, but
were superseded in the fifteenth

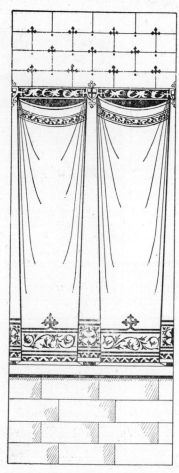

FIG. 163. DETAIL OF THE MURAL
PAINTING OF FIGURE 162

century by tapestries, which, though they were often very beautiful,
are apt to be stiff and formal.

The same idea has determined the decoration of the Sanctuary of
the church of St. Louis at Vincennes (fig. 165) ; but one device here is
peculiar. The curtain is not hung against the wall of the apse, which is

wider than at Tibi-dabo ; consequently a very convenient passage has
been left between the outer wall and the low stone partition, in which
metal rods are fixed ; these are connected by transverse rods from which

FIG. 164.   ROSE-RED HANGING ROUND AN APSE
The altar and the metal work stand out well against this great
monochrome curtain.   (*Church of Tibi-dabo, Barcelona*)

the old-gold coloured material is hung. It makes a very beautiful scheme
of decoration for the sanctuary, provides a dignified setting for the
altar, and separates off a quiet space which is an advantage both from
the artistic and from the devotional point of view. Besides noting the
way in which these long curtains are hung, we must mention that they

PLATE IV

THE SANCTUARY OF A LITTLE CHURCH (FILEY, YORKS)

Illustrating the use of a hanging. It is in a furnishing velvet of a carmine red, and is hung from the roof by its middle and two ends, thus draping more artistically than the usual vertical folds

are not made of silk ; it is not always possible to provide *cortinae sericae* of large dimensions for our Lord in the Blessed Sacrament. The hangings are made of a mixture of silk with cotton or wool ; they are rather full and draped in wide folds, and look very well. The material is not figured, but a row of plain bright-coloured bezants forms a kind of frieze round the lower edge.

FIG. 165. CHURCH OF ST. LOUIS, VINCENNES
Excellent use of old-gold plush hangings. The canopy over the altar partly
made of stuff of the same colour

The next altar of which we give an illustration (fig. 166), is not placed in the sanctuary of a church but in a small chapel, and consequently the framework designed to carry the curtains is very different from the one just described. It consists of four slender pillars surmounted by candle-bearing angels, two at the back and two in front, which pillars are connected by metal rods from which the curtains are hung. The altar with the curtains hung round it in this way reminds one of a triptych with the panels fastened open. The curtains depart from the type we have been praising by being covered with a very ornamental pattern but at any rate the pattern is dignified and is of one plain colour on a background also of one plain colour. The sound proportions and the simple colour scheme combine to produce a harmonious whole which is well fitted for its place in a church. The essentials of decorative art are there, plainly to be discerned in the frontal, the lateral riddels, and the dossal above the pretty retable. But, to revert to our thesis

FIG. 166. ST. WILFRID'S, HARROGATE
A beautiful altar with frontal and riddels, and a dossal above the
retable

concerning the beauty of simplicity and the practical economies which we may effect by pursuing it, we do not find this altar perfect in that respect. Although its general idea is good and although the parts are judiciously correlated, yet the whole thing might be very much simpler, and not lose a bit in effectiveness.

Let the reader turn once more to the Fort Augustus altar (fig. 157); there it is easier to follow the direction and connection of the main

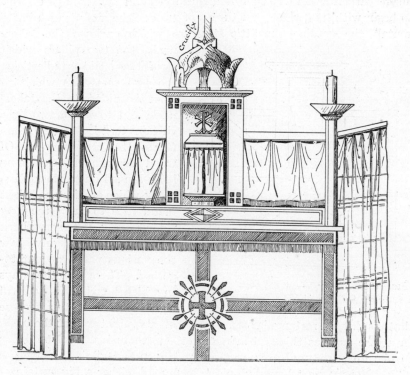

FIG. 167.   ALTAR OF A POOR PARISH
The altar, gradine, tabernacle house, pillars and candlesticks all of wood.
Everything simple, inexpensive and liturgical

lines ; a glance is enough to take it in as a whole and to find pleasure in it.   It is true that the altar is covered by a marvellously ornate canopy ; but this elaboration enhances the perfect simplicity of the draped frontal and of the dossal and riddels, while they in their turn make a foil for the ornamentation of the canopy.   Now, in the Harrogate altar the decoration extends uniformly over the altar and its constituent parts ; compared with the Fort Augustus altar, it displays a certain poverty of imagination and a deficient sense of the more delicate interrelations and contrasts that go to make an harmonious whole ;

before the one the mind is distracted, before the other it is called to recollection and peace.

Fig. 167 may afford hints to those who are looking out for a wooden altar with hangings. It can be very economically put together by any village carpenter and is thoroughly liturgical in spirit and in form. To begin with, the whole structure is of wood. The altar (which has a frontal), the gradine, the little structure which encloses the taber-

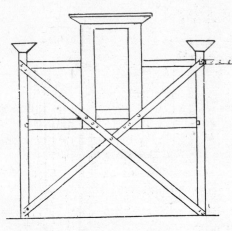

nacle, the two pillars which form two solid candlesticks, the two cross-bars which go from the pillars to the tabernacle and to which two light curtains that form a retable are fastened, all are of wood. Of wood also are the two strong laths hinged on to the pillars, along which are fastened light metal rods to carry the long riddels. Fig. 168 gives a back view, showing roughly how the various parts are put together. There are other ways in which hangings may be of signal service. Let us suppose

FIG. 168. BACK VIEW OF THE FRAME-WORK OF THE ALTAR OF FIGURE 167

that you have a rectangular sanctuary with a straight wall at the back. In a case such as this and in many others, there is a fatal tendency to pile up sculptured ornaments, or paintings and gilding, above the altar. Now a great hanging on the back wall, either a big curtain of upholstering velvet, or a linen sheet dyed red, or some other suitable colour, might be substituted with advantage, especially if it is well draped, and a great economy would be affected, which would allow other expenses to be met. Given an altar, a canopy, and a fine but not too large retable, and all the brass ornaments stand out very well against a plain colour.

If we have to do with a great church in which the altar is placed in the centre of an apse, it is easy to place a curtain immediately behind it ; but, once again, the curtain should be of one plain colour. A rich and complicated scheme of decoration has to justify itself, and it cannot be justified in a hanging because it actually prevents the desired effect from being obtained. We have had a chance of verifying this assertion

FIG. 169.   HIGH ALTAR OF A CATHEDRAL WHICH HAS A SEPARATE ALTAR OF
THE BLESSED SACRAMENT

The designer has given unusual prominence to the impressive crucifix. The
composition very simple and the effect more striking than a complicated
mixture of sculpture and painting

in a fine cathedral which has a separate Blessed Sacrament altar, and
a high altar without any tabernacle or gradines (an arrangement which

is liturgically most correct), and behind this high altar a great hanging

Fig. 170. Bluish Hangings used to Curtain off a Small
Chapel

magnificently figured in gold.   But, just on account of the richness of
this decoration, the crucifix and candlesticks are so lost against the

gold of the hanging as to be scarcely visible.   Fig. 169 shows how this defect may be corrected ; every detail has been carefully studied so as to yield the desired effect of clarity and proportion. Let the form of the crucifix be changed if that is desired, though it is surely splendid and most uncommon in its combination of the Byzantine and the modern. Any style of crucifix, so long as it is well-shaped and of plain metal-work, will do ; but, if the altar is to be truly beautiful, the main proportions must be preserved. The beauty of the whole will depend upon the frontal and upon the things actually required by the rubrics, but also upon the dossal, which sets off the decorative qualities of the ritual objects. If the dossal is done away with and unnecessary accessories are introduced, such as flower vases, candelabra, sculpture, or architectural designs in wood or in gilded bronze, the altar will often be wrecked. Its true importance will be falsified, or rather diminished, and the result will be a confused jumble of forms and colours. Whereas a simple and digni-

FIG. 171. HANGING USED AS BACKGROUND
FOR A CRUCIFIX

fied scheme of decoration emphasises the supreme importance of the altar and gives the crucifix the value that is its due.

Figs. 170 and 171 show two other uses to which hangings may be put. It is not always possible to have a baptistery separated off from the rest of the church ; in this instance two long, ash-blue curtains serve to partition off the space required for the font.

Fig. 171 shows a crucifix placed against a panel of red material ornamented with plain gold lace and draped somewhat after the fashion of a banner. It is certain that the respect due to a crucifix, or the honour which we wish to give to some particular picture, is satisfied by giving them a hanging for a background instead of fastening them directly against a bare wall. We remember being struck by this fact in the private chapel of Cardinal Gasquet, then Abbot President of the English Benedictine Congregation. A beautiful picture of Blessed Thomas More occupied a position of honour, and the devotion which the Right Reverend Abbot had for the martyr was expressed by a fringed red hanging, against which the portrait of the saint was reverently placed.

Only one objection can be made, in our opinion, to the use of hangings. namely, that dust lodges in their folds and accumulates there. This is true of materials that are looped up in various curves, but not of hangings that are draped in vertical folds, still less of plain panels. All hangings should from time to time be taken down, brushed, or rather, shaken out, and replaced. The added beauty they give to an altar, a sanctuary, a devotional picture and so forth, is well worth a small amount of trouble, such as we willingly expend on many other things.

CHAPTER XII

CANOPIES AND VEILS

"THE liturgy of the Church which is the creation of reverence, of piety, of the spirit of order and of tradition," [1] requires that the altar should be covered either with a *ciborium* or with a *baldacchinum*. In using these words and in distinguishing between them we are following the *Ceremonial of Bishops*, the *Thesaurus Rituum* of Gavantus and other standard authors. But since the distinction may be unfamiliar to some readers and the very words to others, we shall begin with a short explanation. The word *ciborium* here designates a permanent structure of metal, stone, or wood, erected over the altar of sacrifice and supported on columns ; and that is the standard meaning of the word, as for instance in the *Liber Pontificalis*. [2] The high altars of the Roman basilicas are invariably covered with such structures.

As distinguished from such a *ciborium* the *baldacchinum* (Italian, *baldacchino*) is a canopy of cloth on a wooden frame. We may be allowed to call this covering a "canopy" as that word is more familiar to English ears than "baldacchino." A sub-variety of this canopy is known as a "tester," as shall be explained later.

What is the purpose of the ciborium or canopy ? And why do we expect the altar of the Blessed Sacrament in every church, and the high altar of a cathedral to have either a ciborium or a canopy ? "The real and only purpose of both is the supreme honour given to the Son of God present on the altar during Mass, or apart from Mass in the tabernacle." [3] The thrones of kings are surmounted by canopies, and bishops too have the same honour shown to them ; why then should we deny a like privilege to the King of kings ? The ciborium is more monumental

---

[1] P. Batiffol, *Leçons sur la messe*, Avant-propos, p. 1.

[2] ed. Duchesne, Lib. I, p. 261, 262, 312, 323, 324, 375. The eucharistic vessel commonly called the "ciborium" in England is known to the Ritual as the *pyxis*, and we might very well call it the "pyx," giving to the tiny vessel which now enjoys that appellation the name of *custodia*. Each would then have an appropriate and distinctive name.

[3] Mgr. X. Barbier de Montault : *Le dais de l'autel du Saint-Sacrement* (*Revue de l'art chrétien*, 1895, p. 306).

and so more solemn than the canopy. We may note that when either is present there is no need for any special canopied throne for Benediction or Exposition of the Blessed Sacrament.

Some have said that a ciborium or canopy is unnecessary when there is a dome over the altar, or even when the church has a well-conditioned roof, because then the priest and the altar are protected from "dust, sun and rain." The reason is false and naturalistic. A canopy or ciborium is in no way merely a protection, neither is it merely an ornament. It is all this, but much more besides. It concentrates our attention on the altar where the Sacred Mysteries are enacted, and is a mark of supreme reverence for the sacred Presence. Nothing can take its place. If we have strayed from the letter and spirit of the liturgical rules, there is nothing for it but to return to them.

This return to the past, in favour of traditions which are in the highest sense perfectly logical, is daily more and more in evidence. Zealous priests are desiring to have their altars covered with a ciborium or a canopy, and the best architects are sending yearly to our public exhibitions designs which provide for one or the other. The great cathedrals of Westminster and Marseilles have superb ciboria. The new church of St. Louis at Vincennes (Paris) has a canopy over its altar ; as has too the Abbey of Fort Augustus, in Scotland. Not every church can aspire to have the relatively more costly ciborium, and we shall speak chiefly of the simpler canopy.

STRUCTURE AND LITURGICAL QUALITIES OF THE CANOPY.—It is necessary first of all that the canopy (and the *ciborium*) should cover the altar (*mensa altaris*) completely from end to end, and that it should extend also in depth over the tabernacle, the altar and the predella. Other structures, therefore, which do not fulfil these conditions, are not liturgically correct, however ingenious or decorative they may be. A tester with valance such as that at the London Oratory is certainly correct, if it fulfils these conditions ; but it sometimes gives rise to anxiety. We wonder, as we look at it : " Is it going to fall, or will it stay firm ? " Our minds are troubled when we see this somewhat mundane piece of furniture poised in mid-air without any obvious means of support. It would perhaps be better to have a true canopy, supported on posts, or one fastened to a back structure, of which the proper adjustment can be divined. That would be simpler, more complete, more decorative, and more reverent. Look back at fig. 157 and you will see a satisfactory canopy which illustrates our meaning.

We have just mentioned the "tester," which is a well-known and very common form of canopy. In this form the canopy is not supported by any posts in front, but attached firmly to a framework at the back. The framework usually consists of two uprights, A and B (fig. 172), fixed in the ground and to the altar, connected and strengthened by cross-beams C, then a frame bearing the tester and valance ; the latter is attached under the projecting edge of the tester, DD. As the canopy inevitably sinks with time, it is prudent to suspend it by two chains fixed to the two front corners and fastened to the ceiling, as has been done at Vincennes (Church of St. Louis). That is a straightforward method, and the two chains may become decorative elements of which there is no need to be afraid. Or again, rectangular pieces of metal at E may be used to strengthen the joints and keep the canopy in its horizontal position. At Vincennes, the canopy is raised somewhat in front, thus forming an obtuse angle with the uprights ; this gives a good effect, and is more pleasing than the strictly right-angled adjustment.

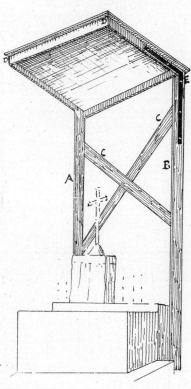

FIG. 172. DIAGRAM SHOWING THE FRAMEWORK OF ONE SPECIES OF CANOPY

For the frame, metal (bronze, brass or iron) may be preferred to wood, as shown in fig. 173, where lofty metal posts, fixed in the ground and to the altar, support the canopy frame, which is made of metal rods slightly curved on the three sides.

PORTABLE CANOPY.—The fixed canopy naturally suggested the movable structure, the so-called processional canopy. When this can be put up and taken down, it usually consists of a tester, and four or six poles connected at the top by cross-bars, over which hangs a valance ; these poles are sometimes connected also, about the middle, by horizontal rods, and have handles which, by means of hinges, can be lowered or

FIG. 173.   A COMPLETELY LITURGICAL ALTAR AND ITS APPURTENANCES
Observe the position of the tabernacle, and its complete veil

held at right angles ; which is very handy for the bearers.   Or else the
canopy is a flexible one ; that is to say there are no cross pieces at all,

and the material of the tester undulates and oscillates according to the movement of the supporting poles (fig. 177). The first canopy (fig. 176), is an ingenious arrangement, but it is fixed and unyielding. The second, being flexible, falls and undulates more naturally.

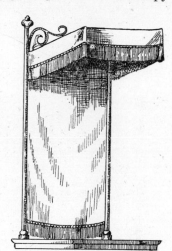

We may here draw attention to the valances of these canopies and of their smaller fellow, the *ombrellino*, which we need not stop to describe. Too often these valances are scalloped elaborately and then adorned with a riot of those flourishes which are so beloved of mercantile art and bad taste. An example of the sort of thing we mean is given in figure 175. Others may be seen in abundance in the catalogues which are scattered year by year to the four winds of heaven. Turning quickly from these horrors, we offer the reader a reproduction of an ingenious tent-like structure, which we do not altogether

FIG. 174. A MINIATURE CAN-
OPY, FOR EXPOSITION
Very simple and more digni-
fied than many one sees.
Compare with figure 96

FIG. 175.   A VALANCE OVER-DECORATED WITH RUBBISHY DESIGNS

commend (fig. 176). We have already commented on its rigidity. But the canopy of fig. 177 wins our suffrages for its flexibility and simplicity of decoration. That simplicity of decoration is a welcome

M

contrast to the usual medley of commonplace motives : monograms

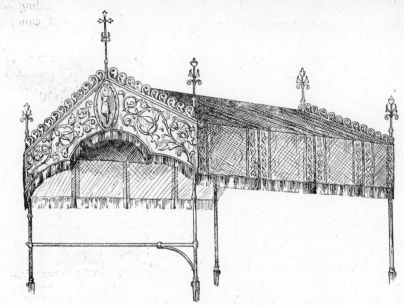

FIG. 176. PROCESSIONAL CANOPY OF ORIGINAL STRUCTURE
The roof material hangs over the sides to form the valance. (*Poussielgue-Rusand, Paris*)

FIG. 177. A FLEXIBLE CANOPY WITH SIX POLES
The simple geometrical ornament of the valance is far superior to an orgy of scrolls and flowerets

sunbursts, spirals and volutes of the most wearisome sameness and lack of artistic vitality.   A better effect may be obtained by simple squares, short lines and other elementary but important units. But they must be drawn and arranged by artists of great experience, who understand how to obtain a beautiful effect by simplification.

TABERNACLE VEIL.—The liturgy requires that the tabernacle should be covered with a veil, and we may now say a few words about that "canopy." The rule of the Ritual is plain when it speaks of the tabernacle as "decently covered with a canopy" (*tabernaculum conopaeo decenter opertum*). This veil, which gives the tabernacle the semblance of a tent (*tabernaculum*), is "the most certain sign of the presence of the Blessed Sacrament."[4] The lamp which burns before the tabernacle— and often also in other parts of the church—is not so certain an indication of the Presence. The liturgy is so convinced of this that the place of the veil "cannot be taken by images painted or sculptured on the door of the tabernacle . . . and the *conopaeum* is required even when the tabernacle is made of precious material, such as gold or silver."[5] If there be no veil, then the tabernacle is bare and poor, however rich its material ; for it lacks that which it ought to have.

The objection that the veil hides the tabernacle has no force against the letter and spirit of a liturgical rule.[6] If this little edifice is to be beautiful, it should be so for its Divine Guest far more than for the eyes of beholders. And surely the curtains contribute a very proper character of awe and reverence which must impress the beholder. The matter is one of obedience to liturgical rule, and also of care and zeal for our Lord's eucharistic dwelling. What is veiled from sight is often much more revered. "Common things that can be had without difficulty meet with contempt," says S. Basil, "while we are naturally inclined to seek after those which are set apart from the common uses of men."

It must be owned that the desire to obey the rubrics meets with very great difficulties in a number of existing tabernacles ; for, having been planned and constructed apart from any liturgical considerations, their

4 *The Eucharist*, by Canon Durieux, translated by Father O. Delphin, Chicago, 1926, p. 221, n. 424.

5 *ibid.*, p. 221.

6 The Sacred Congregation of Rites has been asked this point several times and has always given the same answer (21st July, 1855 ; 28th April, 1866 ; 7th August, 1880). See for instance the answers of 1st July, 1904. The S.R.C. was asked : "May the custom of not using the veil be kept ?" It replied : "The custom may not be kept ; the Roman Ritual and the Decrees should be observed." (*An servari possit consuetudo non adhibendi conopaeum ? Negative, et serventur Rituale Romanum et Decreta.*)

transformation is almost impossible. How, for instance, cover completely or even surround with a veil a tabernacle which is embedded in the thickness of a reredos or of stone gradines? That is what comes of trusting blindly to those who know indeed their own arts, whether

FIG. 178. A TABERNACLE WHICH BEING SEPARATED FROM THE STRUCTURE OF THE UPPER-ALTAR CAN BE COMPLETELY VEILED

of architecture, sculpture, or metal work, but who do not know the very special, and most legitimate exigencies of Catholic worship.

A wise author has lately written on this subject: "The liturgical prescriptions should be observed rigorously, to prevent bungling and incompetence on the one hand, and artistic extravagances on the other." Our architects shall make us new altars and new tabernacles, not as they like, but under the direction of priests who know the liturgy. How, indeed, can we ignore the laws which express the Church's reverence for the Blessed Sacrament? Now the tabernacle, according to these laws, first, should be covered with a veil, secondly, should not be simply a stand for the crucifix, and thirdly, should not have a throne permanently upon it.

Here is a tabernacle which is faithful to these rules (fig. 178). The crucifix is then placed behind the tabernacle, on a shelf, a pedestal, or, if the shaft of the cross is long enough for the figure of Christ to be plainly seen, on the table of the altar. Also, this tabernacle rises directly from the *mensa*, and is slightly separated from the super-altar. It is easy to hang the curtains, or to fix a rod for this purpose, and easy also to slip these curtains between the super-altar and the tabernacle so that they cover the sides entirely ; it goes without saying that they must cover the whole of the front. The top of this tabernacle, that is to say the ball and its base together with the fringed material, is detachable, and may be removed if it is desired to place a throne on the tabernacle for Exposition of the Blessed Sacrament. And for the same reason the veil proper may be made to cover the tabernacle completely, the top as well as the sides, the detachable top going above it. Such a tabernacle may be octagonal, hexagonal, rectangular, or circular in shape ; but its great quality is that it has solved the problem of making the veil a true covering, really enveloping the tabernacle. And let that covering be a really "decent" one. I have seen tabernacles with dreadful contraptions on them. *Decenter coopertum* does not mean covered with an old bag or sack ; it means covered in a graceful and becoming manner.

The tabernacle of figure 179 is noteworthy for its crown, which seems specially appropriate now that the Kingship of Christ has been proclaimed anew by the Holy Father and consecrated by a special feast. Here also, as in the last example, the top may be moved and room made for a throne, if desired. The veil in the illustration covers only the sides of the tabernacle ; but it could be made to cover the top also, going under the crown.

The veil should be divided in the middle so that the door may be opened easily. Moreover, being a veil it should be of sufficiently ample size and sufficiently supple material to fall gracefully. Let us not be stingy in the matter. If we allow the material to be twice the perimeter of the tabernacle it will not be too much, and a skilful worker will be able to make a really good veil. But let there be no lining to destroy the suppleness of the veil. A fringe or galloon may be added, and a veil is often completed by a valance round the upper portion, which serves to conceal the method of hanging and also the gatherings in the stuff which help it to fall into good folds.

FIG. 179. A VERY LITURGICAL ALTAR SURMOUNTED BY A CIBORIUM
The veil surrounds the tabernacle completely

Lest anyone should be misled by fig. 102 of the *Guide pratique,*
which shows the door and the whole interior of a tabernacle lined with
padded silk, it should be remarked that such a lining is quite unneces-

sary. It suffices that the inside of the tabernacle and door be covered
with white silk.

But to return for a moment to the veil, there is the serious question
of its colour in regard to the colour of the vestments of the day. To
some it appears a great nuisance to have to change the veil, but we

FIG. 180. AN EXCELLENT
VEIL OF CIRCULAR FORM
DRAPING VERY GRACEFULLY
Observe the curtain behind

FIG. 181. EUCHARISTIC DOVE
AND CANOPY, XIIITH CEN-
TURY (*Laguenne, France*)

do not grumble at having to use different vestments, and why should
we refuse to vest the tabernacle properly? We should provide four
veils, one for each of the liturgical colours so used; for at black masses
the tabernacle is veiled in purple. And let us change them with our
vestments. We shall not then be vexed with glaring contrasts of colour
and we shall be in harmony with liturgical law.

VEILS OF CIBORIUM AND MONSTRANCE.—The veil used to cover the
ciborium—by which we here mean the pyx in which the Blessed Sacrament is reserved—derives in direct descent from the veils which covered
the doves and pyxes that used formerly to hang above the high altars

in cathedrals and other churches, serving the purpose of our tabernacle.
(Fig. 181.)

The ciborium, then, must be covered with a white veil, *"albo velo"* ;
so also the Eucharistic monstrance. Notice that the ciborium cover is
a *veil*, and not a kind of case made of four pieces of stuff joined together
at the top, like the cover in fig. 182, which is first cousin to our

Fig. 182. Ciborium
Cover, Stiff and badly
Decorated

Fig. 183. Ciborium
Cover, Light, Simple,
Ample and Draping
Gracefully

board chasubles. Neither is the cover of the monstrance a kind of
bonnet—such as is seen, happily, in few churches—with which the
monstrance is covered as a tea-pot with a tea-cosy. These two veils
naturally differ in shape, since they belong to two very different
eucharistic vessels. The ciborium veil is rightly conceived if it be made
perfectly circular, with a small round hole in the middle for the cross
or knob at the top of the ciborium lid ; if the material is very soft and
light, this sacred vessel will be gracefully draped and fittingly covered
by a veil thus conceived and executed. (Fig. 183.)

It will be thought, perhaps, that we are picking a quarrel with the
Guide pratique, because we correct it again for suggesting a lining for
this veil, as well as for that of the monstrance. We are merely fulfilling
what we believe to be our duty ; because more than one error might be
imbibed together with the excellent advice of which there is so much

in that work. We insist then on this ; a lining serves for nothing but to add weight and stiffness to small veils. We have said, and we repeat, that the beauty of these veils is in their folds, which are their leading characteristic and chief decoration. A monstrance veil, in length nearly twice the height of the monstrance, and of a silky material, will fall in most graceful folds ; it is a great mistake to spoil it with lining. The veil, then, must have no lining, and above all, no decoration. The same thing holds good for the ciborium veil. People have a passion for decorating it elaborately, often with motives abominably arranged (fig. 182), paltry symbolical designs, or texts appropriately chosen—so it is imagined. But, even if this be the case, it is still more true that these trifles are out of place on these small veils. We shall explain our meaning further in Chapter XV.

Fig. 184. A Very Simple Silk Veil which Covers the Monstrance Excellently

The hem of the ciborium veil may be finished with a fringe ; and it would be well to have another round the small central opening ; this latter would facilitate the handling of the veil, and is much better than fine loops of silk or gold thread, which become entangled in the arms of the cross that surmounts the lid.

The Altar Cover.—What is required of the altar cover save to cover and protect the altar? We have seen, in Chapter II, an ideal altar cloth completely covering the *mensa*, reaching exactly to the edge in front, and falling to the ground on either side. The cover also will fulfil its duty if its hem reaches the edges of the altar ; it is quite unnecessary that it should hang down over the cloth at the ends. To this hem, a fringe may be added or not ; but, above all, let us avoid altar covers with valances, which are considered necessary, while they are only detrimental superfluities. These bands of stuff are generally a miscellany of meaningless scalloping, fancy work, upholsterer's fringes and tassels, insipid and wearisome designs. Even were all this well-chosen, well-designed and well carried out, it would still be a superfluous display, for the outline of the altar table which is used for the divine mysteries is always preferable.

These criticisms lead us to close this chapter with a sorrowful comment which is, however, no cry of despair. How many people of taste, how many sincere and intelligent Christians, would like to pray before what is beautiful ! But, like a certain man of faith and learning, they find that they must keep their eyes closed when they kneel before the altar, the more easily to raise up their souls to God, undistracted by vile productions.[7]

[7] So have I read of the celebrated Don Vincente de la Fuente, who found himself often compelled to act thus in the churches of his beloved Spain.

CHAPTER XIII

THE archiepiscopal cross, the seven candles, ring and crosier do not enter into our subject, since we are treating only of vestments. We shall consider, in this chapter, gloves, sandals and shoes, mitre and pallium. The illustrations are numerous because these insignia are less known than chasubles, copes, etc., and because the designs we give will (as we hope) be practically useful. Our labour in this matter will be repaid if our desires are realised.

A bishop wears many vestments which are worn also by priests: amice, alb, girdle, stole, maniple, chasuble ; but he has two vestments which distinguish him from the priest-celebrant, viz., the tunic and dalmatic which he wears under his chasuble. The same is true of an abbot when he pontificates in his own church. In Chapter X we treated of the tunic and the dalmatic ; those used by bishops and abbots are generally of very light stuff without any ornament and without lining, characteristics the value of which may be readily appreciated.

GLOVES.—Gloves are a very ancient item of vesture, since history tells us that they were used by Persians, Greeks and Romans. The hands of the Sarmatae on the Column of Trajan are gloved. [1] But liturgical gloves were not introduced in the Church until about the ninth century. Mgr. Batiffol tells us, in fact, that in the liturgy of the seventh-eighth centuries the Pope did not wear gloves, and that they are not worn either by the bishop in the Romano-Carolingian liturgy, described and commented by Amalarius at the beginning of the ninth century. "The most ancient liturgical gloves on record occur in the inventory of the abbey of St. Riquier under the year 831 : *Wanti castanei auro parati*. It is thought that the liturgical use of gloves by bishops was introduced in France, to all appearance during the course

---

[1] H. Leclercq has written a documented study of gloves in antiquity and the early Middle Ages, in the article "Gants" of Dom Cabrol's *Dictionnaire d'archéologie et de liturgie*. Mgr. X. B. de Montault has published an essay with the title : *Les gants pontificaux* (*Bulletin monumental*, 5th Series, Vol. IV, 1876).

of the ninth century." [2]   *Wantus* is a low Latin word denoting a glove. The word *chirotheca* is of Byzantine origin and occurs in many medieval inventories : *"Par chirothecarum," "chirothecas pontificales,"* etc. [3] It is this word that is still used in the Latin liturgy to designate a glove. A few examples of ancient gloves have been found in the tombs of bishops. Their decoration, which consists of embroidered medallions, or of metal discs on which are depicted the Cross, the Lamb of God and the *Dextera Dei*, does not provide much that is useful for us. Plaques of metal, often enamelled, were additions of too heterogeneous a sort for gloves

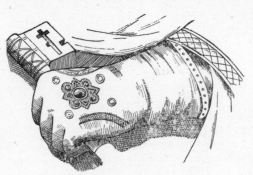

FIG. 185. GLOVE WORN BY ST. PETER IN
STATUE AT VERONA
After Rohault de Fleury, *La Messe*

sometimes made of skin, commonly of cotton or silk.[4] We are justified therefore in not following the Middle Ages in this matter.

C. Rohault de Fleury had the happy thought of reproducing (from a statue at Verona), the hand of St. Peter covered with a glove (fig. 185). The ornamentation is imperfect, but frank

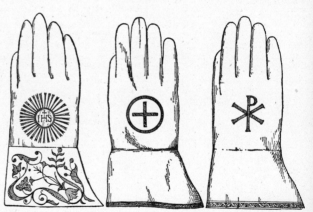

FIG. 186. A SUN IN METAL GILT ON A GLOVE, AND SOME
VERY USELESS VULGARITIES ON THE CUFF
FIG. 187. A SIMPLE DESIGN IN COLOURED SILK ON A FABRIC
OF WHITE SILK
FIG. 188. A MONOGRAM WHICH MAKES A SUITABLE AND
HARMONIOUS ORNAMENT FOR A GLOVE
Also in silk

2 P. Batiffol : *Rites et insignes pontificaux, Revue des Jeunes, XIX*, No. 8, p. 135
3 V. Gay, *Glossaire archéologique*, Art. *Gant*.
4 E. Rupin has published three of these enamelled medallions in his fine work :
L'Oeuvre de Limoges, Paris, 1890, Vol. II, figs. 639, 640, 641.

and vigorous, and it is a relief after what one sees on most modern gloves, especially the ill-designed and ill-embroidered motives, very useless also, which one finds on the cuffs (fig. 186). The shops provide even episcopal gloves ready-made, and they are generally bought just as they are.   A cross inscribed in a square (fig. 187), or, better still, a cross alone, or a monogram, embroidered in *silk*, then simply a band also of *silk*, to border the lower part of the cuff, would satisfy the requirements of practical taste (fig. 188). Embroideries in gold, and oftener in metal-gilt, produce an unpleasant roughness which, by rubbing against the vestments, helps to damage their material.   Moreover, ornamentation in silk is more distinguished and more rational, that is to say, more in harmony with the silk fabric of which the gloves are made.   That is a principle, too, which ought to be more generally followed for many vestments. But we do not wish to exaggerate and to seem to exclude gold ornament altogether, for if placed with discretion it goes very well with embroideries.   What we protest against is the indiscriminate employment of inevitable gold ornament of an insipid character, notably on gloves. Our vendors could seem to have but one idea, to make them expensive and to give them a gorgeous appearance.

CALIGAE.—The readers we have in view will probably not be much interested in the history and description of liturgical hose ;[5] but since they appertain to the insignia of bishops and abbots, we may remark that liturgical language knows two terms in particular for the designation of this item of pontifical attire : first *Udones* and later *Caligae*. Caligae are mentioned in an *Ordo* of Corbie (tenth century), in the treatise of Ivo of Chartres : *De rebus ecclesiasticis*, and in the *De mysteriis missae* of Innocent III, as things which should be put on the bishop (or abbot) before the sandals.   And they say expressly that the *caligae* should reach *usque ad genua*.

Finally, a decree of 1822, approved by Pius VIII, is not less explicit with regard to these two insignia, *Caligae et sandalia*.   Therefore the two are quite distinct, and high boots which are neither sandals nor stockings do not satisfy for these.

In our present-day liturgy we have the word *caliga* and the thing which it signifies, a stocking that covers foot and leg.   The Sacred Congregation of Rites has decreed that the stockings should be of the

5 See, if desired, the articles *Caliges* and *Chausses* in Dom Cabrol's *Dict. d'archéol. chrét. et de liturgie.*

same colour as the vestments of the mass. The same rule applies t ›
sandals and gloves. In masses for the dead the bishop uses neither
caligae, nor sandals, nor gloves.

SANDALS.—There are at least ten varieties of footgear known to have
been in use among the Romans during the first six centuries, varying
naturally according to classes and circumstances. But there are scarcely
more than three that concern us here. The *soleae* worn by bishops, their
ministers, and various sorts of people, were sandals, very much the same
in kind as those still used in certain religious orders ; they consisted

FIGS. 189, 190. BYZANTINE CAMPAGI, FROM MOSAICS AT RAVENNA

of soles with fastening straps.   The *calcei* covered the whole foot
and corresponded to our shoes ; they do not appear to have been
in liturgical use before the twelfth century.   The *campagi* were
intermediate between sandals and shoes.   They were made of a
piece of leather, more or less shaped, turned up at heel and toe ;
straps, fixed to the sides, passed over the top of the foot and
were often wound round the leg (figs. 189 and 190).   A famous
mosaic of S. Vitale at Ravenna shows, on the left of the
Emperor Justinian, Archbishop Maximian (fig, 2), a deacon and a
sub-deacon, all wearing *campagi*. The same is true of S. Apollinaris
in his church at Ravenna (fig 50), of S. Maurus and other personages
in the Lateran baptistery (fig. 4). Sandals of this sort were not reserved
exclusively to the use of bishops and their ministers ; but since they
employed them on certain public occasions we may infer that they used
them also at mass. However, they very soon became entirely liturgical,
and down to the twelfth century they kept at Rome their name of
campagi ; sometimes also they were called *subtalares*.

Fig. 191 represents a very interesting *campagus*, that of Honorius I
(626-638) ; it is reconstructed after a mosaic of the Church of Santa

Agnese *fuori le muri*. The sandal attributed to Pope S. Martin is another typical specimen, with its broadly-conceived ornamentation (fig. 192).

FIG. 191. *Campagus* OF HONORIUS I (626-638)
After C. de Linas, *Anciens vêtements sacerdotaux*

FIG. 192. A SANDAL PRESERVED IN THE CHURCH OF S. MARTINO AI MONTI, ROME
After C. de Linas, *op. cit.*

It is certain, as may be seen from the illustration, that we have here a true sandal, for it must have had side-pieces and straps, which have now disappeared.

FIG. 193. A *Campagus* OF S. EGINO
Bishop of Verona (†802)

It is not so easy to find correct designations for the different types that the Middle Ages have transmitted to us. If anything they are *campagi* ; and the soled shoes, very common from the thirteenth century on, are *calcei*. However, both have been called *sandalia* and the name has remained in the liturgy. But it is clear that footgear with proper soles, which covers the feet completely and is equipped with *taeniae*, laces or tapes, fastening in a knot or buckle, is not the sandal. We have here a shoe, whether the material be leather, silk or velvet.

Campagi and shoes began, in the eighth century, to receive

FIGS. 194, 195, 196. WELL CONCEIVED ORNAMENTS FOR LITURGICAL SANDALS
IXth, XIIth, and XIIIth centuries

ornamentation which the ancient Roman taste, much more sober than ours, did not admit, even for the more important vestments. The first example (fig. 193) is a *campagus* in red leather, of S. Egino, bishop of Verona (†802). There is nothing complicated here. A tongue shaped like a spear-head, reminding one of the tongue of a modern shoe, lies up along the instep over which the leather straps were knotted. The ornamentation consists of a stem from which spring two branches bent back, and which terminates in a sort of trident at the toe. The illustration shows clearly enough the strong and perfectly decorative character of this design. A shoe of the twelfth century, preserved in the church of S. Martino ai Monti (Rome), has its upper divided lengthwise by a beautiful galloon supported by four-leaved rosettes (fig. 194) ; this again is in good style and inspired by a just feeling for ornamentation. Another specimen is not an illustration of

FIG. 197. A MARVELLOUS LITURGICAL SHOE, XIIITH CENTURY
After Rohault de Fleury, *op. cit.*

an actual example, but has been drawn after a miniature (fig. 196). The galloon, with its two branching members, would be a sufficient ornament without the other curves.

The twelfth century marks an advance on those which preceded it, in what regards the richness of the footgear. The most remarkable example which it has bequeathed us is the shoe of Arnold, first arch-bishop of Trier (†1183) ; it is in fine red skin, covered with embroidered foliage. But the thirteenth century seems to have produced the master-piece. You can see, in figure 197, that the *campagus* has become a true soled-shoe, and that it has scallops and tongues fastened by laces. Observe the marvellous arabesques in gold thread laid on to a dark ground, and the jewelled band which divides the upper of the shoe into two parts. The shoe has not survived entire ; but beautiful fragments were found in a tomb of Lausanne Cathedral and have allowed of this reconstruction, which has been effected with intelligence and fidelity. Though our days naturally desire to do better than the past, it is probable that we shall not be able to equal this magnificent achievement. But, after all, it is not either useful or necessary ; and very true and satisfactory effects may be attained by well-designed motives in appliqué-work and beautiful galloons thoughtfully arranged. But how difficult it seems to be to have no other but these simple aims !

MITRE.—We pass now from foot to head and deal with the *mitra*, the distinctive head-gear of bishops. But the word was in use long before to desig-nate a species of feminine headdress, a fillet of some material, an Asiatic headdress, and the Phrygian cap. The liturgical mitre, the pontifical and Roman headdress, is first mentioned in the year 1049, in a bull of Pope Leo IX to Eberhard, Archbishop of Trier : *"Romana mitra caput vestrum insignivimus"* ; and, according to Braun, it is depicted for the first time in two miniatures which date from the beginning of the eleventh century.[6] We recog-nise it especially in a minia-ture, which represents St. Gregory the Great in pontifical

FIG. 198. ST. GREGORY THE GREAT AFTER A XTH CENTURY MS. IN THE BRITISH MUSEUM. The mitre in its origins

vestments and wearing a cap with two lappets.[7] This must certainly be the primitive form of the mitre (figs. 198 and 199). We must, however, admit, in the face of certain examples antcrior to the thirteenth century, that it is sometimes a question whether the papal headgear of frescoes and miniatures is intended for mitre or for tiara. We know in fact that the origins of both have been much debated and that they seem to run together. But since Leo IX speaks of a "Roman mitre" as granted by him to Eberhard, it is pretty certain that this mitre was, as it still is, a piece of dress which the pope himself used. We are therefore authorised to regard as mitres both the skull-cap with convex top of

6 *The Catholic Encyclopaedia*, art. *Mitre*.
7 Cotton MS. Claud A., III, f. 9 *recto*.

N

which we have just spoken and also the semi-spherical cap (fig. 200) worn by S. Gregory in a miniature reproduced by Braun in his article

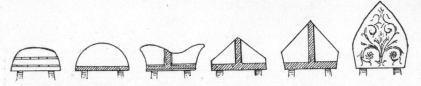

199   200   201   202   203   204

DIAGRAMS SHOWING THE EVOLUTION OF THE MITRE FROM THE XTH CENTURY
TO THE XXTH

Fig. 199. After a xth century miniature. See fig. 198.   Fig. 200. After two miniatures of the xith and xiith centuries.   Fig. 201. Mitre of Eulger, bishop of Angers, xiith century.   After an enamelled plaque.   Fig. 202. Mitre of Bishop Mauricio of Burgos, xiiith century.   After his sepulchral statue.   Fig. 203. Mitre of the xvth century.   After examples still preserved.   Fig. 204. Modern mitre, more and more falling out of favour

Tiara in the *Catholic Encyclopaedia*. Moreover the learned author introduces the same spherical cap into the very instructive scheme of forms given under his article *Mitra* in the same work. A headdress of

FIG. 205. HEADGEAR OF A POPE *Lower Church of S. Clemente, Rome.* The tiara in its origins

much the same character may be seen on the head of Pope Paschal II in a miniature of the *Chronicle of Ekkehard de Aura* (twelfth century, Cambridge).

Some paintings of the eleventh century in the lower church of San Clemente at Rome present another form of liturgical headgear, that has also been identified with the Roman mitre (fig. 205). But this headgear, which occurs thrice in these frescoes, a cap of conical form slightly rounded at the top, recalls much more the undoubted tiara worn by S. Silvester in a fresco of the church of the Quatuor Coronati at Rome,[8] and by S. Peter on the North porch of Chartres Cathedral. But with this statue of the first pope we have reached the thirteenth century, and we have now abundant documentary representations beginning even in the twelfth century. We need not therefore pursue this investigation.

8 In one of these frescoes the pope wears the conical cap, the tiara, and he is accompanied by three bishops in two-peaked mitres. In another of the frescoes he has a mitre like those worn by the bishops.

After the period of somewhat uncertain origins and developments of the mitre, it emerges in the precise form with which we are familiar. This mitre consists of two pieces which form a circle at the bottom and rise to two peaks; in the twelfth and thirteenth centuries these points were obtuse or right-angled, but they became acute later. The two parts of this headgear are united by a piece of material which covers the head.

Mitres of the twelfth century are very rare; but we have at least the mitre of Blessed Uberti (†1133), made simply of white linen and without the least ornament. We reproduce it after an etching of C. Rohault de Fleury (fig. 206). On the other hand, mitres of the thirteenth century are plentiful enough. They are not higher than the preceding one, but they are ornamented with designs or figures which evince a charming freedom of conception, a quick and fresh vigour of understanding and execution.

FIG. 206. MITRE OF BLESSED UBERTI, XIITH CENTURY Made of white linen. After Rohault de Fleury, *op. cit.*

FIG. 207. MITRE CALLED OF ST. THOMAS OF CANTERBURY. *Sens Cathedral*. After Rohault de Fleury, *op. cit.* Decorated with bands of geometrical design and superb floriations. A noteworthy mitre

We have, moreover, a very agreeable variety of mitres of this period. Some few examples only have been selected for reproduction. Among those not given here we may mention a mitre preserved at Sens, which has been attributed sometimes to Cardinal Stephen Langton, Archbishop of Canterbury, sometimes to that other Archbishop of Canterbury, St. Edmund, whose relics are at Pontigny. Covering the whole face of one side of this mitre is a representation of the martyrdom of S. Thomas Becket; on the other side is the martyrdom of S. Stephen.

Figure 207 shows another mitre, also preserved at Sens, and so well

known that it is unnecessary to insist on its superlative merits. It has been perfectly copied many times; efforts have sometimes been made to modify the design, with a view to improving it; but the improvement has been retrograde when, instead of the bold and strong curves that are so admirable in the original, we are given embroidered scroll-work of too mincing a character. The broad galloons with their repetition of geometrical ornament form a very happily-conceived contrast to the robust volutes in gold.

FIG. 208. MITRE AT S. MARTINO AI MONTI, ROME, XIIITH CENTURY
After Rohault de Fleury, *op. cit.*

It is obvious that the ornamentation of the mitre may be inspired by other ideas. The external contours of the two faces are fundamental; the band which surrounds the lower edge gives it a consistency that it needs and completes it very naturally. But the vertical band (titulus) is no more necessary now than it ever was. Its absence gives you space and allows of the composition of some scene that

FIG. 209.   A MODERN MITRE
Inspired by the preceding one; showing the good use that may be made of an ancient model

may stand out very well if the figures are treated in a very sober and almost convention-alised fashion. But there remains always a danger of confusing the effect if you depict a scene ; and it is therefore better to be content with a Christ in Majesty, a seated Madonna, or some other saint. The subject must obviously be carefully worked up, but it can be presented in quite a legible manner. Figure 208 expresses this idea and might serve as an inspir-ation for a better achievement. Such was the attempt of the designer of the mitre in figure 209. He has suppressed the orfrey along the upper edges, which gives the mitre a heavy effect ; the slopes of the angle, set off by a very narrow braid,

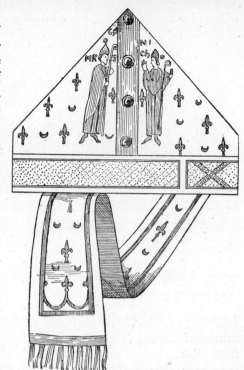

Fig. 210.   Mitre of Anagni, XIIIth Century
After Rohault de Fleury, *op. cit.* Somewhat stiff and thin ; but the idea is good. With certain modifications the decoration might be excellent

Fig. 211.   Design for a Mitre found among Montfaucon's Papers in the Bibliothèque Nationale (Paris)

give more lightness ; more-over, the shape is better. Yet we should not, for all that, despise the mitre of S. Martino ai Monti ; its stars, tiny angels, and above all, its Virgin Mother, all in gold on a dark-blue ground, must produce a beautiful effect. Other mitres of the middle age show us a differ-ent arrangement. On the mitre of Anagni (fig. 210), for instance, there is a figure on each side of the vertical orfrey. The whole composition is rather dry and meagre ; it again could do with improvement. The mitre which is figured in some papers of Montfaucon at the Bibliothèque Nationale (Paris), has a more solid and ornamental character (fig. 211). The band round the lower edge is similar to that on the so-called mitre of S. Thomas of Canterbury. Above we have floriated curves intertwined ; and on each side of the vertical orfrey a flaming star ornamented with a jewel.

Fig. 212. Mitre Decorated with Medallions
Lyons Cathedral. After Rohault de Fleury, *op. cit.* Gold medallions, if skilfully placed, may make an attractive decoration

The Lyons mitre (fig. 212) with its metal medallions is rather uncommon ; and the following one (fig. 213) is no less original. We have all seen so many mitres of a close family likeness, dictated by a sort of modern tradition and achieving banality, that fundamental differences in type of ornament must give us great pleasure. Now, if we only let ourselves be inspired by the two mitres just given, we shall have two varieties and inevitable difference. With some gold medals thinly scattered over the surface, or rather some jewels, or in default of these, rock-crystals, pearls, coral, etc., which cost much less than precious stones, we might often

Fig. 213. Design Inspired by a Mitre in the Treasury at Monza
Stones, well chosen and well arranged, may take the place of the ordinary ornaments

get results far more attractive and original than by our little figures or tiny designs in embroidery. But we must be careful when we give the order and set the artist to work ; we must limit him to a reasonable number of stones, have them well spaced and arranged in a judicious manner. If they are small and all alike, they may follow one upon another and produce a good effect, as in the mitre of figure 216; if they are somewhat large, they had better alternate with others of smaller size, as in figure 213. And then care must be taken to let them appear only here and there and in their proper place ; we shall thus obtain a restful and well-balanced effect. This object has been aimed at by the artist in his design, which is based on a mitre in the Treasury at Monza. The bands of the reversed T in which the jewels are set are bordered with a scrolled galloon. The two triangles of the ground are of white damask ; the two lappets of the same damask and bordered by two narrow galloons side by side. Although these *infulae* are in the nature of accessories to the mitre, yet they obviously have their importance. Only one ancient example is privileged to appear here (fig. 214), because it differs completely from those we generally see and because it manifests rare good sense, and a selection and curious combination of very diverse elements : a long fringe, a circular medallion in a square, and then simply three parallel galloons. It is certainly superior to the scroll-work, inscriptions and coats-of-arms which ornament so many modern lappets.

FIG. 214. MITRE LAPPET FROM THE TREASURY AT MONZA
Very superior in effectiveness to those lappets decorated with coats of arms, inscriptions, or other trifles

The reader will be disappointed if he expects from us a summary account of the changes which the mitre has undergone in the different periods. It will suffice to say that its evolution and that of the chasuble have followed contrary directions. In the period when the form of the mitre appeared to be precisely determined (twelfth century), the chasuble was of ample form, since it clothed the whole person of the priest ; and the mitre, being a headdress only, had proportions in accord with its purpose. It was low in height and was easily fixed on the head, forming a delicate ornament to it ; it was indeed a sign of moderation, harmony and distinction. But when art suffered shipwreck in Europe and the sense of beauty in liturgical things disappeared, especially in the seventeenth and eighteenth centuries, the chasuble was everywhere diminished, while the mitre, on the other hand, suffered portentous exaggeration ; and its ornamentation went parallel with that of the worst sort of chasuble.

We are now abandoning these errors of taste, in conformity with the liturgical movement which is manifest on all sides. As has been explained in Chapter V this movement began in the nineteenth century, and here (fig. 215) we have a mitre typical of it, probably the most artistic one produced by the Gothic Revival. It was given by the Catho-

FIG. 215.   SUPERB MITRE OF MONSEIGNEUR FREPPEL
Bishop of Angers.   Yet one may be allowed to prefer a
clean edge without embroidery, less richness and more
simplicity

lics of France to Monseigneur Freppel, Bishop of Angers, a member of the French parliament and a valiant defender of the Church. Twelve figures, admirably embroidered, are depicted on the principal face. It is a charming and refined piece of work, in one sense a marvel, a mitre very expensive at the time it was made, which would now cost a goodly number of pounds, supposing the other face embroidered in the same way and the lappets each adorned with an embroidered figure, as were those of this mitre. We should not like to say : *Ut quid perditio haec?* yet it is a well-known fact that sometimes, for want of knowledge, as much money is spent on a single item of liturgical vesture or liturgical furniture as would suffice to furnish a whole sanctuary, to make ten vestments, or ten mitres of perfect good taste and far more original than the mitre which has just been mentioned. However, it was made about forty years ago, and our present

FIG. 216. A CHARMING MITRE FOR ALL ITS MODEST PRO-
PORTIONS
Precious without preciosity. Made for Cardinal Mercier by a
London Artist

decorative renascence, which was certainly much needed, and which is inspired by a more profound logic, makes us prefer less numerous elements, better distributed and inter-related, a better structure, a greater sobriety, in fine, well-defined forms and those not bristling with gold embroideries as in the Angers mitre.

A regrettable example is often contagious, and since then we have had mitres with protruding metal floriation attached to their edges, and at the summit now a flower and now a cross or a statuette, also all in metal. But why set a cross on top of a mitre, as on top of banners and all sorts of things? Isn't it enough that the bishop has a cross on his breast? And as to a statuette perched on the summit of a mitre, we shall be having next a niche for it and little turrets of metal.

FIG. 217. A PRETENTIOUS CONSTRUCTION, BADLY SHAPED AND MUCH OVER-DECORATED
The face is not a portrait

Even without these exaggerations we have had mitres made with their two faces like the gable-ends of a Gothic monument. It is always the same story: a simple, beautiful form and an appropriate ornamentation do not suffice; we must needs add, and complicate, and pervert.

After this tiresome criticism here is something to calm, instruct and delight us, a mitre very well-conceived and exquisitely designed, made for Cardinal Mercier by a London artist (fig. 216). Look at it well; one glance is sufficient for you to grasp the whole composition and its ornamentation, for the whole is clear and the motives are well arranged. You will not need any argument to convince you that this mitre is a masterpiece of distinction, in modest and exact proportions. You will notice that there are no figures on it, and that the whole cost of the decoration is put into the rows of pearls, well-arranged and spaced, and the two conventional branches. It is a precious mitre, but one without preciosity and without showiness.

Pass now to the mitre of figure 217, an edifice very insecurely set on its foundations. It seems to say to us: "Take care! I am going to fall on you. But am I not lofty and decorative and exceedingly beautiful?" But this monument, with its Babel-like pretensions, is none the less a monstrosity of bad taste, in spite of its mass of embroidery, quite well-designed but lavish to a degree. The laity judge and condemn these things ; the clergy endure them ; but happily the vast majority of bishops are more and more discarding them, rightly fearing to be abased by these erections.

Before leaving the mitre we could wish that we were able to put before the reader a reproduction of one designed by a very modern artist, which is a thing of beauty. But we must be content to describe it only. To begin with we may say that it is somewhat hard for many of us, so accustomed are we to paltry imitations of the Middle Ages, to understand what the modern artist is aiming at. We are not abusing all imitation. Excellent models may be copied and it is good for the general taste that they should become well-known. But when we copy we should choose the best examples and we should interpret them skilfully. The modern artist, however, does not propose to imitate. The spirit of the contemporary movement is to make new experiments and to dream of new conquests. These experiments have been made in the case of some vestments which were mentioned in Chapter VII, and we there expressed our criticism quite freely. But to criticise is not to condemn all the productions of the new art. That art has naturally had not a few failures ; it has had also its successes, and these sometimes quite extraordinary ones. In the case of the vestment to which we have alluded, vegetable forms seem to have obsessed the artist, and he has revenged himself on them by inflicting horrible distortions. But the artist who made the mitre of which we are speaking was not trammelled in this way, as will appear, though imperfectly, from our description.

The first thing that would strike us is a standing figure, thoroughly in place, on the vertical band. Instead of a number of tiny figures of saints, which must be reduced and diminished, here we have one solitary figure, majestic and important. Although the broad band which runs round the lower edge calls normally for ornamentation running with its own lines, yet the series of juxtaposed rectangles of various heights, which stand on the border, are quite in harmony with the nature of the mitre, for this band also is set up on the prelate's head. A species of spiral, or rather a letter G which recalls a manuscript form, is set in the vacant upper spaces. Why are they there ? Doubtless because their curves connect the angular forms and, correcting the severity of these, give a pleasing variety to the whole. There is in all this no reminiscence of any familiar type or manner or style. The ornamentation may seem simple enough ; yet for its invention and disposition was required no small dose of reflection and audacity. The ground of the mitre above the band is in silk with a strong pattern. And it is a low mitre, something of the same size as the mitre of figure 206. Indeed, the lines and proportions of this master mitre are so good that they give one a feeling of balance, stability and comfort. And isn't it obvious, we ask, that such a mitre will be easy to use ? Look back now at the monster we considered previously (fig. 217). Your opinion, or rather your conviction, will be quickly formed. On the one hand you will

FIG. 218. DETAIL OF THE
SEPULCHRAL STATUE OF DON
MAURICIO
Burgos Cathedral. Showing
a very low mitre

FIG. 219. DETAIL OF A
STATUE OF THE WEST FRONT
OF RHEIMS CATHEDRAL
Again a mitre of small height

recognise moderation and sincerity, on the other extravagance and pretentiousness. Yet some minds will be tempted to think : "Yes, it is a good mitre, but it is too low." And why ? Just because we are accustomed to what are called "prudent" forms, and because we have not studied the early mitres and observed them when they had achieved their perfect form. Now, as a matter of fact, they are no higher than this mitre, as witness the mitre of Don Mauricio, bishop of Burgos (fig. 218), the mitre on a bishop over the porch of Rheims Cathedral (fig. 219), and the mitre of S. Firminus of Amiens (fig. 6). Let us be glad that the artist has gone back to the golden age of Gothic art. Yet the mitre in question is none the less a product of the new art and of a consummate art. It is also a revolutionary work, one that preaches a radical reformation in the character of ornamentation. Indeed, the technique of this orna-mentation is truly remarkable, at least in the case of a mitre ; for the mitre has been a sort of happy hunting-ground for every sort of small and mincing ornament. In the case before us only the standing figure is in em-broidery; the rectangular ornament is appliqué-work and is in vigorous relief.

THE PALLIUM.—We might have omitted the pallium from our book, for our aim is to promote a practical knowledge of beautiful things. And the pallium is not in fact manufac-tured by any known firm, but made at Rome from the wool of two lambs, blessed each year on the feast of S. Agnes in the Basilica Nomentana. The *pallia* are then placed on the Confessio of S. Peter, and the Sovereign Pontiff sends them, as tokens of jurisdiction, to the Patriarchs and Metropolitans of the Catholic world. The reason we give their history here is because they derive from a vestment.[9]

FIG. 220.　PALLIUM OF ARCHBISHOP MAXIMIAN
Mosaic of S. Vitale, Ravenna, vith century

The pallium, in Roman antiquity, was a large piece of material that was placed on, and draped freely over, the tunic. If we examine statues and bas-reliefs we may speak more definitely and say that generally this garment covered the back and passed over the left shoulder, from which it hung down by the side of the breast. The other end was brought from the back under the right arm across the breast and then

[9] Various authors have treated of the pallium, notably Mgr. Duchesne : *Les origines du culte chrétien* (Paris, 1889), pp. 373 *sqq.* ; C. Rohault de Fleury : *La Messe*, Vol. VIII, pp. 45 *sqq.* ; Father H. Thurston : *The Month*, Vol. LXXV, May-Aug., 1892 ; and Mgr. Wilpert : *L'Arte*, Vol. I, pp. 100 *sqq.*

FIG. 221.   GREGORY OF AGRIGENTUM,
WEARING THE GREEK PALLIUM
Arranged as on figures 220 and 222.   After
G. Millet, *Daphui*, pl. x.

passed over the left arm.[10]
Since it is thus represented
about the year 400, we may
conclude, when we find it
first mentioned, in the fourth
century, that this shoulder
garment was worn in the
same, or an analogous way
by the Greek bishops, with
whom it was a symbol of
the pastoral office. "It was
the cloak of the shepherd,
of the good shepherd."

The first figured monu-
ment that displays the pallium clearly, as one of the
pontifical insignia, dates from
the year 547, or thereabouts.
Already it is transformed
into a folded cloak, more
precisely into a long white

band, arranged as shown in
figure 220. This represents
the pallium of Archbishop
Maximian, in S. Vitale at
Ravenna. It is represented
in the same manner on Bishop
Ecclesius in the apse of the
same church (fig. 49), and on
S. Apollinaris in the church
of S. Apollinare in Classe, also
at Ravenna (fig. 50).

10 The pallium and toga are not
always easily distinguishable, when
one studies the monuments and
the authors who have spoken of
this garment. We have described
the pallium as it is represented
on Serena in Dom Cabrol's *Dictionnaire d'archéol.*, etc., art. *Dip-
tyque*, where this garment is called
palla, which means the same as
pallium.

FIG. 222.   INNOCENT III, FRESCO OF THE
XIIITH CENTURY AT SUBIACO
The arrangement of the pallium again recalls
the arrangement of the preceding pallia

The pallium is mentioned a few times before S. Gregory the Great. We know precisely that during his reign it became one of the papal insignia, and that the "Pastor eximius" granted it to bishops whom he wished to honour. A little later we find it being conferred on archbishops, and it became their special badge.

The pallium, such as we know it from the above-mentioned works, anterior to S. Gregory, was depicted by Greek mosaic-artists. And we cannot doubt but that they represented the pallium as worn by their own bishops. So this is the Byzantine pallium. During the course of

Fig. 224. Detail of a Bas-Relief in Ivory
IXth century. Preserved in the Fitzwilliam Museum, Cambridge. The Roman pallium is attached to the chasuble with a pin

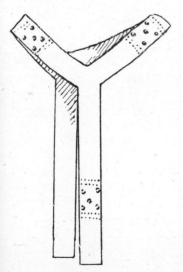

Fig. 223. Roman Pallium on the Palliotto of Milan
IXth century. After Rohault de Fleury, *op. cit.*

the seventh century it was not represented any differently, witness the pallia of two bishops in the church of S. Agnes *fuori le muri*. Witness also the pallium worn by Bishop Maurus in the oratory of S. Venantius in the Lateran (fig. 4).

We observe the pallium, arranged in the same manner, in other works entirely Byzantine but of later date, as for instance in a miniature of the famous Menologium of the Vatican (end of the tenth century), which

represents bishops assembled in council, and in some mosaics of Daphni, which are of the twelfth century. The pallium had then reached a considerable width, to which the Greeks remained faithful, and it is ornamented with very large crosses (fig. 221). As to the portrait of Innocent III (fig. 222), which has no connection with the Byzantine tradition, it provides us, along with that of Gregory of Agrigentum, with two rare survivals of pallia arranged in the way we have just described.

But we ought to fix our attention on the figured testimony that goes back to the century of Justinian and the one which followed, for these examples give us the first typical pallia, Byzantine and also Roman. In the eighth or ninth century a notable difference manifests itself, as may be seen in the case of two archbishops, of whom one is represented in a fresco of S. Maria Antiqua, and the other on a German ivory,

FIG. 225. DETAIL OF AN IVORY PANEL
On which is represented the consul Areobindus (506), wearing the *loron*. In order to display this ornament in its entirety, the artist has removed the folds of stuff which in the original completely cover the consul's knees

a detail of which is reproduced in figure 224.   The pallium has no longer got one end falling straight from the left shoulder, but meets in a V on the breast and from this point the band falls down the middle of the archiepiscopal vestments. So it has now taken the shape of a Y. There is a pallium of the same sort, but without the fold at the point of junction, on the palliotto of Milan (fig. 223), which likewise may be attributed to the ninth century.   We see it also on four personages represented in

mosaics executed during the pontificate of Pope Innocent III (1130-
1143), in the apse of S. Maria in Trastevere, on two mosaics by native
artists in the cathedral of Monreale,
and on frescoes of the lower church
of S. Clemente at Rome.   These
pallia differ from the Milan example
in being ornamented with a cross.

In the tenth century the arms
of the pallium began to be curved
and soon reached a circular form
(fig. 198).   Down to the fifteenth
century these two forms (the circular and the Y form) existed simultaneously and occur on many works
of art representing popes and
archbishops. But the movement in
favour of the circular form prevailed;
while the *omophorion* or Greek
pallium continued faithful to the Y.

The opinion which we now give,
while differing in part from the
conclusion of several authorities,
is based upon many comparisons.
Here it is : (1) The pallium of the
Ravenna form derives from the
palla or civil pallium which we described on page 205. That civil pallium suggested the arrangement of
the band; and this idea developing
produced the first *pallia*, with a
slight difference in the method of
arrangement.   (2) The Y-shaped
pallium derives from the *loron* of

Fig. 226. The Archangel Gabriel
Wearing the Loron
Detail of a bas-relief of the xiith
century. After *Monuments et Mémoires*
of the Académie des Inscriptions et
Belles-Lettres, Second fascicule, Vol.
ix, pl. xx

the Roman consuls, which itself is nothing but the civil pallium, folded
and made into a sort of orfrey. These magistrates wearing the *loron* are
represented in ivory diptychs of known date (400 to 541). Here, in
figure 225, is one of these bas-reliefs, representing the consul Areobindus
(506). In the original ivory panel the end of this scarf passes underneath
the tunic ; but in our illustration we have deliberately made the scarf
hang down on the right of the figure, so as to display the whole of the

loron. This garment is found a little later on Byzantine emperors and

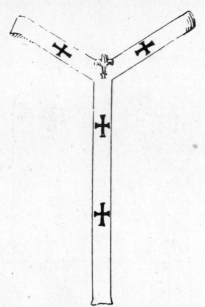

empresses, on four archangels in the apse of the cathedral of Cefalu, in Sicily, and on two other archangels represented on a steatite bas-relief (fig. 226).

If we reduce both the consular *loron* and the pontifical pallium to their simplest terms, that is to say to their bare lines, we reach a Y. But the pontifical pallium was not so wide as the *loron.* And the varied decoration which it received in the early Middle Ages, as also the abundant decoration of the consular *loron,* were replaced by crosses set far apart. Finally, instead of being crossed over the breast as was the *loron,* the three bands of the pallium became joined so as to make an ornament of one piece. Such is the

FIG. 227. A PALLIUM OF THE XIIITH CENTURY
With brooch-pin. MS. of Cividale·
After Rohault de Fleury, *op. cit.*

pallium as it is represented on a great number of personages depicted in miniature, fresco, statuary and other arts.

Figure 227 shows one of these pallia. Observe the pin with fleur-de-lys head by which the pallium was fixed to the vestment. The pallium on the great chasuble of S. Peter in the North porch of Chartres Cathedral is still longer than this, and also has four crosses on the front. We have already seen the pallium on the statue of a pope at the Lateran (fig. 53), and on

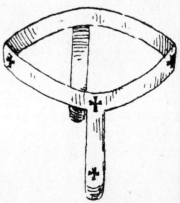

FIG. 228. THE MODERN PALLIUM
After H. Thurston, S. J., *The Month,* vol. LXXV, May-Aug. (1892)

the sepulchral monument of Martin V (fig. 54) ; but in this last there is that· extra measure of ornament which is characteristic of the

Renaissance. The pallia of these two popes have the circular form and seem to be falling from the shoulders ; they must have been held in position by pins. The design of the modern pallium is taken from an article by Father Herbert Thurston.[11] It is scarcely necessary to point out that it has not got the beautiful dimensions of the *pallia* so unceasingly represented in the art of the Middle Ages, and even in the period of the Renaissance.

While the writer was busy with this chapter a friend of his suggested to him that he should express the desire : "Would that the diminished pallium of our days might return to its former dimensions, to its integral beauty !" But that is a matter which appertains to the pastor of pastors ; it is his to decide whether such service should be done to this magnificent emblem, so venerable and so rich in symbolism.

11 In *The Month*, Vol. LXXV, May-Aug., 1892.

CHAPTER XIV

FAULTS OF TASTE AND THEIR CURE

THE title will seem a pretentious one to the point of audacity ; but our intentions are quite modest and unassuming. The purpose of this somewhat discursive chapter is simply to point out certain errors into which the designers and makers of vestments commonly fall, and to demonstrate the possibility—nay, the duty—of attaining a higher standard in liturgical vesture.

Let us begin with the ornamentation of altar linen and of vestments. Here the possibilities are extremely varied and almost boundless. That being so, people have thought that any kind of decoration would do, and these articles have too often been designed, embroidered, and made up without any previous study or real knowledge of liturgical art. The producers of plays at the best theatres do not dream of proceeding in this haphazard fashion ; they call in specialists, men who have made a study of costume, ancient and modern, and artists according to whose designs and under whose direction the clothes worn by the actors and actresses are executed.

Here, again, Mgr. Batiffol strikes the right note in the lecture we have already quoted : "Orfreys," he says, "embroideries, braids, all the fashions of Carolingian, medieval and Renaissance times, all the things which your inventiveness and ingenuity delight to superimpose on the naked simplicity of the actual material—these are excrescences, and they too often imitate festoons or plaster mouldings. You will return to the good taste of ancient times only when you have repudiated all such excrescences, all ornament for ornament's sake, all that imitation of decorative mouldings which smacks so strongly of the wedding-cake. And if it is really too much to ask of you that you should renounce embroidery altogether, let it be discreetly used so as to be lost to view in the folds of the chasuble and not flaunt itself on our backs like a showpiece in a shop window ; let it have a touch of the symbolic and nothing more ; but this involves a radical change in practice." These are true and sound ideas, but we need not carry them to excess ;

there are ornamentations that are wholly unfit for church use, but there are others which may enhance the beauty of vestments.

Let us begin by way of elimination and rule out all white fringes and galloons used with black vestments—too crude a contrast—all gold and silver galloons, edged, scalloped, or fringed along the edge with metallic thread work, all guipures and fringed edgings, in fact all the showy work which disfigures so many trade-catalogues and not a few sanctuaries (figs. 229, 230, 231). Closely related to these horrors is a whole tale of commercial products: small monograms, tiny hearts, other little symbols and patterns, all badly designed, badly embroidered and surrounded with sprays of flowerets or more often with rays made of spangles, exactly like those which glitter on the jerseys and tights of acrobats ; in fact, a whole mass of stuff which is cheap and nasty ; these things are wholly unfit for use in church ; they debase the taste of the public, and, what is worse, debase their religious sense. Unless some little pattern and its inevitable rays adorns the centre of a cross

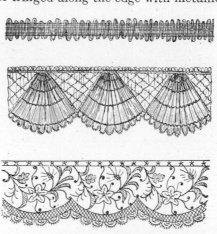

FIGS. 229, 230, 231. EXAMPLES OF CHEAP AND UGLY TRIMMINGS OF LACE AND TINSEL

FIG. 232. A HIDEOUS GALLOON OF A WRIGGLY SHAPE THAT REMINDS ONE OF THE TWISTED COLUMNS OF THE XVIITH CENTURY

or of a cope, there are good souls who cannot say their prayers in peace.

And even worse devices have been advertised, which do not really deserve either further publicity or further condemnation ; but as both have been accorded to them, the present writer will allow himself to express his indignation in a few sentences which would not find a place here if the dictum "*quomodo audient sine praedicante*" (how shall they hear without a preacher ?) did not on this occasion urge him, not only to the spoken, but to the written word. A bare statement of these devices is enough to show their nefarious character.

(1) Albs mainly of tulle on to which there are applied large flowers, cut out of old muslin curtains such as have now gone out of fashion.

(2) Banners on to which flowers of the same kind are applied after their chain-stitch embroidery has been dyed with some liquid gilding material bought at the chemist's.

(3) Chasubles of white silk on to which the design is applied by stencil and the outline then embroidered over.

It is enough to make one doubt one's own accuracy and wonder whether these grotesque devices are not the figments of some nightmare.

As, however, these suggestions have actually been made in print, it may be as well to quote the criticisms which have been made on them. *L'Ouvroir liturgique* (25th Jan. and 1st Feb., 1925), rejects the second suggestion and does not look kindly on the first ; it says : "However, if the tulle is coarse and consists only of a strip not more than eight or ten inches wide at the most . . . and if the pattern should chance to be suitable for church use . . . it might be allowed." No, it must not be allowed. Big muslin flowers cut out of old curtains now out of fashion are only fit for the rubbish heap. There is a want of reverence in the idea of using them to decorate so dignified a vestment as the alb. What those of the clergy who care for the beauty of simplicity desire is the true *linea*, the white linen alb, quite plain, very white, very dignified. [1]

As to allowing white silk chasubles to be painted by means of a stencil, one is shocked to read : " If the design be suitable, the plan of applying the design by means of a stencil and embroidering the outline of it is not to be condemned ; on the contrary, if good embroidery cannot be had for lack of workers or of money, this method may be recommended and should be brought to greater perfection . . . we should like to see special stencils of real artistic merit designed for this purpose." The consequences can be imagined; nuns and ladies, old and young, the readers of this little magazine, are thus encouraged to produce these vile ornamentations, while other folk look on with mixed feelings of derision and pity, unless indeed they are roused to a state of righteous indignation. And what of our manufacturers ? They do indeed produce some articles that are poor enough, but at least they know what the proper processes are, and when all is said and done, they are glad

[1] The reader is referred to what is said about linen vestments in Chapter II.

to make ornamentation that is suited to the nature of the material used and to the sacred purpose to which the vestments are to be put. They also will be misled by such advice.

This stencil process is all very well for the walls of restaurants and assembly rooms, but we ought to be ashamed of using such an inferior kind of work for vestments, which belong to an altogether higher order of things. The mere thought of the honour due to God and of the respect with which we should treat liturgical fabrics and all that approaches the altar, makes us abhor this vulgar device, which is only used in order to produce a showy effect and to produce it quickly and cheaply.

If we are told in reply that many stuffs used for furniture or for women's gowns have patterns thus applied to them, we make answer :

(1) That in the processes used in their manufacture, in market-value, and in the uses to which they are put, these stuffs are altogether inferior to ecclesiastical materials.

(2) That the ornamentation of textiles should only be effected by the actual weaving of the pattern into the material, if a durable and dignified material is aimed at, such as is worthy of our *vestes sacratae*.

Again it has been said "that the dyeing of a specified area of a material is no more to be condemned than the dyeing of the whole piece, or than the covering of the same area with embroidery or applied work." But this is a mistake. The colouring of a whole piece of material is the natural result of using coloured threads in the weaving ; the colouring of patches of a good material by the odious device of stencilling (which is not dyeing at all), is a purely artificial process and quite uncalled for. Embroidery and applied work on silk are at least of a material closely allied to the fabric, and when the fabric is decorated with patterns actually woven into it so that they form one whole, the material used is identical, namely silk thread, and the process of manufacture is all one ; in short, the fabric and the pattern are inseparable. To stencil a painted pattern on to a silk fabric is quite a different thing.

The kind reader will, we hope, excuse us for dwelling so long on mistaken theories and practices which one would have expected to be universally condemned ; it is startling to find that they are approved in certain quarters, for they are a danger to liturgical art. When confronted with suggestions of this kind, we have, throughout the present work, appealed to the principle of simplicity in the processes to be used, and rather than put up with mediocre ornamentation produced by paltry devices, we have preferred to go without any ornamentation at all. A white chasuble or cope keeps its simplicity and dignity if the silk of which it is made remains unspotted; and it is spotted by having a painted design stencilled on to it. Having ruled out all bad materials, designs and processes, we must revert to the danger referred to at the beginning of this chapter by competent authority, the danger namely of thinking it necessary to ornament every sort of altar linen and vestment. Why should they be ornamented? It is just an idea that is in the air, a convention accepted without having been thought out. Every pious person with any self-respect thinks herself obliged to make lace or embroider something for the church. In reading various handbooks and little magazines one is struck by the important position that is given to ornamentation; nothing, it seems, is to be excepted: not the altar cloths and covers, nor the communion cloth, nor the purificator, nor the finger-cloth, nor the corporal; of course, not the pall, nor the collecting bag used at benediction which has to be particularly resplendent (one wonders why), nor the cover of the ciborium, nor the cloth on the missal stand, nor the cover of the missal, nor even its markers; yes, even the markers! "At about the middle of the markers," says one author quite seriously, "some text about the Blessed Sacrament can be painted or embroidered, not too richly." But why? The passages of Holy Scripture chosen by the Church and the great prayers of the missal are under the eyes of the priest during mass; surely they suffice. Far from helping, such superfluities as texts on ribands only distract and annoy one. And yet there is another example of ornamentation that is even more outrageous. We have before us a catalogue showing eight of these markers, each of them adorned with little crosses, little chalices, little crowns, little clouds, rays, and lastly, stars! The intention is unmistakable; the unfortunate priest must be tempted to buy and to buy nothing that is not ornamented. Taken by itself, the above list of things to be ornamented sounds bad enough. It is a pity for the public taste and the public purse that such a noise should be made in order to advertise ornaments that are always useless and worse than useless.

Trade prospectuses and catalogues are denounced here and elsewhere on the ground that they pander to the bad taste of the public by offering for sale ready-made chasubles, copes, stoles and so forth, which too often are vulgar gewgaws and ugly trappings, an insult to God and His Church. The best firms do not issue catalogues, they supply photographs of their work to intending purchasers; they are ready to suggest ideas for a great variety of vestments and to quote prices, which also vary greatly according to the material used and the amount of ornamentation. A journey, too, may be made on occasion for seeing works of interest with one's own eyes, for choosing materials, galloons and so forth, for asking the advice of competent judges in some actual workshop, and so getting what one really desires.

It is obvious that aberrations in liturgical art are encouraged by publications, reviews and catalogues which, with too liberal an appeal to "all men of good will," print quite uncritical assortments of illustrations and suggestions—on one day, good ideas ; on the next, different or contradictory ones ; on one page they describe some excellent process and on another some very inferior one, such as the stencilling of painted patterns against which we have just recorded our protest. Under cover of these invitations to "all men of good will," a host of people are seized with the desire to try their talents and hasten to send in a profusion of designs for "light embroideries" for every kind of church cloth, or photographs of ornamentations which they fondly believe to be most original or at least very pretty. If these contributions are printed without any serious and impartial criticism, these publications do not serve to educate the taste of the Catholic public, which needs educating badly as we shall show further on. Meanwhile, what we wish to impress on these willing needle-women may be summarised thus : there must be a really good scheme for a vestment, good cutting-out and mounting of it ; there must be ornamentation which is fitting and also well-drawn and well-executed, whether it be embroidery or simple applied work ; there must be correct proportions, outlines, arrangement of the pattern, colours and shades of colour, and an appreciation of the relative importance of the background and the pattern. And again, there must be a genuine talent, a skilled hand, a practical eye, the critical faculty, the technique and tricks of the trade. All these things make up an aggregate of necessary gifts, knowledge and accomplishments which are to a great extent the fruit of a severe, persevering and prolonged training in a good school. They are all to be found in certain select workshops where there are designers, embroideresses and needle-women who know their craft, or rather their art ; but for the most part really good artists with no axe of their own to grind and inspired by deep religious feeling are few and far between, *rari nantes in gurgite vasto* ; and other persons are too apt to think they can very quickly become designers, embroiderers and even foremen or forewomen.

We are distressed to have to make the above remarks and others which will follow in the present work, because they will cause pain to many zealous workers in the house of God. But is it not best to point out the malady and do one's best to cure it ?   Should a sick man not be grateful to him who takes a deep interest in his well-being ?

We shall only delude ourselves if we speak of "attempts crowned with success," when we refer to workshops that have only been going for six months ; this kind of talk may encourage young beginners— which is quite right—but it involves awarding the victory to those who have scarcely entered the battle and who will proceed to rest on their laurels and to make vestments as unsuitable for our churches as were those that went before.   A fair number of these workshops are so very new and so full of confidence for the future, that it would do them good to grow old a little by looking back and becoming acquainted with some of the many works of past ages.   That might have a salutary influence on the character and technique of their work.   Look at the marvels of polychrome art dug out in recent times from Egyptian tombs, or at the friezes of spearmen and lions and at the rose work of Persian art, or at the stalwart bas-reliefs of the Assyrian sculptors, or at the simple but fascinating art of the early Christian ages, or at the glories of the Middle Ages displayed in so many vestments that have been preserved in our museums or in the sacristies of our churches. Study their shapes, the fabrics they are made of, their ornamentation, and the ingenious and varied processes used in the execution of them. Fill your mind with these great examples, copy little or nothing, and keep a watchful eye on those best works of the present day, which are paving the way for the decorative art of the future.

Again, firms and workshops of a rather earlier date should transform themselves and renew their youth ; a thing which many have done, both wisely and courageously.   If directors and designers do not cling obstinately to their old styles, but are ready to accept what is good in the new art, if they do not stiffen their backs when they meet with criticisms and opinions which may be painful to them, but are far more helpful than insincere praise ; if, on the contrary, they receive such criticisms with the intention of profiting by them, then indeed these directors of old established societies, firms, and workshops will make proof of the true wisdom and humbleness of heart, which are the distinguishing marks of the truly good and singleminded artist ; their work will live and inherit a blessing.   "But," they may say, "we have experience behind us ; our business has been in existence for a long time." All honour to them for that. Nevertheless, the saying *humanum est errare* holds good at all times, and in all places ; and it would be a mistake to believe or to force oneself to believe that all that one's firm does is well done and that one's own views and methods can be forced upon other people. It may be that other people's views and methods rest upon quite different principles, or at any rate, on a change of taste which is not devoid of solid foundations. Such a frame of mind weakens one's hold on the realities of life and sterilises artistic production, and it is only too probable that firms with this outlook will sooner or later have to yield pride of place to others which are prepared to walk boldly along better paths.

Let us take some instances which are not purely imaginary. We may put on one side the buyer who merely asks for vestments of a given shape, colour and price, and expressly disdains any further knowledge of the subject, being ready to leave all that to the manufacturer, who is free to choose the quality of the fabrics and the style of ornamentation. On the other hand there are priests who are not without some knowledge of the subject. They make their own observations and form their own judgments. They state their opinions and ask for advice ; they ask to see patterns ; they discuss things with the manager of the firm or of the workshop and come to an agreement with him. The manager is generally glad to help his clients ; if he has had ten or twenty years' experience, he has a wide knowledge of business. What good service he can render, what enlightenment he will effect in the realm of liturgical art, if he adds to this invaluable experience the still more valuable gift of complete single-mindedness ; and also of a broadmindedness which refuses to be exclusive ! With these qualifications the manager will occasionally be able to produce vestments which could not have been conceived except by a person possessing an exceptional knowledge of the art, such as none of the workpeople actually employed by the firm could lay claim to. We know of a Lyons firm which has produced a real work of art ; but the composition and colour scheme were the work of a very great artist of the same town, who had never before worked for the firm. A Paris firm did another bit of work, something really perfect, but it was no member of the firm but a clever artist who made all the drawings, chose all the materials for the ornamentation and settled the exact processes to be used. By putting oneself in this way into the hands of really competent men, one can occasionally have the great satisfaction of producing a work of real beauty.

In their own province judicious priests can insist on a style of art which is in keeping with their churches. "My church is not Gothic and vestments of no particular style do quite well for it." The answer he gets is "Gothic is the correct ecclesiastical style; our firm stands by the Gothic style ; we work from none but first-class Gothic designs and use an exclusive line in textile fabrics which is our patent." [2] And the priest goes elsewhere. The lesson is hard but well-deserved. Another priest said to the manager of a workshop : "My parish church is dark ; I want a set of vestments of a bright red colour." He is quite right, and if the manager tries to force a deep crimson upon him, because he has it in stock, he is certainly in the wrong. Or again, "Our church is very big ; and the woven galloon that you are showing me for the two crosses of a chasuble is very narrow and would look like a shoe-lace when seen from the back of the church." This priest's argument is quite reasonable ; his request should be attended to and a suitably wide galloon shown to him. Another priest knows that small veils, e.g., the cover of the ciborium, the canopy of the tabernacle and the veil of the monstrance, should hang loose in order to look really well and should consequently be made of soft material and not lined ; he asks to have them made as he wishes, but the manufacturer insists on a lining, to make them last longer he says. This is not right ; but the priest is right to want veils that will last well—some years at least—and which are up to a certain standard of beauty.

We have indicated certain dangers and errors, and have suggested certain remedies. It is difficult to say what are the best remedies for that great evil, the rampant commercialism of the present day. Something resembling the medieval guilds of craftsman, but on a larger scale, has been suggested ; but these unions were the spontaneous creation of their own period and cannot be reintroduced at will in an age in which social conditions, modes of thought and methods of work are very different, especially in the face of a strongly entrenched commercial system. There is, however, one solution of the difficulty which may be suggested and which seems to be both reasonable and practicable.

Let us begin by supposing a workshop in which there is a division of labour such as is generally found in the workshops which produce the various vestments in use. It is obvious that the people who design the vestments and get them made by the manual workers must be persons of sound good taste. It has been well said, and agrees with some of our previous remarks, that: "the unlucky thing is that everyone imagines that he himself possesses that quality of good taste which, in the realm of the beautiful, occupies the position which belongs to good judgment in the realm of reason—innate faculties both of them,

---

[2] I know two important firms, the one in London and the other in Paris, both of which may have to close down "for Gothic reasons."

but capable of development by practice and study. They require a clear vision, deliberate choice and the power of drawing the particular out of the general. Now who will own to being deficient in good judgment or in good taste ? The conclusion is that the aesthetic part of the work should be allotted to persons with aesthetic gifts and training."[3] If such are not to be found, let the managers be well assured that no pious wishes, no amount of goodwill, or of ingenuity will fill the void. So to begin with there must be some natural talent, and it must be educated ; not only in the masters and mistresses, but in the workpeople under them. How can they take an intelligent interest in art or attain a high standard of taste unless they are educated up to these things ? It is therefore a prime necessity that they should attend classes in decorative art, independent and non-official classes. Private tuition, if competent, may take the place of classes ; but the teaching given by one master, and in his individual style, is not the equivalent of the teaching by several masters in an art school. Supposing that the young person who aims at the noble work of making church vestments has received a year's education in a school of decorative art, and that he or she has been taken on in some workshop. As the work is highly specialised, the learner will get a supplementary education by concentrating on that work, because the master or mistress of the studio, who, we must suppose, has a sound knowledge of his art, will direct the apprentices. This is the method of art teaching that was practised by the great masters of old, and there are artists at the present day who do the same thing. In this vestment studio the master will teach, but will take care that the apprentice should do the work himself ; he will give explanations, but chiefly by way of demonstration and of correction ; truly a disinterested vocation, a lofty task, and a laudable devotion.

There is no insuperable difficulty in re-introducing this system. What is necessary is that those who have commissions to give for designs or works should give them to artists and not to factories or tradespeople. The artists would get clients and so be able to reduce the cost of production ; they would take assistants or promising apprentices to do the more elementary kinds of work—and there you have re-emerging the system of the old masters who produced such wonderful results.

But the clergy also need educating, and for this they should, while in the seminaries, have some lessons both theoretical and practical,

[3] *L'Ouvroir liturgique*, 12th and 19th Dec., 1926, p. 170.

not so much on the different styles as on aesthetics and the liturgical arts, on the theory of the beautiful and on sincerity in art. Church vestments would naturally be dealt with in these lessons. Slides showing vulgar vestments with tawdry ornamentation, and then by way of contrast, simple vestments in perfect good taste, or richer ones with distinct and well arranged designs should be shown ; and a commentary, explaining why the former are to be condemned and the latter admired, would serve to form the good judgment and taste of the students and be an important part of their aesthetic education. The necessary studies in seminaries are very exacting ; but surely an hour might be found once a month throughout the five years for a lecture on art by some competent authority. Candidates for the priesthood would un-doubtedly take a great interest in such lectures, which would help them to see the necessity of everything in a church forming one harmonious whole, and also to realise that this desirable end cannot be attained by haphazard buying of articles manufactured by wholesale methods. They would learn to go to the right firms and the right artists, and there would soon be a supply of such firms and such artists in response to the demand—and so the thing would be done !

So far we have dealt with art strictly so-called in relation to the designing of vestments ; but we take it for granted that the details of the work, which have their own importance, such as the cutting out and sewing of the material, the application of orfreys and of galloons : that these things also require specialists in their line, women that is whose skill and taste have received some training. We must all have had a feeling of repulsion at the sight of certain badly mounted chasubles, copes, banners and so forth, the work of various companies or firms which sell every sort of church ornament : statues, gold and silver work, stained glass windows, iron work and vestments. It is all very well to help the workmen of one's own firm by giving them the work, if they can really do it well and if this family spirit is not pushed to extremes ; but it is sad to know of real artists who live in poverty, suffering and isolation, "like rocks beaten by the waves of stupidity and ignorance." 4

It is not, be it observed, that we wish to protest against any and every form of co-operation, or against the work produced by many hands ; for it is the case that a workshop specially for vestments, if it be independent and well-organised, in fact a small guild in itself, is, generally speaking, capable of producing better work, because the

4 Aug. Cochin : *Les Sociétés de pensées, Correspondant,* Feb. 10th, 1920.

expert knowledge of some and the skilled workmanship of others are more readily concentrated on the work in hand—the making of church vestments. It may be objected that in every separate workshop belonging to a great firm, the same expert knowledge and the same craftsmanship can be applied to the work of that particular workshop, and in theory this is true. But in practice the manager or chairman of a company cannot unite in his own person a thorough knowledge of so many arts, and it will be very difficult for him to select really competent heads for each department, and a spirit of loyalty to his men will lead him to make some appointments that fall short of the best. Take for example the mounting of vestments to which we have just referred. In a special workshop with a high standard of craftsmanship, this work is generally well done; with a company or firm that undertakes many different kinds of work, there is a tendency not to supervise this part of the work as carefully as is necessary.

Fig. 233. Detail of a Badly Mounted
Chasuble
All puckers and creases

I have seen some shocking instances of this carelessness. I should like to stress this point, for this work of mounting is not so simple as one might suppose. First, the cutting out has to be done with the utmost accuracy, and then comes the art in itself of stitching together, by hand or by machine, several layers of stuff—the principal material, the lining, ornamental strips or orfreys, not to mention cords of various kinds, fringes and tassels. If the needlewoman is not sufficiently skilled she will sew on strips, orfreys, etc., in such a way as to form puckers and creases that ruin the whole look of the vestment (fig. 233). No self-respecting tailor would turn out a suit of clothes like that. What the *Practical Guide* says very truly of the sewing on of galloons (p. 43), applies equally to the orfreys and bands of silk or velvet that are often used instead : "A galloon is well applied when it is firmly attached to the vestment, when it does not look at all as though it had been merely stitched on, and lastly when its edge forms an absolutely straight line." Our advice to the reader is that if he has suffered disappointments in this matter, he should turn to those firms and workshops which mount their vestments to perfection. Vestments ought to be mounted properly and we ought to see that this is done.

Allow me in bringing this chapter to an end to describe two very different experiences that have befallen me. I have visited some work-shops whose walls were disagreeably bare, though even in a workshop absolute simplicity, even if somewhat disconcertingly severe, is to be preferred to bad or mediocre pictures, which one feels are only put there to fill up the walls. Art-mistresses, I cannot call them artists, were acting as forewomen and five or six young girls were working hard at their sewing and their ugly little bits of embroidery ; young slaves I thought them, grinding at a sordid task. I was so sad at heart that I could not have uttered a word of praise with any sincerity ; on the contrary, I made so bold as to point out a nonsensical mistake in the process used for tracing patterns. "You are quite right," I was told, "but it is a trick of the trade." I went out saying to myself that I would never have a vestment made there. Their hands toil, but their only aim is to make money ; the Christian spirit is lacking. When one considers how many purely commercial workshops of this kind there are, one understands how it is that one sees "our Mother, Holy Church, horribly attired . . . she who is all beautiful within. All this work only ends in making her grotesque. . . . Artists have put heart and soul into her adornment ; then vanity and commercialism step in, and she is dressed up like a doll and becomes a laughing stock." These are the words of that man of taste and true Christian, Mons. C. Dulac (in a letter of 25th June, 1897).

And I have also seen a model firm where nothing but vestments is made. The superintendent and all the workers, some of them artists, others people of sound good taste, down to the girls in the office and behind the counter, are all at one in a truly Catholic outlook, but one and all free members of a guild, independent each in his own sphere and all sharing in the privilege of a true artistic tradition. The superintendent had been trained for thirty years or more under her father, who was deeply versed in liturgical studies ; it was her duty to look at all the work being done, to make suggestions and issue directions ; then came half-a-dozen men, real artists, working in their own studios ; one of them undertook the designing of ornamentations for vestments ; others were embroiderers ; I noticed one of them, with his little crucifix in front of him, embroidering a head of our Saviour most beautifully; others were making orfreys in good, strong, clear patterns. In another studio were a dozen women and girls, also doing embroidery and apply-ing velvet patterns on to satin. Very good work was done in this women's workshop—but the men did still better ; the superintendent remarked on it herself. "Men have more feeling for decoration and do work that is accurate to the last detail without being finicky," she said. The walls were covered with hundreds of illustrations of first-class works chosen among those of antiquity, the Middle Ages, the Renaissance, and the most modern times. Every day these great models could be seen at leisure, studied and assimilated. Then, and this is important, the best works executed by the firm were on show in another place where they could be studied every day. I have never seen such practical and effective aids to education. And how well the masters and mistresses carried out their function ; to let the beginners actually do the work, to demonstrate, to correct, to teach by setting an example. During the week that I was there, an American bishop, an English priest, some Belgian priests, and a French monk came to give orders. During the last few years hundreds of vestments have been designed and made in this studio, for cardinals, bishops, priests and religious orders. This is the result of really good work, the fruit of Catholic piety and zeal, of a proper study of the liturgy and of the training of intelligence, of eyes and of fingers.

It is to be hoped that studios and apprenticeships of this kind will take the place of the ordinary commercial workshop. And let us be allowed to utter this devout prayer : that such Schools of Sacred Art may meet with the practical support which they so richly deserve. Then, and not till then, will church art be rescued from the decadence into which it has so unhappily fallen.

P

CHAPTER XV

THE USE OF SYMBOLS

THE originals from which decorative designs can be drawn are multifarious ; they include springs of water, rivers and seas, the firmament of heaven with the sun, moon and stars, animals and flowers, the human figure, geometric figures and arabesques. Most artists draw largely from these sources when they undertake symbolic decoration. The practitioners of the latest modern art do indeed not infrequently aim at some intelligible meaning in their designs ; but as they are apt to use extremely abstract ideas, their works have little or nothing in common with that type of religious symbolism which consists in suggesting a relationship between certain abstract ideas and certain familiar objects or scenes. The value of such symbols varies greatly according as they are drawn from the Scriptures, from an accepted tradition, or from subtle affinities discovered by the unaided imagination of the artist. This last kind of symbolism is apt to be frivolous ; Dom Beauduin has rebuked its "misdeeds," and a lady of much discernment in liturgical matters has written as follows on the subject : "The pushing of symbolism to excess has always been a mark of spiritual impoverishment in the Church ; this feature alone is enough to show the student of liturgical subjects that he is dealing with a period of decadence." [1] But perhaps we are actually at one of these periods ? Ingenious and would-be symbolic designs are, in fact, more the fashion than they were in the much abused nineteenth century. The nimble fingers of many a Martha ornament vestments and church linen galore with these symbols ; and priests, though accustomed to a more robust diet, take a pious pleasure in these sweetmeats. From an artistic point of view the result is that this infatuation for symbols and symbolic designs is endangering the true beauty of liturgical vesture.

The primary aim in the designing and making of a vestment should be the production of a thing of beauty, and this can be done without any use of symbols. Simplicity, proportion and clearness of line will produce

[1] *L'Ouvroir liturgique*, 17th and 24th Oct., 1926, p. 152.

an immediate and forcible impression of beauty ; whereas a vestment adorned with symbols presents a twofold difficulty. For first the artist has to produce a thing of beauty, and at the same time endeavour to provoke ideas of a spiritual nature in virtue of a preconceived convention ; and then the layman has to be thinking out what the work he sees is supposed to represent. [2]

The reader must not jump to the conclusion that symbolism should be altogether banished from our vestments ; on the contrary, there are occasions on which the use of symbols may quite rightly be desired ; but even so, those subjects only should be chosen which are susceptible to the most simple expression and the most decorative treatment, and which, by their use in the earliest Christian period and ever since, have been consecrated by tradition, if not officially by the Church.

We will now deal with a few well-known iconographic subjects ; we cannot do so in any detail, but we trust that our remarks, whether laudatory or the reverse, may be of use to persons of independent judgment who do not wish to adhere to unsuitable subjects, and desire that the best subjects, real or imaginary, should be had in honour.

Some living creatures are already used as symbols in Holy Scripture : the lamb, the lion, the dove, the serpent and others ; and similarly, the anchor, the crown, the cloud of incense, tongues of fire, the heavenly bodies and so forth. But the number of these symbols is not in reality very great ; and though their number was slightly increased in the early Christian period, this was only done with great caution ; scope for fancy and ingenuity was chiefly found in the use of the word Ichthys, in the treatment of which both learning and reverence were displayed. The real mania for emblems did not set in till the Middle Ages. The wise course is not to re-open the flood-gates of fantasy ; not to accept all that the writers of the Middle Ages chose to imagine ; not to add to the list of emblems they have bequeathed to us, nor to continue to give purely fantastic explanations of the symbols used. Common-sense should lead us to restrict ourselves to the symbols used in the Scriptures, with the possible addition of a few emblems which express in some striking manner ideas that are worth expressing. There will always be those among the faithful who will have difficulty in understanding

[2] The philosopher and theologian, Jacques Maritain, in his criticism of the symbolistic system of Maurice Denis, says : "Because it makes the beauty of the work consist in its power to storm the affections, this system aims too much at the onlooker. . . The artist must be as objective as the sage, in the sense that he must not think of the onlooker except to give him beauty, as the sage thinks of the listener only in order to give him truth." *Philosophy of Art*, tr. O'Connor, p. 97.

symbols, however restricted their number ; their meaning should be explained from time to time ; an occasional instruction on this subject could be made both interesting and edifying.

The symbol of the Lamb is so plainly used in Holy Scripture that there is no need to dwell upon it there. The paschal lamb, standing upright with its flag, the sign of victory, or again the lamb, standing "as it were slain," a living sacrifice ; these offer very beautiful subjects for artistic treatment. J. Speybrouck, in the *Bulletin paroissial* has drawn a whole-page illustration representing the Lamb of God, in Heaven, surrounded by the four beasts, emblems of the evangelists, and adored by the elders. (Fig. 234.) An interesting eucharistic emblem, which has apparently not found a place on our vestments, is the Lamb on a hillock, standing in front of a shepherd's crook, from which there hangs a jar of milk. There is an ugly design which represents the symbolic lamb lying dead, with its belly facing the onlooker and its legs stretched out in front. The Lamb shown lying limply on a book made its appearance late in the history of religious art, and it has been repeated as vexatiously as the pelican, by cheap and tawdry processes, on copes and the veils of monstrances.

And why should only the Lamb be pictured ? The seer of Patmos has told us that "the Lion of the tribe of Juda . . . hath prevailed." This subject surely lends itself to heraldic and decorative treatment ; show the lion crowned if you will, embroider it in gold on a red ground ; be bold. As the principal figure, this subject may perhaps be an innovation ; but its use as a symbol is amply justified by the Apocalypse.

Very ancient representations are extant of two harts, quenching their thirst at the four rivers of the Earthly Paradise, which are shown springing from a hillock surmounted by the monogram XP (Chi-rho, as on fig. 239), or by the Lamb, and a very fine composition might be designed on these lines, where there is sufficient space. I have seen it attempted on too small a medallion—at two yards off it could not be made out at all. It might, however, do well on an altar frontal.

Many of us are familiar with the figure of the two stags and the seven rivers ; one sees the idea but it is unscriptural, and quite modern. Then again, there are the two stags by a fountain of living waters. Both of these compositions are allowable ; but surely the preference lies with the four rivers of Eden, which have been traditionally recognised as symbols of the four gospels carrying the grace of Christ to the four quarters of the world. The thought is simpler and has the fragrance of the Early Christian era.

Of birds those most commonly depicted are the dove, emblem of the

FIG. 234. THE LAMB, THE EMBLEMS OF THE FOUR EVANGELISTS,
AND THE ELDERS
A fine symbolic composition by J. Speybrouck

Holy Ghost ; the dove bearing the olive-branch ; doves emblematic of the souls of the faithful ; the pelican ; the phoenix ; and the peacock. There are good designs of the dove, showing the back with the wings and the tail feathers outspread, which are very decorative (fig. 235). Where it is the breast of the bird that is shown, the treatment is usually trivial and unsatisfactory ; so too sometimes the effect produced when it is represented in flight (Fig. 242). This difficulty is inherent in the subject ; but an artist can overcome it if he works out his design with thoroughness, neither endeavouring to keep too close to ancient conventions nor to pursue novelty overmuch.

Designs have also been made showing doves drinking from waters springing from the rock which is Christ; but experience has shown, as in the case of the stags, that the subject is too complicated for use on a medallion. At a distance, two little white dots show, which are the doves, the springs of water are scarcely visible, and the rock not at all.[3] As for doves insinuating themselves among the branches of a vine the better to reach the grapes, they nearly always spoil the lines of the composition ; the eucharistic vine is a sufficient symbol without them.

FIG. 235.   MEDALLION WITH DOVE
Unity, clearness and decorative feeling

The "pious pelican" is rather an ugly bird, but its symbolism is well established in Christian tradition, and we must therefore respect it. At the same time we may recognise that the story that it opens its breast to feed its young is pure fable, an invention of the Middle Ages. And when this bird is represented surrounded by its progeny feeding from its torn breast, the whole thing becomes rather complicated and repugnant. The pelican standing with its feet close together like

[3] *L'Ouvroir liturgique*, 21st and 28th Feb., 1926, p. 122.

a soldier on parade, and with its long neck all arched, is just as bad (fig. 237). On the whole it would be better to leave this bird in its native haunts.

FIG. 236.   THE DOVE BY SPEYBROUCK

Truth of line and attitude.   An ideal dove and a beautiful composition

The phoenix has been taken as a type of the risen Christ, or of the resurrection of the dead, because he is supposed to be consumed by fire and to rise alive from his ashes. Another legend, and a very pagan one ; a suitable emblem perhaps over the gateway of a crematorium.

The peacock only deserves attention on account of his feathers with their beautiful metallic colours ; he shows himself off in them as who should say, " Look, what a fine bird am I !" Imagine two big peacocks with tails outspread, one on each side of an altar crucifix, and pity the poor priest who has these emblems of pride before his eyes. [4] I have also seen two peacocks, likewise strutting in full majesty, on a stole ; the effect was lamentable ; there was no proportion between the narrow space that there is—or isn't—at the two ends of a stole and the two "feathered fowls."

[4] L'Ouvroir liturgique, No. 2, p. 9.

I shall no doubt be told that peacocks are to be found in very early sculptures and even among some of the frescoes in the Catacombs. But they are just depicted, as other birds are, for decoration's sake, and there is no ancient or valid tradition attaching any symbolic meaning whatever to them. Nowadays great efforts are made to explain the presence of these showy creatures, and if they are depicted anywhere near a vase surmounted by XP we are told that "the symbolic birds are about to feed and they cast a glance of supplication,

FIG. 237.   A FRONTAL WITH NO SENSE OF SPACING AND PROPORTION
AND NOT IMPROVED BY ITS SYMBOLISM

adoration, and gratitude to the Christ to whom they owe their food." To attribute "supplication, adoration and gratitude" to two birds is a faulty and pietistic interpretation. Their heads are raised in the direction of the monogram and that is all.

Once started on this slippery path, it was difficult to stop and, in fact, proved impossible. To the peacock was assigned the singular honour of representing the risen Christ, because, each year, it "loses its feathers as winter comes on and grows them again in the spring, when nature seems to rise from the grave." But we have reached the climax when we read : "As the tail of the peacock when spread out displays its long feathers full of eyes, it came to symbolise the beatific vision which the faithful will enjoy in heaven."[5] To print such nonsense can only provoke the critical reader to laughter. It is another example of that ingenuity which is on the look-out for explanations that it may

[5] *L'Artisan liturgique*, April-May, 1927, p. 58.

presently promote to the dignity of dogmatic truths. But when all is said, we have nothing but a lamentable diet of pietistic fancifulness.

If, therefore, symbols are to be used, we should wish them to be founded on scriptural use, or at least backed bv some sound reasoning.

Even so not every emblem can be readily transposed to textile fabrics, nor adapted to such limited surfaces as medallions, palls, or the coverings of ciboria. Let us take as examples two of these small veils, illustrated in we will not say what periodical. One of them displays seven solid Roman pillars, in reference to the text, "Wisdom hath built herself a house . . . she hath hewn out seven pillars." But it is not true wisdom that has built a portico on this veil ; it is the hankering after symbolism rather than the love of beauty ; and the result is an architectural design where it is wholly inappropriate. On the other ciborium veil we see the five wise virgins all depicted with identical gestures and attitudes. Female Saints, also in identical attitudes, make a grand decoration on the

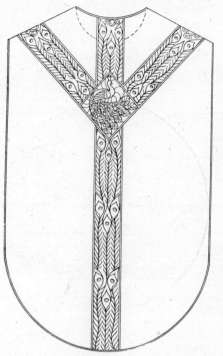

FIG. 238. FALSE SYMBOLISM OF THE PEACOCK
The decoration of the cross bad because finicking

walls of Sant' Apollinare Nuovo at Ravenna; but there the artists, having a large flat surface at their disposal, have treated each Saint in a manner worthy of herself, whereas on the veil of a ciborium there is no space to draw and embroider the figures properly. *Non erat hic locus.*

Here is another example—the brazen serpent lifted up as a symbol of our redemption. A Speybrouck might produce an original pen and ink composition on this subject ; but the needle, silk, and gold thread of an embroideress are another matter. I have seen once, and once only, a medallion in which the serpent was depicted lifted up on a Tau ; the drawing was poor and the colouring tasteless.

Bad results can also be produced with the fish, but it can also be artistically treated.   The subject seems to lend itself more readily than many others to satisfactory lines, colours and proportions, whether as a monogram or in conjunction with the basket of loaves, as witness the illustration which we owe to the *Société liturgique de Nîmes*.   (Fig. 239).[6] Nor must we forget the sacred Fish on the trident, and the design of two fishes on either side of the anchor of salvation.   (Fig. 240).[7] Why not try a frieze of dark waves and fishes worked in silver thread or in grey lightened with white, all centring in the Ichthys ?   But that only, as we have said before, if there is space enough, and if the vestment or part of the vestment adapts itself to such treatment.   Another example of a ciborium veil will illustrate the danger to which we allude.   On this one little veil there are worked a river, several little fishes, one big fish (the sacred Ichthys), the basket of loaves, and finally a text that no one can decipher. Does not this show that symbolism pushed to excess is a delusion and a snare, and produces trivialities, not to say caricatures ?   It should be observed how these little things kill the big things; in the case before us the real beauty of a ciborium veil that is quite plain and falls in graceful folds.

FIG. 239. THE ICHTHYS
A good design. (Liturgical Society of Nîmes)

So much has been written about flowers that on this occasion we shall limit ourselves to citing an extreme example, and we invite the reader to peruse the following list.   " . . . the crocus symbolises joy ; the snowdrop, confidence ; the hyacinth, power, peace ; the tulip, prayer ; the dahlia, splendour ; the anemone, carefulness ; . . . the myrtle, the state of virginity ; the honey-suckle or the rose of Jericho, the Blessed

[6] Inspiration might well be sought from an excellent drawing by Speybrouck of the Fish and the Basket. Treated more simply and quietly—it is too full of action to be suitable for textiles—it would make a good composition.

[7] I have tried to give a brief account of the iconography of the Ichthys and of the fishes, which symbolise the faithful, in the *Month*, May, 1921, pp. 414-421, with six illustrations.

Virgin Mary ; hawthorn, hope ; the balsamine, hastiness ; the buttercup, celibacy ; . . . the hortensia, instability ; the jessamine, friendship ; . . ."[8]   "Enough," the reader will cry, and we hasten to obey— there is no need to go over the same ground again. We will limit ourselves to one short story about lilies and roses ; it tells of a great artist working on a beautiful vestment. His name was Armand Caillat. He was once asked to set to work and design a red velvet chasuble. The best goldsmith in France, in the nineteenth century, was given one of those orders which are a joy to lovers of the beautiful.   " Put lilies and roses where you like; arrange them as you please ; that is all; go ahead." He, who had been accustomed to filigree

FIG. 240.   TWO FISHES AND THE ANCHOR OF SALVATION

Simple and clear arrangement

work, to delicate enamels, to working in the precious metals, left minute work behind him. "The large surface of a chasuble of mag-

FIG. 241.   A FRIEZE WHICH IF SIMPLIFIED WOULD MAKE A GOOD ORFREY

nificent velvet calls for a design on a large scale ; I will make lavish use of unconventionalised lilies and of well-characterised roses ; I will place them alternately, connecting them with very formal arcs of

8 *Church Symbolism*, by M. C. Nieuwbarn O.P., tr. by J. Waterbury, London, 1910, pp. 142 and 143. The author accepts and teaches true and false symbolism without discerning between them. All manner of symbols are also allowed by X. B. de Montaut : *Traité d'iconographie chrétienne*, 2 vols., Paris, 1890.

gold." The effect was superb ; I shall never forget it ; but more was
due to the genius of the artist than to the symbolism of the flowers.

Real flowers are things of beauty ; but their beauty which, in a state
of nature, is fully realised, ought in a work of art to be in some way
heightened. If they are drawn and embroidered *au naturel* they are
only copies and do not come up to the originals. In other words, they
must be transmuted and glorified, first in the mind of the designer, and
then by careful delineation, faultless proportions, clear spacing, and
finally by the embroiderer's art, in such a way as to reveal their beauty

FIG. 242.   A FLOWERED FRONTAL—PUERILE WORK

more clearly than nature does. How far from this ideal are the miserable
lilies, the flowerets and the pitiful foliage of figure 242. It is, on the other
hand, well illustrated in the lilies shown in figure 243 ; they are drawn
in a way that is true to nature and at the same time give an impression
of serenity, simplicity and power which enhance their natural beauty.

We come next to emblems derived from fire, clouds, rays of light and
stars. Tongues of fire did indeed figure forth the consuming fire of the
Holy Ghost, and clouds may rightly symbolise heaven ; but both the
one and the other as drawn on recent chasubles, are most uninteresting
innovations (figs. 244 and 245). There is none of that feeling for the
decorative in this kind of work, which is so manifest in the civil and

ecclesiastical costumes that one admires in public and private collections. At the Musée de Cluny, in Paris, there has been preserved a vestment which is covered with very beautiful flames, so widely dilated that one would think they were alive, and so skilfully idealised that they seem to have a character of their very own. The little tongues that one sees on some modern chasubles are commonplace and vulgar compared to these flames, which if used with discretion, could even in these days be employed with good effect on church vestments. As for the clouds shown in one of the illustrations of chasubles, a priest, who had been examining the photograph attentively, said to me: "But what are these? are they misshapen eggs?" And yet it should not be difficult to attain a degree of humility at which one would be willing to seek inspiration from the conventionalised clouds which figure in certain quasimedieval fabrics. It is a sign not of weakness but of courage, sometimes to swim against the stream instead of letting oneself drift idly with it.

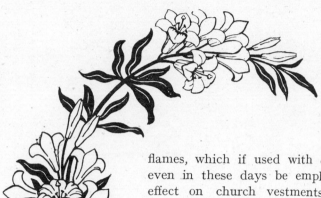

FIG. 243. A SPRAY OF LILIES, NATURAL, AND YET IDEALISED

The artist has brought out the essential character of this beautiful plant

As we are speaking of the firmament, it may occur to the reader to inquire why some specially brilliant star is not singled out to represent Our Lady, Star of the Sea. It would look very well for instance on a chasuble, at the intersection of the arms of the cross and the upright. If you are not afraid of adding some rock crystals[9] to this star it will shine all the more brilliantly to the glory of Mary, our Morning Star (fig. 247). For heaven's sake pray give up those five-

[9] The next chapter deals with imitation precious stones, which often serve very well for the decoration of some details in a vestment.

pointed stars whose profusion often nauseates us ; take the trouble to

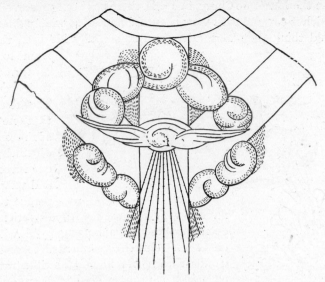

FIG. 244.   THE UPPER PART OF A CHASUBLE
Dove, rays, clouds : too many things

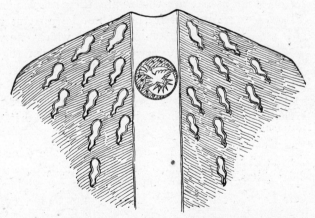

FIG. 245.   ANOTHER CHASUBLE
The column too wide, the dove too small, the tongues of
fire grotesque.   An example of the evil wrought by symbolism

give them more and better defined points.   If discreetly spaced, they
might form a worthy accompaniment to the principal star.[10]

[10] This scheme of decoration would remind one of an arcosolium in the cemetery
of St. Callixtus (de Rossi, *Roma Sotteranea*, Vol. III, plate xxxv.).

Rays should also be treated as artistic elements. They are so accommodating that they get put anywhere and anyhow, especially in conjunction with rows of little metal discs, shameful gauds which, happily, any self-respecting workshop would be ashamed of nowadays. On the contrary, it requires no small amount of skill and labour to work out a design in rays thoroughly well from start to finish. Each separate ray must be accurately drawn, the length and width must be measured, by eye at least; they must all

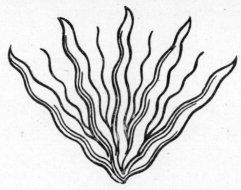

FIG. 246. A FINELY SPREADING FLAME WHICH IF SENSIBLY USED WOULD MAKE A GOOD DECORATION

be drawn alike and arrayed symmetrically, or the shapes and grouping must be varied so as to produce the effect of a sharp edge standing out upon a clear background. Too often these details are so muddled and confused as to become meaningless. On the other hand, the colours and outlines of a good design are sufficiently clear without any representation of the light given by the rays, though such may indeed be required by the space to be covered, and is capable of effective treatment in the

FIG. 247. A RICH STAR THAT MIGHT SYMBOLISE MARY
Stella maris and *Stella matutina*

hands of really skilled designers and embroiderers. It is disastrous to make use of such things just to fill up a space or to introduce symbolism. The *Ouvroir*, in the article to which reference has already been made, gives eight drawings of palls, all equally commonplace : one shows "a sun, emblem of the risen Redeemer" ; another "the sealed tomb and the Paschal Sun (Christ) rising" ; and a third, an ugly fat cross with once more, "the rising sun, emblem of paschal joys." Surely there are more suns than enough in spite of the explanatory notes which attempt to screen the author's puerile designs under a cloud of symbolism.

Too often one sees hosts and hideous chalices on common lace, as

FIG. 248.   RAYS

Detail of a well worked out glory by J. Speybrouck

well as on veils, chasubles and copes ; this is derogatory to the holy host and to the most sacred of vessels. As both are present on the altar of sacrifice it would show a proper respect not to depict them. The designers and embroiderers should confine themselves to the true eucharistic symbols—the vine and the ears of corn.

We shrink from dealing with the most awful of all mysteries, and symbols representing the Holy Trinity have therefore been left to the end of this chapter. After having made a rapid survey of designs emblematic of the Word and of the Holy Ghost, it must be owned that it is more difficult to find any emblem that will express both the unity and the trinity of the three divine Persons. None of the symbols in ordinary use can claim any great antiquity ; as however they are in use, we may point out that a triangle inscribed with the ineffable name, or with a great ugly eye, is not a satisfactory design. Besides, if the Church made the creative Trinity the patron of the ancient builders, yet the freemasons have adopted the triangle as the badge of their secret society, and that is a reason for not using the triangle on vestments. In Ireland the three-leaved shamrock is looked on as a symbol of the blessed Trinity. There is, however, a design which from the point of view of drawing, composition and meaning, is superior to any other ; it consists of three complete circles or rings, interlaced ; they are un-mistakably three and at the same time one in a symbolic figure complete in itself (fig. 249). There seems to be no better way by which to symbolise the unity and trinity of the incomprehensible Deity. The three circles are all that is required ; on a dark background, they stand out well ; and any addition of the names of the divine Persons (e.g., *Pater*), or of their initials P.F.S., or of the name of God in Hebrew, or of trefoils or scrolls, is unnecessary com-plication.[11]   The mystery of the Trinity is so great that it requires to be treated with the utmost simplicity, if only to recall the perfect simplicity of the divine nature.   I have seen a full chasuble made for a cardinal which has no decoration except the three circles placed near the top of the cross.   They are in gold on a velvet ground and can be discerned clearly from some distance.

FIG. 249.   THREE INTERLACED CIRCLES
An excellent emblem of the Holy Trinity

The large area of an altar frontal would allow of the three circles being joined lengthwise. *L'Histoire du Canon de la Messe*, by Dom G. Lefevre, has an excellent design by J. Speybrouck (p. 6), in this form. The middle circle has the XP on a cross ; one of the lateral circles has a hand raised in blessing, *dextera Dei*, and the other has the dove. By suppressing the clouds and limiting the number of rays, a very beautiful frontal might be made.

Although much that is fascinating has been written about symbolism, it is as well to repeat our admonitions.   Be on your guard ; attach more importance to the general lines of a vestment and its constituent parts than to far-fetched conceits, which may catch the eye of a few of your friends, but which are too apt to deprive chasubles, copes and

11 See for example the four medallions shown in *L'Artisan Liturgique* (April-May, 1927); these designs cannot be recommended.

Q

church linen of the virile character they should possess. At the same time we admit that well-chosen symbols, sparely used, symbols which are correct in themselves and put in their right place, which are simplified and rid of all complication—these will be appreciated as are other precious and stately ornaments.

The designing of vestments, their ornamentation and especially the symbols used in their decoration, should be the work of persons of talent. But talent is not always to be found, and then we must look to those who have love ; by which we mean a genuine love of the things of the Church. But let us insist on this: there should also be a foundation of sound knowledge. It is possible to possess undoubted talent, to design symbolic ornamentation of a touching beauty or of unusual depth of thought, and yet lack that width of imagination and sense of proportion which we have noted in the chasuble designed by A. Calliat.

Let us lift up our hearts and be more hopeful and more confident. Creative talent inspired by piety and affection will not fall a prey to subtleties, quaintnesses, over-elaboration and love of novelty ; it will produce an art that is strong, simple and stately. And then we shall see true works of art and an art that is truly religious. What matter if they excite less remark from the members of some society or other, or from those who visit exhibitions ? There will always be souls *pulchritudinis studium habentes*, who will value them justly. At least the artist will have the satisfaction, before God and man, of having worked for the beauty of the things that pertain to Catholic worship.

CHAPTER XVI

ORNAMENT IN GENERAL

WE now enunciate for the last time a principle which in a slightly different form has been expounded in several chapters, namely that sincerity and strength in liturgical art can only be attained by constantly bearing in mind the qualities which are essential to good vestments and good vesture. If they are wholly adequate to the use to which they are to be put, if, that is to say, they are of the right shape, the right dimensions, and the right texture, then they fulfil their purpose ; and an extreme simplicity is no defect in them, but rather an added beauty, or even an essential part of their beauty.

Nevertheless there is no need to push one's puritanism to extremes, or to assert that each and every vestment should be wholly unornamented. It is all a question of degrees and it is possible to have an ornamentation which is well designed and well executed, which emphasises the main lines of the vestment and is not out of keeping with its purpose. These qualities are the justification of any ornament and the lack of them condemns it.

As altar-linen has been dealt with in Chapter II, we shall treat here more particularly of the ornamentation of silk vestments and accessories. By ornamentation we mean the art of arranging the various elements or ornaments, and hence the words proportion, design, structure, and composition are frequently, and often interchangeably, used in this book. "Ornamentation" is used both of the process of combining these elements and of the completed result. [1]

Every design consists of lines, straight or curved, or of the two combined. Let us take first the case of straight, parallel lines, such as usually determine the orfreys of our vestments and more especially the crosses of our chasubles. The distance between these lines determines the width of the orfrey and is a matter of some importance; one sees offered for sale designs in which the orfrey takes up as much as a third of a narrow chasuble and produces a cross of disproportionate size, or else orfreys

---

[1] F. S. Meyer, *A Handbook of Ornament*, Introduction, vii-viii.

of moderate width such as those which go to make the cross on the beautiful vestment shown in figure 75, or again orfreys of the most meagre proportions. Take another look at the chasuble shown in figure 84 and you will note how the well-designed width of the orfrey contributes

FIG. 250.   AN OLIVE ORFREY   FIG. 251.   ANOTHER OLIVE ORFREY
        A poor design   Much better than the last

to the balance and harmony of the whole. This orfrey is woven of threads of divers material, but we have previously shown that a plain silk ribbon or a strip of cloth of gold lace, of velvet, or of plush, if well cut and neatly stitched, is quite suitable for a chasuble. The beauty of the chasuble will depend very largely on the due width of the strips of material which are used for the orfreys, and hence the importance of the lines which bound the cross and mark it off from the rest of the chasuble, which we will assume to be also designed on good lines. The most important point is simplicity and clarity of design ; next in importance come the correct dimensions and relative proportions of the parts and the way they are put together. It is these things which give a vestment its proper character, what Clive Bell calls its "significant form" ; thus the beautiful lines of the chasuble and its cross will help to bring out the inner meaning of the vestment.

And what is the good, generally speaking, of aiming at anything more than this ? Further elaboration may at the outset delight certain zealous souls, but generally ends in disillusion for themselves and for the priest for whom the vestment is being made. Here is an example which is not just a flight of fancy. A priest, who in this is only representing the desires of many of his colleagues, asks for help in making artistic vestments and for suggestions for ornaments that are not too difficult for his altar society. By return of post, he receives a pattern for an orfrey, which stands condemned by its forced symbolism and poverty of design (fig. 250). The spear-shaped leaves, which bear no resemblance to olive leaves and which are supposed to be embroidered on a blue ground, produce a graceful effect, but it is so graceful as to be weak and feeble. Besides, this design requires a degree of skill and accuracy in the making to which many women do not attain. "Well then, buy the orfrey ready made." No, because it lacks the essential quality of visibility ; and besides the idea is to find work for the sewing-party. What then ? Use a woven orfrey or a strip of velvet which will look much better and cost one-third the price. Or, if more work is required, choose some geometric pattern, good in itself and properly spaced on the strip of material—you will find some examples given further on (figs. 262, 263, 315) ; or else attempt an olive design remodelled as shown in fig. 251. The leaves and fruit should be embroidered in a pale greyish green, which is their natural colour, and will show up well on a dark red ground.

GALLOONS of small, or rather small width, are very much used as bordering. Many of these galloons are made of silk, others of gilt or silvered metal, others again of cloth of gold.

This bordering also will have its width determined by the width of the vestment. It exists in many varieties and it would not be a bad thing to start by throwing a great number of the old patterns on the rubbish heap. And we should welcome new ones, if they are well worked out. Some modern patterns seem to be determined to copy the cubists.

See the squares and rhomboids of figs. 252, 253 and 254. We have
already mentioned these patterns, but will take this opportunity to

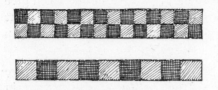

FIGS. 252, 253, 254.   GALLOONS IN THE
MODERN STYLE
Hard and fatiguing to the eye

reaffirm our opinion that the
juxtaposition of these small
figures involves too many broken
lines, sharp angles, and math-
ematically equal spaces, and that
the multiplication of them is as
wearying to the eyes as the
squares of a chess-board.
These patterns show a great
poverty of invention, and others
that are more restful to the eye
should be chosen. If we must
have squares and rhomboids, let
them be better spaced. Patterns

in which curved and angular forms are combined produce a less
stiff effect (figs. 255 and 256). Other
patterns consist of leaves or flowers,
either drawn from nature or conventionalised, woven in a light
colour on a dark ground or vice
versa (fig. 257). Patterns of the
same colour as the background but
woven differently so as to stand
out bright on a dull ground have a
softer and more pleasing aspect; done

FIGS. 255, 256.   BETTER SPECIMENS OF
A LESS ARID STYLE

in yellow they can well be used
instead of gold braid. Less
marked patterns, for instance
simple net-work or parallel
lines which scarcely show at
a distance, are suitable for
narrow galloons, which are
used merely as an edging and
produce the desired effect
more by their colour than by
their pattern.

FIG. 257.   GALLOON WITH A YELLOW MOTIVE
ON A VIVID RED GROUND

FIG. 258. GALLOON IN GOLD, RED AND WHITE

The use of galloons varies
according to their width and the inventiveness of the designer. A
good orfrey can be made with an unedged strip of material on to

which parallel galloons are carefully stitched (fig. 259), and other arrangements can be easily devised.   The same idea is used in fig. 262, but there strips of material are used instead of galloons. In the figure shown, the red square and the four black strips that surround it, leaving a small space between, serve to break the monotony of the straight strips. The three parallel strips are of a thin red material, carefully cut and applied on the white damask of a cope. It is not a heavy ornamentation and is more interesting than orfreys with patterns of arabesques or foliage.

Very wide woven galloons are sometimes used instead of orfreys. If they are woven in elaborate patterns and in three or four colours besides that of the background, all this elaboration detracts from the proper character of the vestment. The chasuble shown in fig. 84 has a cross made of a galloon woven in two colours only, and the effect is excellent.

In general it may be said that much more originality is shown in the treatment of the simplest patterns if these are carefully thought out and made on purpose for a parti-

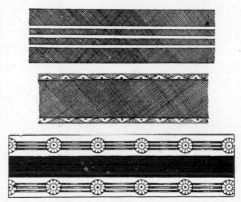

FIGS. 259, 260, 261. VARIOUS WAYS OF USING
GALLOONS

cular vestment, than by the use of galloons woven in hundreds of yards. These are the product of the machine, while the former are the fruit of individual thought and care which give them a charm or even a forcefulness which cannot be got by weaving. Fig. 263 is an example of this : squares of red velvet are quite plainly edged by narrow galloons and well spaced on the white and yellow silk of which the cope is made ; these rows of squares are related to the hood, which has a jewelled cross edged with the same narrow galloons; the effect of the whole is shown in fig. 147. The idea of this orfrey may seem to be a little crude, but its merit is that the effect, being produced by very simple means, is much more striking than the finicking devices in silk and gold, whose wearisome reiteration is familiar to all of us.

CORDING AND BRAID are often employed, as for instance as an edging to applied bands ; but in this case they have a prominence

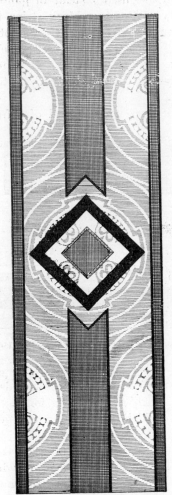

FIG. 262. BRICK-RED AND BLACK MATERIAL APPLIED ON THE WHITE DAMASK GROUND OF A COPE

FIG. 263.   AN INEXPENSIVE AND VERY DECORATIVE ORFREY Squares of red velvet framed in a gold galloon

which the "spirit" of the materials could well dispense with, and they are stiffer than galloons of pure silk. If these latter are in one colour only, they produce a far neater effect, which is a result of that uniformity of colour and of their flat surface. Let us suppose a red cording used to edge a green velvet laid on a green damask. The result will perhaps be satisfying if you look at the vestment from close to, in the shop or sacristy ; but it will be nil, if you look at it in church, at a distance of ten yards or so. On the other hand the outline of the cross will probably be very clear, if it has been edged with a galloon instead of the cording, and though the galloon is of the same colour and width as the cording. However, the use of cording for marking the edges of a pall, chalice veil, stole, etc., is quite a different matter, and these trimmings may then produce a satisfactory effect. And they have the great advantage that they help to secure the outlines of these accessories.

FINGES are frequently used for vestments ; they are used to edge the hoods of copes, stoles and maniples, and have a more elegant and finished effect than plain hems or an edging of galloon ; moreover, in all the three cases mentioned they emphasize the vertical line of the vestment. Silk fringes are soft and graceful ; the effect they are meant to give is enhanced if they

FIG. 264.   A GOOD MANIPLE ENDING IN
TASSELS

Gold braid and blue satin appliqué work. A bad maniple ending abruptly with a square of damask

are not narrow, like edgings of galloon.   These latter may quite well be narrow, but fringes are different and the effect is skimpy if they are so narrow as to look merely like a second edging tacked on to the first. The best firms display very beautiful fringes and also very artistic tassels ; it is true that these latter are more expensive, but they look very well on stoles and maniples.

  Sometimes a hood is made with no fringe but a tassel instead. The two styles can be seen and compared in figs. 301 and 302. Tassels are

also sometimes attached to the top of dalmatics and tunics. Tassels
at the two ends of the cord which unites the two sides of the pastoral
stole are also in common use. Again fringes have been used all along
the lower edge of copes, tunics and dalmatics, and occasionally even
all the way round some chasubles. We consider that these additions
may rightly be objected to.

PEARLS AND GEMS, real or imitation, were much used on vestments

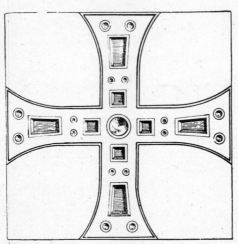

FIG. 265.   A GOOD ARRANGEMENT OF GEMS
          OR WELL-SHAPED GLASS

in the Middle Ages, some-
times with discernment and
good taste, and sometimes
with an unjustifiable prodi-
gality which has been
imitated, especially during
the Gothic revival, with
coloured glass. At the present time a reaction has set
in, and these ornaments are
banned altogether. But this
also is a mistake. Little
bits of blue, red, yellow and
purple glass all mixed together in a small space may
look very ugly and inhar-
monious ; but if these small
ornaments are used with
discretion they will produce effects which are not lacking in charm.
A mitre attractively ornamented with pearls has been shown in figure
216 ; a stronger effect is noticeable in the cope shown in fig. 147. Fig.
265 shows a substantial cross which has been drawn not with any
particular use in view, but simply as a study in the arrangement of
gems of different colours. If in making a cross of this pattern the
larger gems were all of one colour and the smaller round ones were
made of rock crystal there would be no risk of producing an inharmonious
effect.

The champions of sincerity in art will perhaps exclaim : "Genuine
precious stones, perhaps ; but imitation ones, never ! We stand for
truth in all things." That is certainly an excellent general rule to
go upon and it is a cause for which we have often pleaded ourselves.
Let it be admitted at once that imitation gems should never be so used

as to make people believe that they are real ; any more than the Greeks on the outsides of their temples painted white marble with green or red in order to counterfeit coloured marbles ; or were trying to deceive when they gilded the white marble of the acroteria and shields which adorned the fronts of these temples.

They called to their aid these paints and this gilding with the one idea of adding a decorative touch and a heightened splendour to buildings which would otherwise have been too uniformly white. We need not hesitate to follow masters such as these nor to be guided by their principles. If we use little bits of glass or some of the wonderful imitation pearls now made, let us do so because they add a certain charm and grace to the vestment. This effect is produced in the chasuble shown in figure 266 in which the M and the ring round it are prettily adorned with rock crystals ; as also the pendants. I have seen a similar chasuble in which the crystals were replaced by some thick white stitching, and the effect was very poor com-

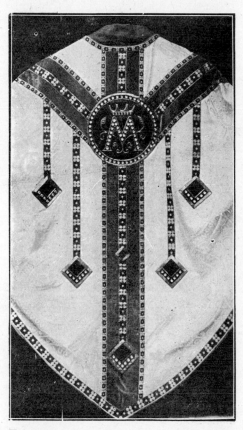

FIG. 266. CHASUBLE REPRODUCED AGAIN
To show the very decorative effect of the
rock crystal ornament. See fig. 87

pared to the other. The centre and the extremities of a cross are the points at which small gems would naturally be affixed. The use of gems in any particular place can neither be prescribed nor condemned ; it is all a matter of taste.

MEDALLIONS are never necessary ; and yet the tyranny of convention and the domination of the manufacturers make them, to judge from the catalogues, an integral part of the cope and of the centre of the cross on the chasuble. No explanation is needed to demonstrate what an error this is, quite apart from the fact that many of these medallions are thoroughly bad in drawing and in technique. If you are looking for variety in design, more especially in monograms, you will find you have no choice ; for ninety-nine per cent. of these commercial vestments have ready-made medallions applied in a way with which we are only too familiar (fig. 267). We must not let our choice and taste be confined by these barbed-wire entanglements, but be well assured that conscientious work can produce something better than copy-book medallions. Let us prefer work that is individual and original, which if it is the fruit of a well educated taste will always have some touch of spiritual beauty, and can also be designed and thought out specially for the place where it is to be used.

FIG. 267. A VULGARITY OF TOO COMMON
A TYPE
Bad style, bad design

Medallions with figures, emblems, or monograms are sometimes—we do not say always—suitable for the hood, which, being an outstanding part of the cope, is well adapted to frame some such subject. The same is true of the point where orfreys join the vertical strip of a chasuble (fig. 268). Objection has been made to the use of this ornamentation because it was unknown to the Middle Ages. This is not reasonable ; we are not living in the Europe of the thirteenth century but in the Europe of to-day. It has been well said in *L'Ouvroir*: "Our ancestors covered their orfreys with pictures and figures ; we can no longer afford such expensive embroideries ; let us then have at least one striking ornamental point, in keeping with the rest of the vestment. If an orfrey embroidered throughout cannot be afforded, let a plain woven silk galloon be used and then a really fine centre-piece will be within reach of our means."

Few shapes are really suitable for medallions ; the circle and the square are the best, the former being perfect in outline and the latter a funda-

FIG. 268. CHASUBLE WITH A BEAUTIFUL MEDALLION
Watts, London

mental figure. Then come the ellipse which is weaker than the circle,

FIG. 269.   A FEEBLE AND VERY
AFFECTED MONOGRAM

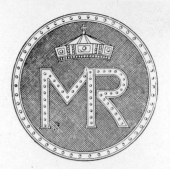

FIG. 270.   AN ORIGINAL AND
VERY DECORATIVE DESIGN

FIG. 271. A WELL-KNOWN MONO-
GRAM
Here clear and strong

FIG. 272.   INTERLACED LETTERS
To be in gold on a dark field

FIG. 273.   A MONOGRAM WHICH
IS A RELIEF AFTER THE USUAL
VULGARITIES

FIG. 274.   MEDALLION SUITABLE
FOR BLACK VESTMENTS

and the figure formed of two arcs meeting along their chords. A square
medallion set square or on one of its angles has been used with success

at the point of junction of the arms of the cross with the vertical strip
(fig. 235). The triangle is not often used ; the space enclosed by it is
usually too small, the three acute angles are not attractive, and viewed
as a symbol it is inadequate.

Finally it may be said in
general that more complicated
geometrical figures, especially
irregular ones, are not satisfactory; this has been proved
by experience and is shown
in figures 276 and 277.

What subjects are suitable
for medallions meant to be
placed on vestments ? Only
a foolish and irresponsible
spirit will answer: "Anything
you like ; anything that will
fit into the required shape."
It is scarcely necessary to
refute this idea. It is obvious
that if these medallions, which

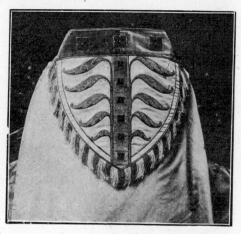

FIG. 275.　HOOD OF A COPE AT AMPLEFORTH
ABBEY
Ornament in gold, old-rose velvet, and black

one can compare to frames, occupy an important position, they should
be used to frame subjects of some importance, for instance, a head of
Christ, or a bust of the Virgin, either alone or preferably with the holy

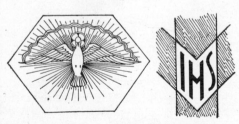

FIGS. 276, 277.　MEDALLIONS OF IRREGULAR
AND UNPLEASING FORMS

Child. We have seen an
illustration of a square
medallion containing a
peacock on the cross of a
chasuble (fig. 238) ; if makers
of vestments take this as a
model they will be led astray,
for this symbol of vanity, as
shown in the illustration, is
extraordinarily complicated
with innumerable feathers
spreading out over the greater part of the square ; this design
is so confused that the subject could not be made out at all from
a little way off. Designs consisting of words embroidered or applied
are similarly out of place on a medallion ; for instance, EGO SUM
RESURRECTIO ET VITA (*l'Artisan liturgique*, 1ᵉ année No. 9). Instead

of an outstanding subject we have here twenty-three letters, that is
to say twenty-three separate and insignificant designs enclosed in a
square which is treated in the style of a memorial tablet.

To be at all tolerable, medallions should therefore have suitable
subjects ; but let it be remembered always that there is no need to

FIG. 278.   COPE OF WESTMINSTER CATHEDRAL
Observe the hood and the unusual position of the monogram. A vestment
of a very artistic Byzantine character

have medallions at all.   Readers who have turned over the pages of
this book will have noticed many illustrations of vestments without
any, and will perhaps have exclaimed with relief : "Here at last are
chasubles and copes without medallions." It must, however, be admitted
that cases occur in which it is difficult to design an ornament for the
point of junction of the arms and upright of the cross on a chasuble
without using a medallion.   One example is enough to illustrate this
point (fig. 279).   The whole effect of this triple branch enclosed in the
orfreys is very stiff.   It is true that the roses, which are conventionalised
on modern lines and seem to have been modelled in square moulds,

add to the stiffness of the design, and we do not lay the whole blame on the absence of a medallion. We are convinced, however, that a single rose on a single stalk, which is all that is needed to give the idea, would be more graceful and more effective, especially if placed within the frame provided by a medallion ; but it must be prettily designed (fig. 280).

Fig. 279. A very Stiff Design with a very Formal Rose Branch

Fig. 280. Shows a Rose very much at its Ease on a Medallion
It might be worked in very pale colours on a dark ground

This criticism is not meant to be taken for a rule ; the white chasuble made at Nîmes has on the back a Madonna not enclosed in any frame, but well fitted to occupy the space where the orfreys meet (fig. 281). And the flame of the chasuble in figure 282 would be spoilt if we confined it in a medallion.

Inscriptions and Monograms.—Since the letters of the alphabet are often used either to compose monograms or to make up a word or two in order to give, for instance, the name of a saint, or again in short inscriptions on the long horizontal band of an altar frontal, it may be well to comment on their good and bad points. We are bored to death with the continual multiplication of Gothic letters with their stiff and broken lines (fig. 267), and no less with interlaced letters in free-hand drawing such as are used in the marking of pocket handker-chiefs (fig. 269). These two seem to be the beginning and end of the

R

designer's knowledge of epigraphy and calligraphy. It is really about time
to put a little more thought into it and so honour the Name which is
above every name and also the holy Name of Mary.   Let original

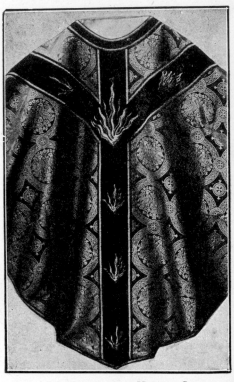

FIG. 281. VIRGIN AND CHILD
not ENCLOSED IN A MEDALLION
And to be used thus on the cross
of a chasuble. (*Atelier des Filles
de l'Église, Nîmes*)

FIG. 282. RICH AND NOBLE CHASUBLE
BELONGING TO CARDINAL BOURNE
Red and yellow lampas ; gold flames on a
velvet cross. See fig. 86

drawings be made ; let the monograms be varied ; let lettering earlier
than that of the Gothic period and also lettering in the most modern
styles be studied and put under contribution (figs. 287-291). There is
an element of intentional ugliness or intentional drollery in some
modern lettering ; but when this has been eliminated we shall still
find plenty of examples of script that is clear, well-shaped, elegant or
forceful, and which anyone can decipher.

THE COMPOSITION or arrangement of the decorative elements in vestments and other ecclesiastical vesture has been treated of at large in this book ; we will now add a few supplementary remarks on the same subject. As before, we give brief criticisms of works of very diverse character, in order to bring out what is faulty in the one or good in the other. It would be easy to comment on a large number of excellent works and on a still larger number of bad ones, for the latter superabound ; but it will be more useful and more practical to draw the lesson intended from a limited number of examples.

FIGS. 283, 284. ALPHA AND OMEGA WELL DRAWN AND OUTLINED WITH-GOLD THREAD

FIGS. 285, 286. THE SAME, LOOKING AS THOUGH THEY HAD BEEN MADE BY A CARPENTER

The principles discovered and the criticisms made, both favourable and unfavourable, can then be applied to other works. But it will perhaps be well, before we begin our review of the works in question, to lay emphasis on a point which will help us to form correct judgments.

In the Introduction to that great publication (still in progress), the *Trésor d'Art Chrétien*, M. Paul Jamot, writes as follows : "Christian art is best inspired by an art that is fully mature, or at least by an art with classical tendencies." The "new art," to which we have had occasion to refer, is not yet mature and stands in need of those "classical ten-

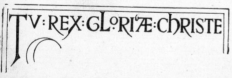

FIGS. 287 to 291. FIVE DIFFERENT TYPES OF LETTERING

dencies" spoken of by the above-mentioned excellent writer. Let us
emphasize this point and demand "a return to classical standards," as
against the impressionism whose votaries, including those of them who

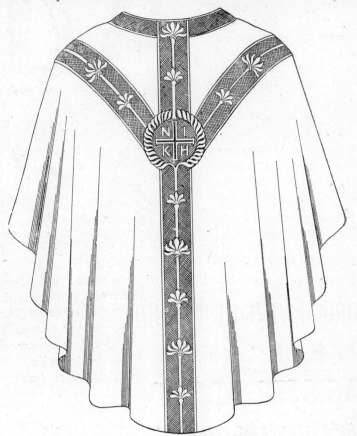

FIG. 292.   A NOBLE CHASUBLE
With a graceful, strong and well ordered decoration

design vestments, persist in looking upon a work of art as a "bit of
nature seen through a temperament," and also against the post-
impressionism, the cubism, and the suprematism which reduce persons
and things to formulae in order to justify wild extravagances of line
and colour. "Classic" art is in the opposite camp to these schools and
its characteristics have been discussed in Chapter VII ; it is the strong
and salutary principle to which we owe it that the best of contemporary
art is already producing some work that is very nearly perfect. Look

for a moment at the chasuble shown in figure 292, and observe how the
scheme of ornamentation rejects all that is superfluous, how delicate and
how well-spaced the formal flowers of the pattern are, and how the spirit
which informs the whole thing is one of sobriety, lucidity and modesty,
qualities which are essential to
a work of art. Everything about
it is harmonious, is subject to
the golden rule of intelligibility,
is, indeed, in the "classical"
spirit. The reader has seen
other works inspired by the same
spirit, and we draw his attention also to the black chasuble
of figure 293. It will give particular satisfaction as a welcome
relief from all that raised embroidery and those broad
metallic galloons of which we
have so much. The chief credit
belongs to the artist who
designed it, but we must con-
gratulate also the nuns who
made it, for their excellent
rendering of the lotus flowers
and the phœnix. All is clear,
well-arranged and very decorative.

FIG. 293. A BEAUTIFUL BLACK CHASUBLE
Made by the Benedictines of Argentan

The majority of decorative
artists, having left the beaten
tracks and being eager to improve
the art of liturgical vesture, have
worked for some twenty years now at their task, but not in this spirit.
Their own spirit is rather hard to define, for their work is rather
complex, and yet we may perhaps distinguish certain main characteristics. But let us observe before we start that liturgical art is not cut
off from all other decorative art, and that there must be much in
common between the respective styles of decoration. However, the
various modern decorative arts have their varying expression, and so
we should expect a special mode of expression in the decoration of
liturgical vesture.

A certain number of vestments are directly influenced by the angular school of art. We have spoken of them in Chapter VII and will only

FIG. 294.   DECORATION OF A GREAT PAENULA
(From *L' Ouvroir liturgique*). Delicacy and grace, but a lack of structure

mention them here. Those who make them, or rather those who conceive and design their ornament, including the figures, consider that the interpretation of nature is an affair of synthesis and that it is proper to represent all forms by angles. We need not say that their works are arid, hard and generally disagreeable. This is a mannerism or a madness and seems to derive from the famous cubist school.

Closely allied to the angular school is another which likewise pays no heed to the qualities or the principles which have been expounded in this book. In this school every artist claims to go his own gait without any care for harmony whether material or spiritual. This is supposed to be a return to nature, either, that is to say, to merely natural forms, or to natural forms modified and distorted in accordance with the catchwords of the modernist school. Examples of this kind of work have been shown in Chapter VII. But there are many different ways of treating geometric patterns, plants, animals and figures. We must repeat that designers of this school, when they come to deal with church ornaments, are too often fascinated by the idea of symbolism and sacrifice more important qualities to this idea. Also, their imagination is not content with beauty of form, nobility of line and simplicity of composition, but likes to toy with dainty effects or to indulge an exuberant fancy in eccentric designs and treatment of even the most sublime subjects. The works to which we allude are not vulgar or merely commercial in character, but they are lacking in balance, construction and individuality. Figure 303 for example shows a design for a stole which has been published recently ; too many different ideas are combined in it and none of them is predominant ; it merely aims at the dainty effects we have just mentioned. A marked contrast is provided by the stole shown in figure 304 ; it also is ornamented with a cross, but the other elements of the design serve to accentuate the form of the cross and the total effect is strong, dignified and well conceived. This composition is classical in spirit.

There are other kinds of modern vestments which differ notably from those we have just mentioned and which derive from special artistic centres. And that is not surprising or unusual. The same epoch often shows such variety, from country to country, and the same formation of various schools. And so it is all to the good that monks and nuns should form themselves into such schools and by the pursuit of their own ideals should transform and purify the art of their time.

In order to understand what has just been said, consider the two chasubles of figures 295 and 296, the hood of Plate V, another chasuble in Chapter VI (fig. 88), and at the end of this book the admirable banner of Plate VI. These are but a few of the works produced by the monks of Marià Laach. All the compositions of these artists are not equally good. Some have a marvellous delicacy, grace and nobility ; others give us dignified hieratic figures amid rather dull surroundings

FIG. 295. CHASUBLE OF THE ABBEY OF MARIA LAACH (RHINELAND)

(fig. 296) ; others again exhibit that multiplicity of detail which is contrary to the classical spirit of simplification. But all are the fruit of

FIG. 296.   ANOTHER CHASUBLE FROM MARIA LAACH
Strong decoration, inspired by the XIIth century

a knowledge and an effort which put them far above most of the productions of those who are inspired by the "return to nature," by impressionism, cubism and the rest.

In fact, the works of such a school as that of Maria Laach belong to that class of works in which the artist considers *before everything* the qualities of the decorative composition, in the clarity of the arrangement and the elimination of useless detail. It is work of a classical tendency, and that tendency is present in the minds that conceive it and the hands that make it. This school is not an exclusive one, for it takes its

FIG. 297.   CROSS OF A FEARFUL COMMERCIAL SPECIES

FIG. 298.   RATHER COMPLICATED, BUT VERY WELL CONCEIVED

FIG. 299.   A DESIGN BADLY WORKED OUT

FIG. 300.   VERY DECORATIVE

inspiration from all sides. You may remark in it the influence of the antique, as also many a trace of the best Byzantine and Romanesque art. And since the works of these two last-mentioned phases of art have an undeniable decorative quality, far superior to the quality of any realistic school, as is admitted by all good authorities, we are not wrong in favouring their influence in the designing of vestments. And there is now something of a reaction against that Gothic art which has been so much and so badly copied, but especially against the styles of the sixteenth, seventeenth and eighteenth centuries.

But there is a long way to go yet before we rescue liturgical art from the domination of bad styles in composition and decoration. The faults of many designs and of the articles made from these designs may be summed up as follows : Lack of good draftsmanship and a sense of proportion ; multiplication of complicated and useless detail ; and, in some very modern work, a fantastic irresponsibility. Let us illustrate this from the use of symbols and monograms. Good makers and good workers welcome monograms and symbols, but use them in moderation.

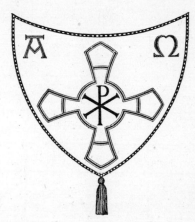

FIG. 301.   CLEAR   AND   WELL   FIG. 302. LESS SIMPLE AND FRANK
          BALANCED DESIGN

They have been used far too lavishly and scattered broadcast in unsuitable places, as for instance at the bottom of albs and surplices. Take the cross, for instance. It has been treated as a commonplace, ordinary motive and repeated *ad nauseam* on galloons, on stuffs, on altar cloths ; and often badly treated in the process. Consider the crosses of figures 301 and 302. The second is too large and too heavy ; the other is larger still since it extends over the whole hood, and yet it is lighter ; each of the parts, the monogram, the circle, the broad and narrow strips, is simple and goes to form a well-balanced whole. Let us consider next two crosses drawn for no particular purpose. One of them (fig. 297) is in the style of the showy decorations which were fashionable some fifty years ago ; the faults in composition are flagrant : four fleurs-de-lis at the end of four sticks and hideous rays made of gilt spangles. Compare this cross with the other (fig. 298), which is drawn in a very careful Gothic style. What a world of difference ! It is obvious that the first cross has gone wrong because different bits of design have been put together without rhyme or reason, whereas the success of the other has been achieved by the sound taste and singlemindedness which have gone to the thinking out of the design and to its careful execution.

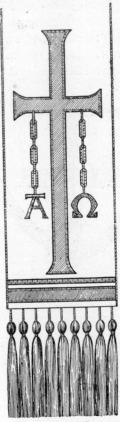

FIG. 303.   TOO MANY ITEMS AND
NOT ENOUGH CHARACTER

FIG. 304.   STYLE, STRENGTH
AND CLARITY
See fig. 130

This beautiful cross is complicated, but if enlarged and accurately cut out it would look well on an altar frontal. The next two crosses (figs. 299 and 300) are drawn within squares : the former has not been well thought out ; its awkward shape, the heavy four-lobed figure round it with the trefoils in the corners combine to form a dull composition ; it sins against the rudimentary principle that the principal subject should be given the greatest importance in a design. The other cross is by an artist at Bruges who is an accomplished draftsman; it is extremely simple, and perfect of its kind. If, on a white background, the cross and the outer strips were done in red and the ground of the inner square in green, the effect would be very good.

As we compared the crosses of figures 301 and 302, so may we compare the stoles represented in figures 303 and 304. The first contains too great a mixture of unlike objects and has too little character of its own ; the other is grave and dignified, with its tall cross, chains carrying alpha and omega, and then the tassels which accentuate its length.

Next, in figure 305, consider a notable example of the naturalistic school. We have indeed returned to nature with a vengeance, in this elaborate mass of fruits and foliage. The design has been entitled: *The Holy Spirit and His Fruits*, and is all grapes and apples. Why not also peaches, strawberries and other delicious fruit ! And why are there not twelve sorts ? Without waiting for an answer, we will give a brief criticism. (1) The design would do excellently for a table piece. (2) The branches, leaves and fruit are too closely

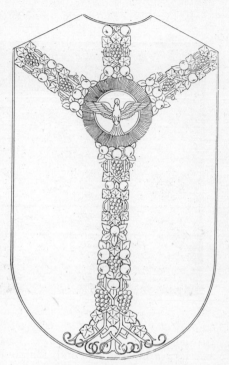

FIG. 305. GRAPES AND APPLES
Too much detail and more suitable for a
dinner table than for a chasuble

packed and the scheme of colour, pale green, dark green, yellow and purple, which is suggested in the polychrome reproduction, would only increase the confusion. (3) The work required in the making would be very great and very expensive. Only think : there are the branches to embroider, besides seventy leaves, forty-six apples and all the grapes to be cut out, stitched on to the red material and outlined in silk-thread ; not to mention that the ends of the maniple and stole and the corner of the veil for the chalice are also decorated with bunches of grapes and apples.

The same modern complexity, naturalism and symbolism are exhibited on the bands of a frontal and a canopy which are also reproduced in *L'Artisan liturgique*. Finally a climax of fancifulness is exhibited in the peacock-chasuble of figure 238. There you have the imperial bird crouched in his medallion, and the orfreys covered with peacock feathers worked in silk. The work is one that required enormous patience, and

FIG. 306. A FRONTAL WHICH IS BOTH HEAVY AND FINICKING
(*L'Ouvroir liturgique*)

yet how useless in the end, for none of its intricate decoration can be distinguished at a few yards' distance. Satin orfreys in the metallic blue of the eyes of these feathers, with a few carefully arranged decorations in gold, would have made a superb cross. But, no; we must have minute detail, complication and multiplicity. Perhaps such examples as these will make the reader favourable to us in our condemnation of extravagant ornament, in our advocacy of a good selection and arrangement of subjects, and in our effort to persuade priests to spend their money on simpler and better vestments.

Let us continue our critical survey. It will perhaps help the manufacturers and even more the designers—on whom a large measure of the responsibility lies—to abandon the errors we have exposed. But at any rate the enlightened public will cease to tolerate them. In figure 306 is an altar frontal which you will condemn without more ado, when you have observed how out of proportion its divisions are, how feeble and yet heavy its ovals, how finicking its spirals, rays, and flowerets. The makers aimed at producing a noteworthy frontal to show at the Paris Exhibition of 1925 ; but they only achieved a work which combines heaviness, affectation and complexity.

If you look up the number of *Les Arts français* which is entitled *L'art religieux moderne,* you will find an even worse *vestis altaris.* I do not think it is possible to imagine a design so over-loaded and so crammed, nor one so wholly wanting in that clarity of conception and that sense of proportion which classical principles demand.

FIGURES.—We now come to designs involving figures, and it so happens that this same number of *Les Arts français* gives an illustration of a chasuble ornamented with a figure of the Blessed Virgin which is unparalleled for mawkishness and affectation. It betrays a complete ignorance of anatomy and of the art of designing, and the Holy Child (may we be pardoned for saying so !) looks like one of those wooden dolls that people knock down with balls at our fairs. Look at them both and you will soon make up your mind ; either you will smile or you will be pained ; and with reason. M. Maurice Denis has said of the art of which these vestments are specimens : "It is one of the most triumphant manifestations of the ingenuity of the women of France, of their taste, and of their artistic activities." Ingenuity and activity, no doubt ; but a humiliating lack of taste, and consequently of achievement. We must have the courage to speak out.

The exigencies of modern taste are pleaded as an excuse for these things. We hear of a keener feeling for originality, and of the right of the artist to give a sincere and vital expression to the modern mind. Poor reasons indeed, and such as do not justify the treatment of the Virgin Mother in the design we have just described, nor the angels of figure 307. Look at them there, packed one on top of the other, shapeless wisps of figures with languishing faces and mere buttons of mouths ; all in the whimsical style of certain ultra-modern advertisements. Nor again do these reasons justify such violent work as that of the cope in figures 309 and 310. Why these odd and tortured designs, these incomprehensible gestures, these mad postures and lunatic expressions ? Are we to be asked to accept these also in the sacred name of modernity ? Many will refuse to do so. They are not hostile to modern art, but they like moderation, they like their figures to have a certain average health and attractiveness, and they like them well conceived and well grouped.

For the sake of such people we reproduce three representations of very different angels, though the technique of these works is not that of vestments (figs. 311, 312, 313). The angels here are different in concep-

FIGS. 307, 308. BANNER AND DETAIL FROM THE SAME (*L'Artisan liturgique*). A mass of languishing angels. Should be much simpler

tion, in design and as types ; they are works of a new art, but of a superior and spiritualised art. They are made by men who possess a profound knowledge of design, and who live by doctrine, liturgy and prayer. From their recollected life they derive the power of portraying adoration. Their work is a prayer and a help to those who pray, whereas the examples given above could only cause aversion and distraction. Doubtless the uneducated man and the worldling and even the good Catholic, being accustomed to the usual banalities, or to the disturbing effects achieved by certain ultra-modern artists, are not disposed to

like designs of so elevated an order ; but many souls of faith and recollect-
edness will value them at their true value.　They are evidently the
productions of art, of religion and of prayer.

Figures have been mentioned many times in this chapter, sometimes
from the point of view of design, sometimes with regard to their represen-

FIGS. 309, 310.　HOOD AND ORFREY OF A COPE
A medley of extravagant gestures and wild expressions

tation in fabric ; and we have just seen some angels in the grand style
and that an eminently religious style.　But for all that we may ask
whether it is really logical to ornament damasks and brocades with
the human form, and to embroider it on liturgical vestments.　At no
period of Greek antiquity were figures displayed on woven stuffs ; and
the same is true of ancient Roman costume, whether civil or religious.
It was later, under the influence of Byzantine luxury, that the habit grew
of decorating such stuffs with figures and scenes.　These pictorial stuffs
were reserved for emperors, empresses and certain high officials ; or
they were given to churches, where they were used as hangings or as
wrappings for the bodies of saints.　But the impetus once given there
followed many "storied" stuffs, from the workshops of Alexandria,

S

Constantinople, Damascus and Tyre. We have examples from the fourth century to the end of the twelfth ; but it is especially in the Gothic era that figures were embroidered on vestments.

Fig. 311.   Angels again, but Depicted with Sure Touch, Finished Art, Deeply Religious Feeling. (Beuron)

Now just as figures are perfectly in place on plain surfaces, in frescoes, mosaics and paintings, when they can be seen without difficulty, so are they unsuitable for stuffs, for vestments, for *insignia*. For either the figures are wholly hidden or else they are mutilated and distorted

FIG. 312. ANGELS TREATED IN THE MODERN MANNER, YET VERY
RELIGIOUS IN FEELING
(Br Notker Becker, of Maria Laach)

—and what pleasure can we find in headless trunks or in random limbs?
And such figures stiffen, complicate and weigh down the stuffs on
which they are placed. Moreover bishops, and even priests, are great

figures in the Church, and what need have they of figures on their mitres
and vestments ?   Such figures enhance the price, but they do not
enhance the beauty of a vestment.   They are appreciated only by a
very few folk who are near them, and from a truly decorative point
of view are inferior to good conventional motives, which, if well-
arranged, form an ornament that is easily perceptible by eye and mind.

FIG. 313.   ADORING ANGEL, IN THE GRAND STYLE
(Tabernacle door, Monte Cassino, Beuronese School)

What we have just said is but a theory, which we advance with all
due modesty. Some will accept it, others will not. To those who still
insist on figures we offer the following advice, which embodies a manner
of dealing with them that is conformable to the principles of religious
and decorative art : Let them have style, yet without any slavish
copying of a particular style ; let them have sobriety and accuracy of
lines, proportions, attitudes, gestures ; and in their expression, strength
without heaviness, serenity without affectation.   Moreover, though
the artist should no doubt keep his eyes fixed on nature, he must not
copy it too closely in these figures ; he may on occasion be deliberately
inexact, disengaging the reality from its accidents and penetrating to
genuinely beautiful forms. In short those figures that are to appear
on liturgical vestments should be submitted to a certain idealisation
and precise discipline, and set in a special mode of being.

CHAPTER XVII

SOME METHODS OF ORNAMENT

SINCE such books as the *Guide pratique* and the *Artisan liturgique* give much instruction in the technique of ornamentation we shall confine ourselves here to some very general notions regarding different processes and their effect. Some such simple general notions of certain processes which are used in the ornamenting of vestments may be of use to priests, and it is for their benefit that we have formulated them. We have already noted that the application of a coloured pattern by stencilling must be abominated (p. 214). Actual *printing* in colour should also be avoided ; it is too much like the printing of wall-papers and muslins. *Hand-painting* is also unsuitable for materials which must above all things preserve the essential qualities of softness and lightness. An exception may be legitimately made for the use of the paint brush in particular faces or details of faces.

We have often had occasion to refer to a technical process known as *application*. It is rarely possible, as it was in the Middle Ages or even before the war, to afford long strips of work or whole figures in embroidery and we must therefore resort to appliqué work. It is economical and can give distinctive and original results if the artist who conceives, let us say, human figures or simple ornamental subjects, does not look on *application* as a mere technical process, but gives his mind to the best ways and means of carrying it out. To explain this point would involve repetitions on the subject of the knowledge of the theory and practice of art and of the attitude of mind which should characterise the artist who designs and makes vestments. Rather we will pass on to explain the process of *application*. The first operation consists in cutting out pieces of stuff very accurately according to the outlines of the design ; next these pieces are *applied* and stitched on to the material which has first been stretched on a frame ; they are then outlined in silk or gold thread, so as to fix them more firmly and to give them a higher degree of finish. Geometric patterns can give very good effects of line and of colour so long as they conform to correct principles of drawing, proportion, arrangement and so forth. But it is not enough to fall in love with this process of application, which looks easy enough, and to stitch on rectangular or round figures with the idea of making, let us say, an orfrey, or of ornamenting a stole, saying to oneself, "This is on modern lines, it is decorative art," just because it is appliqué work. The Red Indians of North America can do that much.

Figure 314 shows an ornament which has been very carefully thought out. The dark elements are of red velvet ; the light parts are made of a yellow material. Five rock crystals add their lustre to this pendant, which is sewn on to a red and yellow silk of a pure Byzantine style. The effect has been described as "splendid and thoroughly pontifical" ; and in fact it is a detail for a dalmatic, which is one of a complete set of vestments for use at pontifical masses. Another illustration (fig. 315) shows a strip of white satin ornamented with circles and monograms ; the lateral orfreys are connected by yellow satin bands on which are applied small transverse strips of red velvet. All this is done in

FIG. 314. A PENDANT APPLIED ON A BY-
ZANTINE VESTMENT

appliqué work. A third specimen is shown in figure 319. This tall Madonna, which has been cut out in order to be applied on to a background, is very well conceived. The eyes, the nose, the mouth, and the hands are worked in embroidery, and a narrow silk cord, fixed to the foundation by means of silk thread, is used to mark the folds of the drapery.

Tapestry work, or cross-stitch, is done on open-work canvas woven in squares. The operation consists in covering this canvas either with silk, or, more often, with wool ; when it is finished it looks like a mosaic of small squares of silk or wool. This work was very fashionable in the first half of the nineteenth century, when many vestments were worked in cross-stitch. The only really beautiful cross-stitch work I have seen was at the house of Hudson, at Paris, and these were geometrical patterns very well conceived both in line and colour; use had thus been made of the only kind of ornamentation that is suitable for a process which is based entirely on a square. In another workshop I have seen the most frightful and nonsensical mixture imaginable. It is true that the idea of it came from California. A parish of those parts gave the manufacturer his orders ; the garments of the figures were to be made in fine embroidery and the faces and hands in cross-stitch. The result was horrible. A righteous judgment on people who asserted their views in a matter of which they were utterly ignorant.

EMBROIDERY may be called colouring in needlework on a solid ground of linen, silk, satin, or velvet. Embroidering on white linen with red thread has been mentioned in Chapter II. We will now speak of embroidery in silks with which gold thread is nearly always used also. An attempt to explain the great variety of embroidery stitches would carry us too far afield and would be of no service to the majority of priests ; we refer those who are interested in these very multifarious operations to the *Guide pratique*.

During the Middle Ages ornaments were done almost entirely in embroidery ; after the Renaissance appliqué work was extensively used, often in conjunction with embroidery. Many ancient embroidered vestments still exist. Instead of giving a list of the more important of

FIG. 315.   A BEAUTIFUL ORFREY FOR A WHITE COPE The bands in yellow satin; the circles and monogram in red velvet are represented black in this illustration. Cf. fig. 148

these, I will call attention to a single English cope (*opus anglicanum* as the inventories call it), which I went to study and to get photographed at the museum of Vich, in Catalonia, on behalf of L. de Farcy, author of the great folio work : *La broderie du XIe siècle jusqu'à nos jours.* Arches, interlaced curves, foliage, and shields are displayed all over this cope which also exhibits some fifty human figures and as many angels with outstretched wings ; and yet, as by a miracle, all these details are admirably arranged ; every bit is clear, graceful, and alive ;

FIG. 316.   A TAPESTRY PALL
Dreadfully clumsy design

and moreover the embroidery in which all these figures and ornaments are worked is characterised by the simplicity and directness which the craftsmen of the thirteenth century used to put into their work. Without seeing them oneself it is difficult to imagine the beauties of these embroideries in silk and gold thread.

Some firms in England, France, Germany and especially in Belgium, produce very beautiful embroideries. I have seen and admired various copes, chasubles, and mitres, and I am bound to say that the embroidery was perfectly done and beautifully finished in style ; the colours embraced every conceivable shade, graduated, combined, fading into one another or contrasting the one with the other, some sober and soft, others brilliant and resplendent, like the beautiful sunlit glass of our old cathedrals. And yet, though all this work is undoubtedly sincere and displays a wonderful knowledge of the various stitches used in embroidery, one does sometimes sigh after the directness of design, the simplicity of modelling and the primitive draping of garments which are so essential to decorative art. We have criticised adversely the figures on a hood and on an orfrey shown in figures 309 and 310, but it must be admitted that the style in which they are drawn, namely with a few strong lines to mark the folds of the garments, is not devoid of merit. After all, this is the principle which has been followed by the vestment makers of Nîmes in making the two Madonnas shown in figures 281 and 319. The artists did not aim at being antiquarian revivalists, but

FIG. 317.   DETAIL FROM THE VICH COPE
Catalonia ; end of xiiith century

in fact they have partly followed the technique and conventional forms of the Vich cope. The folds of the tunic and mantle of St. James are there depicted by means of fine cord sewn on to the embroidery (fig. 317) ; this fine cord is worked over in silk which is not done in the two Madonnas of Nîmes, the execution of which is very much simplified and at the same time very effective. This technique may be looked on with favour; intelligently used it gives good results. The principle we deduce is that very little drapery should be worked in embroidery stitches; if the garments are very dark, a pale silk cord or two gold threads will do to mark the folds; if the garments are light in colour, dark lines of stitching or of silk cord will outline the folds. If the garments are cut out and applied, the same technique will serve. The faces can be depicted by a little embroidery as in the tall Madonna (fig. 319); but no hard and fast rule can be laid down. Hatch work rather than mingled shades, or a few shadows in the right place, are obviously often suitable. The directors of workshops know all this well, but the clergy are rightly interested in these economical processes so as to know where they stand in placing orders.

FIG. 318. A WONDERFUL MEDALLION
In very fine embroidery. (A. E. Grossé, Bruges)

The important point in depicting figures is to bear in mind that the servile copying and meticulous imitation of nature are contrary to the rules of an art which does not aim at the qualities of a miniature nor of any detailed painting. The art of embroidery has qualities which are proper to itself and it must be allowed to keep its individuality. If the future proves to be favourable to more simple processes, yet we may be very sure that the art of fine embroidery will continue to supply us with delicate detail and ornament. There will always be skilful embroiderers, men and women, and there will always be wealthy patrons ready to encourage them.

Before ending we offer the reader three examples of embroidered work which show interesting and instructive contrasts. The first is the hood of a cope, showing a majestic St. Peter which has excellent points (fig. 320). The ground is decorated with Gothic ornaments of poor design and ponderous execution, but the very sober fashion in which St. Peter has been treated makes the work a well-conceived one from the decorative point of view. The attitude and gesture of the apostle are correct ; the outline and folds of the tunic and mantle are strongly marked by almost black lines, and the shadows of the draping are well laid upon the white of the vestments.

The second hood is admirable (Plate V). Again we have a single figure, this time the Son of God, all nobility and grace, the most beautiful among the sons of men. One cannot but admire the extremely delicate care that has directed the designing of the figure, the white raiment, the pendant ornaments. We have frequently urged that ornament should consist of a few items only ; well, in this case there is a multiplicity of ornament in the figure, but take note that all the curves, flowers and conventional fruits spring from just two branches. And with what exact and consummate knowledge all is arranged and rendered! The elements have been chosen from nature ; but they have been transformed and made a fit frame for the figure of the Son of God.

FIG. 319. A TALL MADONNA OF MASTERLY
TECHNIQUE

Appliqué work, the folds of the drapery marked by fine silk cording. (*Atelier liturgique, Nîmes*)

The third hood is not less marvellous, but from a different point of view (fig. 321). The grouping of the figures is skilful, their attitudes good, and their gestures not exaggerated. Moreover, the whole is rendered with a perfection of technique that has not been surpassed. The whole cope was one of the masterpieces of the Gothic Revival. But, as we have seen, reason, instinct and a renewed good sense no longer favour the imitation of the thirteenth, fourteenth and fifteenth centuries. And why bring in so many figures, artistic and beautiful though they may be ? Beauty may be achieved with many fewer, or with only one, or even with none at all.

FIG. 320. HOOD OF COPE BELONGING TO BIRMINGHAM CATHEDRAL
Designed by D. Powell. The figure of St. Peter very well treated ; the fringe
too stiff

But what are we to say of the extraordinary effort which has produced an alb and a chasuble ornamented with some thousands of figures ?[1] It is impossible to give a detailed reply, at the end of this book. We will only remark : (1) that the 152 tiny figures in the squares round the edge of the chasuble suggest a row of postage stamps ; (2) that proces-

[1] Both are shown in *L'Artisan liturgique*, 2e année, No. 7 and 8.

PLATE V

A VERY BEAUTIFUL HOOD

The manifold decoration, but wise and well-arranged, is in contrast to the
simple and majestic figure of Christ in admirable vesture. (*Abbey of Maria
Laach*)

sions of figures which may look very well on the walls of a church are
wholly out of place on the hem or wrists of an alb ; (3) that scenes
piled one on another, multitudinous details, national costumes and
landscapes, are the extreme limit of decoration.   By this laborious
and infinitely meticulous process a chasuble becomes a picture gallery,

FIG. 321. A FAR LESS SIMPLE HOOD, BUT OF A MARVELLOUS TECHNIQUE
(A. E. Grossé, Bruges)

and loses its proper character and essential qualities.   There is no more
true art in this than there is in printing the whole Bible in a tiny
duodecimo.   It is a *tour de force* and nothing more.

It looks very much as though the motto was : "The greatest possible
amount of ornament in the smallest space."   To that we are tempted

to retort with "The smallest possible" on small spaces, and even on big ones too. But let the ornament that you have be well conceived, well placed, well made. If that be done we shall no longer have that complicated and distracting ornament, which is sometimes of so prodigious a character that it absorbs all our attention. Rather we hope to see vestments whose merits lie in their shape, their lightness and their colour, and which are consequently worthy vesture for bishops, priests and ministers. Such vestments will have the essential qualities of simplicity and beauty, which two words summarise the whole argument of this book.

APPENDIX

BANNERS

CONSIDERING the title of this book, this appendix is a digression. But since banners are closely related, from the point of view of texture and work, to liturgical vestments, we give them hospitality in these pages. It provides us with an opportunity of showing the reader some very praiseworthy works of art.

The Labarum of Constantine is in date the first standard of a religious character to which our banners may appeal for their ancestry. But the Labarum was not, properly speaking, a Christian banner ; it was really a military standard, the standard which Christ bade the Emperor make, to serve him as a protecting symbol in battle (fig. 322).

The earliest ancestors of our banners seem to be those processional crosses with red streamers, which were used as early as the seventh century in processions in the streets of Rome (fig. 323). But it is hardly until the period of the Middle Ages that we meet any mention of *banners* in ancient inventories ; and they were then small flags, rectangular in shape, often ending in two or three points (as may be seen on the Bayeux tapestry), and fastened by one edge to a staff. There was a flag of this sort, with three points, in a mosaic of the triclinium of the Lateran palace. The mosaic represented St. Peter giving this standard to Charlemagne.[1] These *bandi* or *bandae* carried armorial designs and symbolised the feudal rights of princes, suzerains, and knights-bannerets. So they were not church banners, even when they had sacred emblems on them, as was sometimes the case.

The white pennon of St. Joan of Arc may assuredly be regarded as a religious standard, although for her and for her army it was a standard of battle, a sign of fresh hope and a rallying point for renewed effort. But neither the flags of princes, nor the red *vexilla* hanging from processional crosses, nor even the pennon of St. Joan were banners in our modern sense. And it is of the modern banner that we would treat in this appendix.

[1] Nothing is left of this mosaic, but a sketch of it has been preserved.

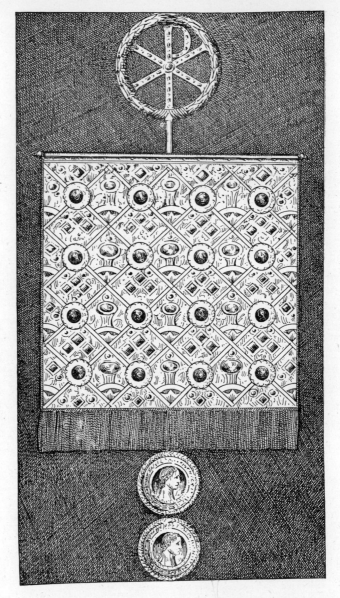

FIG. 322. THE LABARUM OF CONSTANTINE

Reconstructed according to the description of Eusebius and the data provided
by Mgr. Wilpert. The medallions are fixed on the shaft. (*Abbey of Maria Laach*)

Everybody knows the sort of use that is made of pennons, banners and flags on certain feastdays to decorate, or rather to uglify, our churches, even the very best of them. Who has not seen them hanging from the arches, sprawling over the walls, concealing the pillars, invading and hiding the sanctuary ? Let us have discretion and not conceal the lines of our churches with this riot of unnecessary ornament.

FIG. 323. PAPAL CROSS AND THREE PROCESSIONAL CROSSES
DECORATED WITH PENNONS
(From a fresco in the lower church, San Clemente, Rome)

Pennons and bannerets are often made of bands of yellow and white, blue and white, or other colours, on which are applied shields, fleur-de-lis, monograms, inscriptions, and (alas !) gilt-paper stars. For these things, as for many other ornaments, the rule ought to be "a little and good," as St. Francis of Sales recommends. Our churches are not worthily decorated by masses of these cheap bannerets. It would be better to abolish all this trashy stuff and to limit ourselves to a couple of great pennons or flags of good shape and proportions and made of silk or damask. Let them have a simple and good decoration, and then set them at the entrance to the sanctuary. Our folk would soon learn to appreciate them and to prefer them to those countless gaudy objects that are really only suited for a country fair.

Exact proportions of length and breadth, exact balance of design and divisions : these things are of the first importance. And yet they do not seem to worry some of our makers, who produce pennons of an

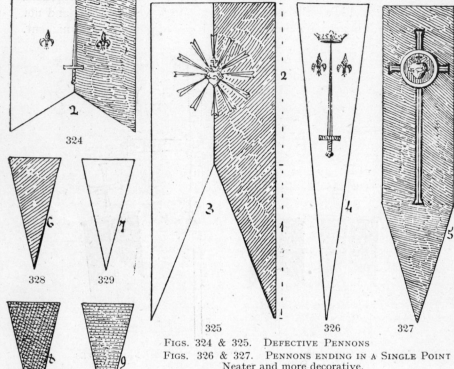

FIGS. 324 & 325. DEFECTIVE PENNONS
FIGS. 326 & 327. PENNONS ENDING IN A SINGLE POINT
Neater and more decorative.
FIGS. 328 to 331. FOUR PENNONS

almost square shape (fig. 324) or others with points that equal in length the body of the pennon (fig. 325). That is all wrong both in conception and in effect. The spirit that presides over these productions is that familiar demon of hurry and carelessness. Anything is good enough for the popular taste—that is the theory—and so anything is produced, regardless of art and beauty.

To those who are not content with this state of affairs, we suggest pennons either of one point only, or pointed for a third of their length ; or better still, long straight flames, cut at a very acute angle (figs. 326 and 327). If we must have a large number of pennons, then let them be very simple and of one colour (figs. 328 to 331), for that will give far better results than those eternal pennons in two or three colours. We have seen in a certain place a mass of single-colour pennons, some in gold-yellow, others violet, rose, white, green, red, sky-blue, turquoise-blue and dark-blue. The mixture was neither discordant nor vulgar ; and the note of joy was excellently conveyed.

According to our modern taste and practice the genuine processional banner is fastened to a cross-bar and kept in a more or less horizontal position near the top of a perpendicular staff. Such a banner offers an obvious canvas on which to display the figure of the patron saint of a town, parish or confraternity. The danger here lies in wishing to have the banners too large, and in not considering what a weight they are when the material and decorations are heavy. Perhaps we have all seen those standards of velvet, or heavy watered silk, loaded with figures in relief and metal ornaments, overwhelming the men or girls who carried them, especially when an untimely breeze sprang up. It is a very unsatisfactory solution of this difficulty to have two

FIG. 332. WELL-DESIGNED BANNER
Entirely given (and properly so) to St. Joan of Arc

bearers, and consequently two poles, which are badly held, and dragged different ways. Let us leave this to those strolling bands in the streets, who give silent voice to their protests or their appeals on long strips of bunting. Let us keep to reasonable proportions, and materials and decorations light enough to allow one person to carry each banner without superhuman efforts.

The length of these banners being always greater than the width, let us consider the qualities of the whole before deciding on the details, not forgetting that full length figures (fig. 332), compartments, bands of material, and decorative designs running lengthways, will be of value in emphasising the two long outer lines. This is only an indication which it is well generally to take into account ; but, indeed, transverse galloons and orfreys diminishing the length may produce quadrangles with equal sides, perfectly suited to receive designs, as is shown in

*

figure 333. Here the square generates four others united by a quatre-foil which encloses a circle ; there is diversity, and yet the different forms support one another. The cinquefoil which, on the banner, encircles a central medallion does not spoil the square formed by the upper part

FIG. 333.   BANNER FOR CON-
FRATERNITIES OF THE BLESSED
SACRAMENT
Good composition.   (Beyaert,
Bruges)

FIG. 334.   EXCELLENT COM-
POSITION
The figure of Our Lady is small,
but stands out well. (Beyaert,
Bruges)

of the banner (fig.334), but is, on the contrary, skilfully formed and adroitly placed in the centre of the background, while the decorative design—palm-leaf and a conventional tree—is needed to fill the spaces. All is clear, well arranged and well thought out. An important detail should be noticed: the little figure of our Lady, prettily set, is indeed small, but stands out well in light colours on a dark ground ; it is better than many figures which are displayed in undue proportions on many banners.

The two examples just described are evidently inspired by ancient styles, which have been put to good use. But there is no rule imposing these styles, nor any fixed form or arrangement ; the essential thing is that an artist, free and independent, having a thorough knowledge of

FIG. 335. VERY INTERESTING BANNER

Original idea and well worked out. One or two imperfect details do not
impair the value of the whole. (After *Die Christliche Kunst*)

art applied to materials, should have a definite end, that the parts of his composition should form a whole, and that all the elements should be subordinate to the whole. Such an artist still exists ; but he is becoming rare ; he is not known nor sought after ; and if people happen to meet him and see his work, the immense majority of purchasers turn away and go straight to manufactured products of the poorest kind.

DONA EIS REQUIEM

FIG. 336. SENTIMENTAL BANNER IN THE WORST COMMERCIAL STYLE

FIG. 337. BLACK BANNER
Enhanced with coloured and gold ornament.
(Beyaert, Bruges)

It is not without repugnance that we show you one of these productions, a black banner (fig. 336), which we beg you to compare with those that follow ; the gradation is easy to grasp and the lesson conclusive. First, the banner labelled "sentimental" is a veritable collection of all that is senile and out of date : three cusps, supposed to be Gothic in shape, two large, crossed branches with languishing twigs, clouds and tears which are ludicrously pitiable. Look at this typically ugly work, and you will at once recognise others of the same family, as sickly as itself, in certain catalogues.

The next example has none of these childish pretensions (fig. 337) ; instead of an exuberance of tear-sprinkled vegetation, we have a large cross of a very decorative galloon which forms the greater part of the ornamentation. Then for the colour scheme we see, not that everlasting white, or imitation silver, on black velvet, but a touch of flame colour and clear yellow on the cross-shaped orfrey, a straw-coloured ground for the medallions, and everything outlined in gold. And why not these discreet touches of warm and varied colour, since they are so effective with black, which, moreover, greatly predominates?

We now come to the third example of the black banner, and, this time, we have a work of superior character (fig. 338). The cross, the intersected

Fig. 338. Beautiful Black Banner
Admirable in design and colour. (A. E. Grossé, Bruges)

curves, the repeated PAX, the greenish leaves, the golden fruit made ruddy by its fastening of red silk, are all good, all in their right place ; the whole is impressive without being heavy, and the arrangement faultless, simple in appearance, but in reality very clever.

It may be said that the designs on these two banners are purely decorative. That is quite true; but the decorative art which characterises them and which embraces all liturgical vestments is not an art of small importance; on the contrary, it is a great and lofty art, and Ruskin has said that there is no art of a higher order than decorative art. Now liturgical art is a decorative art, when it makes use of figures to adorn its banners and vestments. And both, to be works of art, demand a certain power of conception, a certain active energy and individual originality, clear divisions, accurate and decided contours, and careful connection of subject and details.

FIG. 339. ANOTHER BANNER IN THE COMMERCIAL STYLE

With bad design and ornament

It might be thought at first sight that these qualities are to be found in some degree in the many banners displayed without remonstrance in the advertisements of our ecclesiastical furnishers. But that is not so, except in rare cases. These banners have a plan, because there must be one of some sort; but it is conceived apart from any pursuit of art for art's sake or of art for religion's sake. It is not art to design a banner with the aim chiefly of flattering uneducated eyes. It is not art to repeat, without the least creative imagination or higher aspiration, hackneyed and retrograde patterns, such as are commonly employed, because the general public accepts them. It is not art to practise an "emotional style," and to finish off banners, surround figures and so on, with arches supposed to be Gothic, or weak oval curves. It is not art to be perpetually drawing fatuous monograms and meandering and interlaced ornamentation, so as to spread a design, continuous or otherwise, over all available space. Finally, it is not art to put on a banner, at shortest notice and without artistic effort, some effigy which is made to order and which gives little suggestion of sanctity, and then, because there are spaces on either side, to cover them with be-ribboned branches such as any bungler can botch up without talent or reflection.

Diximus. We shall not be sued for having thus described a score or so of trashy banners of which sorry reproductions are before us as we write, because we are not wronging John or Richard, but denouncing commercial art in general. It is not art. What is it then ? It is trumpery work, decoration turned out by the yard. A single example in support of our opinion is here reproduced (fig. 339). There is no serious art in it—nothing but paltry and deceptive attractiveness. And there are other and worse banners. We must draw a veil.

Let a last example now give us something of its strength and tranquillising sweetness. But we wished first to strike a note of indignation, so as to convince our readers, and to give them a distaste for all the confections and fabrications of which we have spoken.

You have now seen several banners worthy of your attention ; look at them again, and examine especially the one reproduced in Plate VI. In form it is large and rectangular, with a fringe at the bottom, and two long straight bands, also ending in fringes, on either side. Horizontal bands reduce the length of the decorated part. The frame in which the saint is set is divided into four regions ; in the corners are concentric curves and conventional fruit. Round the whole is a frieze formed of S-shaped and small bifurcating figures. The decoration is rich, very quaint, and very abundant, but well arranged ; it forms a remarkable contrast with the martyr clothed all in white garments, which are quite simple and admirably draped. In this piece of Catholic art are to be found the grace and nobility of the works of Greek art at its zenith. But Greek art was incapable of producing a face sublime and serene as that of this Cecilia, whose gaze penetrates heaven and whose soul is blessing the Lord : *Benedic anima mea Domino.* We too, leaving this saint, may bless the Lord in happiness and in gratitude, for that he has among the sons and daughters of the cloister His servants and His artists who desire His glory above all things. There, and else-where too, are men and women who can produce works that are the fruit of thoughtful taste, of consummate art, and above all of medita-tion and peace.

PLATE VI

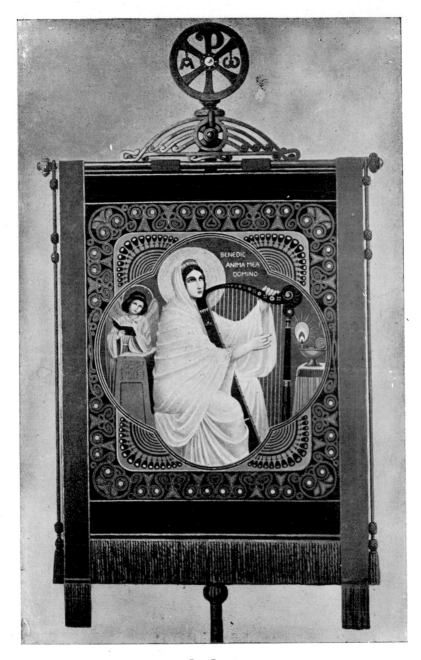

ST. CECILY

A marvellous banner, with broad lines, restful spaces and original
decoration; a virgin saint nobly arrayed (*Abbey of Maria Laach*)

BIBLIOGRAPHY

This is not a complete bibliography of the subject, but a list of those works only which I have used in writing this book.

A. W. N. Pugin : *Glossary of Ecclesiastical Ornament and Costume,* 1844.—Rather out of date, and confined to Gothic vestments.

F. Bock : *Geschichte der liturgischen Gewänder des Mittelalters.* 1856-1871.—Likewise out of date, but valuable.

Martinucci : *Manuale Sacrarum Caeremoniarum,* Rome, 1871.—This book, compiled by the pontifical Master of Ceremonies, has the highest authority.

Viollet-le-Duc : *Dictionnaire du Mobilier.* 1858-1875.—The articles on vestments are still valuable.

Rohault de Fleury : *La Messe,* vols. VII and VIII.—Archæological studies and a great number of etchings of vestments.

V. Gay : *Glossaire archéologique.* 1887.—A careful piece of work, with short articles on alb, cope, chasuble etc., and many citations of inventories. New edition in two vols, 1929.

M. Magistretti : *Delle Vesti ecclesiastiche in Milano,* 1897.—Concerned with the Ambrosian liturgy, but very instructive.

J. Braun S.J. : Articles on vestments in the *Catholic Encyclopædia,* and the two works : *Die liturgische Gewandung im Okzident und Orient,* 1907 ; *Die liturgischen Paramente in Gegenwart und Vergangenheit, ein Handbuch der Paramentik,* 2nd ed. 1924.

L. de Farcy : *La Broderie du XI*ᵉ *siècle jusqu'à nos jours.*—A folio work which is unsurpassed for all that concerns embroidered vestments.

Dom Gréa : *La sainte Liturgie,* 1909.—An excellent little book.

Dom Cabrol : *Dictionnaire d'Archéologie chrétienne et de Liturgie.*

P. Batiffol : *Leçons sur la Messe,* 1920.—Some excellent passages on vestments.

A. Fortescue, D.D., Ph. D. *The Vestments of the Roman Rite,* 1925.—No more than a pamphlet, but full of knowledge and liturgical feeling.

R. James : *The Origin and Development of Roman Liturgical Vestments,* 1926.—A well-ordered archælogical and liturgical essay.

Bénédictines de Saint-Louis-du-Temple : *Guide pratique pour la confection des ornements gothiques.*—Very useful.   Some passages criticised in this book.

L'Artisan liturgique and *L'Ouvroir liturgique.*—These two periodicals are sometimes lacking in judgment ; but readers of formed taste will find in them much valuable information and an abundance of illustrations, in which they will be able to distinguish successful designs from failures. Three of the chapters of this book appeared first in *L'Ouvroir*.

Besides these books, others are cited in the course of the volume.

INDEX

INDEX

Printed by The Stanhope Press Ltd., Rochester, Kent